INEVITABLE
PARTNERSHIP

INEVITABLE PARTNERSHIP

Understanding Mexico-U.S. Relations

Clint E. Smith

LYNNE
RIENNER
PUBLISHERS

BOULDER
LONDON

Published in the United States of America in 2000 by
Lynne Rienner Publishers, Inc.
1800 30th Street, Boulder, Colorado 80301
www.rienner.com

and in the United Kingdom by
Lynne Rienner Publishers, Inc.
3 Henrietta Street, Covent Garden, London WC2E 8LU

Library of Congress Cataloging-in-Publication Data
Smith, Clint E.
    Inevitable partnership : understanding Mexico-U.S. relations /
    Clint E. Smith
    Includes bibliographical references and index.
    ISBN 1-55587-897-0 (hc.: alk. paper)
    ISBN 1-55587-873-3 (pbk.: alk. paper)
    1. United States—Foreign relations—Mexico. 2. Mexico—Foreign relations—
United States. I. Title.
JZ1480.A57M67   2000
327.73'072—dc21   99-088894
                                                            CIP

British Cataloguing in Publication Data
A Cataloguing in Publication record for this book
is available from the British Library.

Printed and bound in the United States of America

        The paper used in this publication meets the requirements
  ∞   of the American National Standard for Permanence of
        Paper for Printed Library Materials Z39.48-1984.

    5 4 3 2 1

To Marilyn Sode Smith

With Love and Appreciation

Contents

Part I   An Evolving Relationship (1800–1994)

**Part 2   The Relationship Today:
Contemporary Issues**

Part 3   Into the Twenty-First Century

Figures

Acknowledgments

A great many scholars, government officials, businesspeople, bankers, artists, writers, students, and others both from Mexico and the United States have helped me over the last few decades to learn about the fascinating and complex relationship between the two countries. Several of these friends and colleagues have written about Mexico and the United States, and their works are to be found in the bibliography that accompanies this volume. These works are rich in insight and represent a broad range of views and approaches to the Mexico-U.S. relationship. I consulted many of them frequently in the preparation of this book. Their works are generally fuller in scope or deeper in focus than this volume, which is intended for the reader who is not already an expert on Mexico or Mexico-U.S. relations. In fact, a principal goal of this study is to call the reader's attention to those works. I recommend those books and hope that the authors will understand the impossibility of singling out individual authors on this page. I also want to thank those former students who have contributed to my understanding in this field.

I am indebted to Kristin Johnson Ceva and Guadalupe Paz, who provided important research assistance during earlier stages of this project and, along with Adriana Perez Mina, reviewed the early draft of this volume. I am grateful as well to Michael Pretes for lending his considerable expertise and good advice on U.S.-Mexico and North American transboundary and environmental issues. I also want to give special thanks to Megan Hendershott, a very talented editor, and, of course, to Sally Glover and Lynne Rienner for their unflagging encouragement and support in the publication of this book. I take full responsibility for any errors that have crept in despite everyone's best efforts.

I also want to recognize William R. Hewlett, chairman emeritus of the board of the William and Flora Hewlett Foundation, for his deep understanding of the importance of U.S.-Mexico policy studies and for his vision and sustained generosity that made possible the development and growth of a significant number of important U.S.-Mexico policy studies centers at leading institutions in both Mexico and the United States. There is no doubt that the collaborative efforts of these institutions have played a critical role in improving the understanding of the complex nature of U.S. relations with Mexico. It was my pleasure to have been closely associated with Bill Hewlett in these efforts.

Finally, I want everyone to know that without the initial encouragement and steadfast support of my wife, Marilyn Sode Smith, it would have been impossible for me to write this book.

—*C.E.S.*

Introduction

The 2,000-mile border shared by Mexico and the United States is unique in its separation of the First World from the Third. Across that border, though, there is a daily flow of millions of economic, political, social, and cultural interconnections that make the two countries increasingly interdependent. This phenomenon—whether welcome or not—binds Mexico and the United States into an inevitable partnership. The challenge is to learn to work in a collaborative style to manage the complexities of that relationship in a mutually beneficial way.

In this book I explore the nature of the interdependent Mexico-U.S. relationship and find that it is essentially asymmetrical. During the earlier years of the relationship, this asymmetry—in industrial and technological capacity, in economic and military power—created an image of a weak Mexico dependent on the "Colossus of the North." Not too long ago a conventional description of the binational relationship would have stressed Mexico's "dependence" on the United States and the "exploitative" role of U.S. and other transnational corporations vis-à-vis Mexico. The reader will discover why this is no longer true, if it ever was.

Perhaps more important to an understanding of U.S.-Mexico relations than economic asymmetries are the sharp cultural and historical differences between the United States and Mexico. As a famous Mexican philosopher remarked, "I as a Mexican am part of a singular paradox—that of Mexico and the United States. Our countries are neighbors, condemned to live alongside each other; they are separated, however, more by profound social, economic, and psychic differences than by physical and political frontiers" (Paz, 1985a).

As Octavio Paz well knew, the United States and Mexico have arrived at their present circumstances by very different paths. Mexico's twin roots are embedded in a great Mesoamerican civilization—Mayan, Aztec, Zapotec, and in *La Madre Patria*—the mother country, Spain. The conflict between the two cultures resulted in a generally unhappy colonial experience and led to a nineteenth-century revolt against Spain—a rebellion catalyzed, ironically, by the growing strength of the *mestizo*, the very product of the two civilizations' interaction. The Mexican Revolution produced a system of one-party rule that has governed Mexico for more than seventy years, and, despite the rapid growth in the strength of opposition parties of the left and right, that party is still seen as a viable contender in the 2000 presidential election.

The historical memories of the United States, which broke away from the Old World earlier and developed a democratic political system more than two hundred years ago, are quite different. The result is profoundly distinct perceptions, from the two sides of the border, of the major problems in the relationship.

Beyond these historical memories, it is important to understand that the last years of the twentieth century have been marked by fundamental reforms in Mexico's economic, political, and social structures. Building on the base of economic stability created by the persistent discipline of President Miguel de la Madrid (1982–1988), Mexico has experienced a dramatic opening to the global economy under Salinas (1988–1994) and Zedillo (1994–2000), and a seemingly unstoppable movement toward political pluralism and the nurturing of a civil society. At the same time, new or changing aspects of U.S.-Mexico relations in matters such as the debt crises, narcotics trafficking, trade and investment, the environment, and migration, have steered the United States in the direction of growing dependence on a stable and prosperous Mexico.

This new era must be described and a fresh look taken at the nature of the U.S.-Mexico relationship in the new millennium. That is the principal task I have set for myself in this volume, which is intended not only for public- and private-sector policymakers, but also for the academic community, students, and the general public in both countries.

Several important early events are described in Chapter 1: the movement of Anglo-American settlers to Texas (then a Mexican state); the Mexican War (or, to Mexicans, the War of the North American Invasion), which ended in Mexico's humiliation and loss of half its territory; the period of liberalization and *la Reforma* (the Reform) as Mexico was rebuilt afterward; and, finally, Mexico's emergence as an industrializing society. (A chronology of important events in Mexico's development begins on page 207.)

The onset of the Mexican Revolution and the long decade of violence and terror as opposing forces struggled for national power is covered in Chapter 2. Names almost magical in Mexican history books—Zapata, Pancho Villa, Carranza, Obregón—fill the pages of the story of this tragic decade (1910–1920). Chapter 2 describes the aftermath of the revolution, the series of Mexican presidents and leaders who shaped the changing Mexican world, and, finally, the tragic events of 1968. There is a focus on the controversial but still much-admired President Lázaro Cárdenas (1934–1940), who is remembered for his efforts at land reform in Mexico's rural areas and for the expropriation of the foreign oil companies.

The story of Mexico and U.S.-Mexico relations through the administrations of Echeverría (1970–1976), López Portillo (1976–1982), De la Madrid (1982–1988), and Salinas (1988–1994) is told in Chapter 3. Special attention is paid to the stabilization efforts of De la Madrid, and to the way in which Salinas opened the Mexican economy, successfully conducted negotiations for the North American Free Trade Agreement (NAFTA), and, only weeks after what appeared to be a successful conclusion of his administration, saw his world fall apart as Mexico's financial bubble burst and serious political scandals involving his family began to break.

Chapter 4 is the first of several chapters that take a thematic approach to the Mexican scene and the bilateral relationship. It contains a description and analysis of Mexico and its role in the global economy. In 1982 a new era of economic relations between the United States and Mexico began when Mexico's central bank ran out of foreign exchange, the foreign debt reached $100 billion, and an outgoing president's nationalization of private banks and massive devaluation of the peso created a financial crisis that reverberated throughout Mexico and the world. Since then, the story has generally been one of rebuilding, with a few dramatic exceptions, including the peso crisis in 1994–1995. The effects of NAFTA on the Mexican economy, the changing patterns in U.S.-Mexico trade and investment, and the dramatic growth in U.S.-Mexico trade, which more than tripled in the 1990s, are described. The chapter concludes with an analysis of the final years of the Zedillo administration and prospects for Mexico's economic future.

Mexico's dramatic political transformation, with growing pluralism and a move toward democratization, is reported in Chapter 5. It is noted that the change from the old authoritarian order became more marked in the De la Madrid administration, and that the forces of social and political progress have continued, with some setbacks, since that time. The clearest steps toward political pluralism and the emergence of a stronger civil society took place in the 1990s, and the chapter's major focus is on Mexico's transformation during this period. Key issues include the reach of judicial reform, public security and the rule of law, electoral reform and the emergence of the Mexican Congress as a political force, and a review of 1998–1999 gubernatorial elections, where each of the three major parties celebrated victories in different parts of the country. The chapter also examines the changing role of church-state relations in Mexico and the impact on social issues of an emerging civil society.

The long history of Mexican migration to the United States, and how the rules of the game have changed over time, is outlined in Chapter 6. There is an analysis of current U.S. immigration policy, and its impact on the bilateral relationship. We discover that immigration should not be seen as primarily a law enforcement issue. Mexican immigrants to the United States have by turns been welcomed with open arms and brusquely discouraged. Their growing numbers make Mexican Americans a dynamic and positive presence in American society—particularly in the key states of California and Texas. The chapter concludes that greater bilateral discussion of migration issues should be a high priority, given the United States and Mexico's rapidly growing economic and social interdependence.

Because of the crime, violence, corruption, social disorder, individual destruction, and international tension it engenders, illicit drug trafficking constitutes a source of great tension between Mexico and the United States. It is likely to remain so into the next millennium. Perhaps in no other area has the intergovernmental relationship been more complex. U.S. leadership through several recent administrations has failed to attack the problem adequately on the domestic demand side. Mexico has been unable to make significant progress in curbing illegal activities, which sometimes involve corrupt civilian, police, and military officials. Chapter 7 concerns the important and always troublesome issue of U.S.-Mexico collaboration to control illegal trafficking in narcotics and dangerous drugs. The chapter criticizes the current, and counterproductive, "certification" process, and suggests alternative ways of better managing collaborative efforts in this struggle.

Chapter 8 reports that after years of neglect environmental issues are now a serious component of U.S.-Mexico relations. The chapter looks at examples of institutional cooperation in improving the environment in North America in the context of the global environmental awareness that began in the 1960s. Included in the study is a discussion of the rapidly increasing population of the U.S.-Mexico border region and the impact of this population growth on environmental problems. The chapter describes how new organizations, springing both from NAFTA agreements and from nongovernmental groups, are working together to achieve common environmental goals in such areas as air pollution, sewage and toxic wastes, and the ecosystem. It also takes a more historical look at existing institutions such as the International Boundary and Water Commission (IBWC) and their track record in managing more traditional concerns such as transboundary water supply and quality. The chapter concludes with an analysis of whether trade and environmental issues should be linked, and highlights the need to strengthen existing governmental and nongovernmental institutions designed to improve cooperation in dealing with environmental concerns.

Chapter 9 identifies and analyzes the two countries' differing perspectives on foreign policy issues, and especially how those issues have evolved over recent decades. A section on "Mexico and the World" traces the course of Mexico's foreign policy from Adolfo López Mateos (1958–1964) to Ernesto Zedillo (1994–2000). There is also a report on how California-Mexico relations are fast becoming a key element shaping California's economic growth and social development. While Mexico's impact is also felt in other states, notably Texas, this sharper focus on a single state, and its special trade, investment, immigration, environmental, and educational and cultural interrelationships, is designed to demonstrate in specific terms how the bilateral relationship has become "intermestic," that is, a combination of international and domestic policy dimensions. The chapter concludes with an analysis of the differing perceptions and changing nature of U.S.-Mexico national-security issues, and the future of U.S.-Mexico relations, between the two countries, with some specific recommendations for institutional and policy changes in Washington that would improve the management of the relationship.

Discussions of economic and social relations between the United States and Mexico are increasingly taking on a North American flavor with the inclusion of Canada in a vision of a united North American community. Chapter 10 explores the origins of the North American Free Trade Agreement (NAFTA), the negotiation and approval process, its impact on the continent's social and economic sectors during its first years in effect, and prospects for the future, including the proposed Free Trade Area of the Americas (FTAA). It notes that the United States has suffered a particularly hard blow in its relations with its hemisphere trading partners: the failure of the Clinton administration to gain approval for fast-track authority. Such authority has been vital for the successful conclusion of international trade agreements. Failure to achieve this approval has global implications, as the world's trading nations move toward a Millennium Round to reform the World Trade Organization (WTO) and create more robust trading, investment, and services opportunities around the world. The volume concludes with a look at the prospects for progress toward creating the mutual understanding and respect—and the institutions needed—to build a strong and successful partnership.

PART I

An Evolving Relationship
(1800–1994)

I

Two Young Countries: 1800–1910

The Colonial Period

During the long period when the inhabitants of the thirteen English colonies and those of colonial New Spain were engaged in their struggles for independence (1775–1783 for the United States, 1810–1821 for Mexico), the two societies were small, and separated from each other by a wide expanse of sparsely populated land.

One might think that relations between the two colonies would have been close and significant, as military confrontations between England and Spain had occurred sporadically since the sixteenth century. Colonists both in English America and New Spain looked on with concern as the major European powers fought, won, and lost wars and traded parts of the New World with one another. Cuba, Florida, and Louisiana, pawns in this great game, were traded back and forth over the decades.

In fact, however, bilateral relations in the colonial period were marked by a mutual lack of interest on the one hand, and pervasive prejudice on the other. While the colonists of New Spain looked askance at the religious reformers and heretics of the English colonies to the north, Cotton Mather prayed for—and even, in 1699, wrote a treatise on—the need for the spiritual regeneration of the benighted inhabitants of New Spain.

Not surprisingly, the two new North American nations took very different paths in their economic, social, and political development. They were guided in large part by two quite distinct beginnings. The American colonies were settled in significant part by Puritans, Quakers, Catholics, and many others seeking religious freedom. They carried with them the seeds of political and economic liberalism that were to explode in the last quarter of the eighteenth century with the Declaration of Independence and the Constitution and its Bill of Rights. New Spain, on the other hand, was created by a process of armed exploration and political, economic, and religious conquest, which the Spanish *conquistadores* extended throughout the sixteenth century to Santa Fe and San Antonio and, over the seventeenth and eighteenth centuries, to Los Angeles, San Francisco, and beyond (see Figure 1.1).

There was another important factor in the two countries' diverging paths toward development. In the American colonies, most of the indigenous peoples typically were driven away, and the villages and towns of the new colonists were largely populated by Europeans. The system of governance established in these towns, an outgrowth of Reformation England and the Continent, spread throughout the colonies and grew more liberal and democratic in nature. The American economy became a free-enterprise system based on private initiative and ownership, in which the state, and certainly the church, played small roles. This combination of liberal political and economic systems proved to be a powerful engine of growth for the new United States of America when it emerged late in the eighteenth century.

In contrast, the missionary priests who arrived in New Spain with the *conquistadores* labored to convert and co-opt the subjugated Aztecs, Mayans, Zapotecs, and other native peoples. Indigenous labor soon became vital to the sugar and wheat plantations, cattle ranches, gold and silver mines, and artisans' workshops of the viceregal economy. Although the social process in New Spain was inclusive in its co-optation of the indigenous peoples, it was also strictly hierarchical. Social privilege and political power were carefully measured by such criteria as one's rank in the Spanish nobility, the Church, the military, or the royal system of *encomiendas,* under which privileged *peninsulares* (Spaniards actually born in Spain) or *criollos* (Spaniards of "pure blood" born in New Spain) were given by the king's order a group of Indians to "care for"— which all too often meant to exploit unmercifully.

Much lower in the hierarchy of New Spain was the rapidly growing population of *mestizos,* those born of mixed Spanish and Indian heritage. While accepted as foremen in the mines, plantations, ranches, and small factories, or as skilled artisans and small merchants, they did not enjoy the social status or power of the *criollos*

Figure 1.1 Extent of the Aztec Empire, Viceroyalty, and Republic

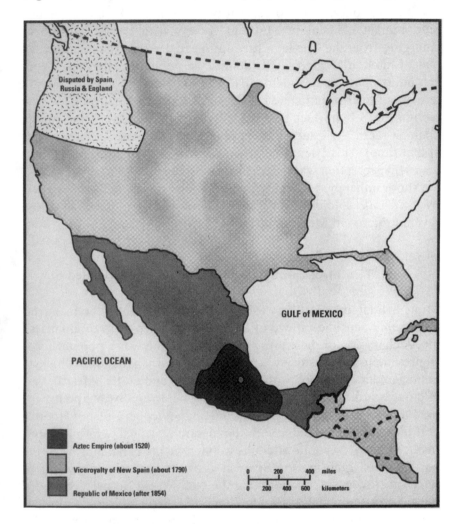

Disputed by Spain, Russia & England

GULF of MEXICO

PACIFIC OCEAN

Aztec Empire (about 1520)

Viceroyalty of New Spain (about 1790)

Republic of Mexico (after 1854)

0   200   400   miles
0   200   400   600   kilometers

or *peninsulares*. In 1800, the Mexican population of about 5 million was composed of some 2.5 million *indios,* 1 million *criollos* and *peninsulares,* and some 1.5 million *mestizos. Mestizos,* while accounting for only about 30 percent of the total in 1800, became the predominant element in Mexican society over the next century, emerging from the Mexican Revolution of 1910 as the central feature of modern Mexico's self-identity—a population that the Mexican philosopher and educator José Vasconcelos was later, in the aftermath of the revolution, to call *la raza cósmica* (the cosmic race, in recognition of the fact that the people represented all the major "human races"—"Caucasian, African, and Oriental"—as perceived at that time). This later view of the *mestizo* as the hallmark of Mexican self-perception was foreshadowed by the role *mestizos* played in the short, unhappy, but vitally important uprising in September 1810 by the *criollo* soldier-priest Father Miguel Hidalgo, one of the most revered figures in Mexican history.

The Mexican Struggle for Independence

Miguel Hidalgo y Costilla was born of *criollo* parents who managed a *hacienda* near the village of Dolores in the province of Guanajuato. A champion of the *mestizo* and the *indio,* he was a popular local figure due to his mastery of the Otomí Indian language and his encouragement and support of indigenous arts and crafts. After Father Hidalgo's ordination in 1776, he briefly held responsible posts, including that of rector of El Colegio de San Nicolás Obispo. His liberal ideas were unpopular with the hierarchy, whose wrath Hidalgo incurred in two separate attempts to improve the economic lot of his parishioners. Ignoring the Spanish Crown's ban on the making of wine or growing of silkworms in the New World (to protect its domestic trade monopoly), Hidalgo imported grape vines on one occasion and mulberry trees on another, only to see them destroyed by royal soldiers. He subsequently faced interrogation by the Spanish Inquisition.

By 1810 Hidalgo's main energies were devoted to conspiring for an uprising that he hoped would lead to Mexican independence. The center of the conspiracy was the city of Querétaro, some fifty miles southeast of Dolores on the road to Mexico City. His fellow conspirators, also *criollos,* planned to organize an insurrection and seize power from the *peninsulares* and their allies. Initially, as a ruse, they would declare their fealty to King Ferdinand VII, but *their* clear final purpose was independence.

Royal authorities learned of the plot and arrested three of the conspirators, including the wife of a former governor of an Indian district (*corregidor*), who nevertheless was able to get a warning to Hidalgo. This woman, Doña Josefa Ortíz de Domínguez (La Corregidora), thereby achieved her own place in Mexican history.

Acting on the timely warning of La Corregidora, the three remaining principal actors in the revolt—Father Hidalgo and two royal cavalry officers, Captain Ignacio Allende and Lieutenant Juan Aldama—decided to move immediately, and for outright independence. The church bells were rung at Dolores early in the morning of September 16, 1810, and the assembled crowd of *mestizos* and *indios* heard a stirring address by Father Hidalgo. He called for the expulsion of the Spaniards and an end to bad governance and the burdensome system of Indian tribute to the Crown.

Propelled by Hidalgo's fiery "Grito de Dolores" ("Cry of Dolores"), the ragtag army of 700 began its march to nearby San Miguel, where it was reinforced by Captain Allende's cavalry. By the time it reached Celaya on its way toward its first major goal—the capture of the strategic provincial capital city of Guanajuato—the tiny revolutionary band had grown to 20,000.

Hidalgo's army arrived at Guanajuato on September 28 to find that the *peninsulares* and their supporters had retired to a well-constructed granary, which they had fortified. At first, royalist soldiers held off the rebels, who attacked in numbers and suffered many casualties. However, the heroism of a miner, who managed to set fire to the main gates of the granary and thus permit a successful entry by the rebels into the fortified building, allowed Hidalgo's forces to achieve victory.

Despite the exhortations of Hidalgo and Allende, the surrender of Guanajuato was followed by violence and pillage by the victorious peasants and miners, who had been exploited for decades. The hated *encomenderos* and *hacendados* (landowners) were attacked and sometimes killed. These excesses redoubled the resolve of the viceroy in Mexico City to put down the rebellion. Hidalgo and his military commanders were excommunicated, and royalist forces were raised to march north and engage Hidalgo's troops. Meanwhile, Hidalgo's rebels had moved south to capture Valladolid and had defeated a small royalist force defending a strategic pass through the hills surrounding the Valley of Mexico.

The beginning of the end for Hidalgo came when, for reasons still not clear, he failed to take advantage of this opportunity to march on Mexico City and, by its capture, to successfully end the war for independence. Instead, perhaps not realizing the weakness of the royalists, he turned back, suffered a defeat at the hands of pursuing forces in Querétaro, and retreated to Guadalajara, where he was well received by the populace. Here he attempted to form a provisional government.

But a well-trained, well-equipped royalist army was soon on the outskirts of Guadalajara. Though outnumbered by the rebels, the army soundly defeated them and forced Hidalgo and his principal lieutenants to flee toward sanctuary in the United States. On their way to the border, they were intercepted by royalist forces, captured, and condemned to death. After their execution in June 1811, their heads were hung on the corners of the granary in Guanajuato as a warning to those who opposed the king of Spain.

While Hidalgo's rebellion was short-lived, his heroism and vision were vital precursors to the subsequent successful battles by another soldier-priest, José María Morelos, and many other heroes of the struggle for independence. This struggle came to a successful conclusion on September 28, 1821, with the ringing of church bells throughout Mexico City and the countryside to celebrate a peace treaty signed by the warring factions, and the installation of General Agustín Iturbide as the leader of the ruling military junta.

Independence: The Early Years

During the first forty years of its independence from Spain, Mexico reached its greatest territorial expansion. Over the same period, however, the country also suffered through more than thirty presidencies and military *golpes* (coups), to say nothing of the somewhat grotesque crowning of the Emperor of the Cactus Throne, Agustín I (formerly General Iturbide), on July 21, 1822, and his overthrow in 1823. Mexico became a republic, adopting the Constitution of 1824, which was based significantly on the U.S. Constitution.

This period was marked not so much by problems with the United States or other foreign nations as by profound internal changes. A power struggle ensued between the established landowners, who had survived the struggle for independence, and reformist liberals, who had a modern vision of the state. The confusion created by the collapse of the Spanish Empire and the emergence of an independent government resulted in weakness and ambiguity, and created an atmosphere of potential conflict between Mexico and its northern neighbor. Indeed, earlier U.S. dealings with the Spaniards, such as the disputes over the Louisiana Purchase of 1803[1] and the Florida Purchase of 1819, had already begun a chain of events that in a few decades was to bring the two countries to war.

The boundary between Texas and the Louisiana Territory was a major source of irritation. In 1812, the United States declared war on England and announced the annexation of Florida. This action raised questions about the territory lying between the United States's Florida and Spain's Texas. It was already becoming apparent that the strength of the Spanish Empire was waning in the New World and that the United States was in a strong position to negotiate transcontinental frontiers. Finally, on February 22, 1819, a treaty was negotiated according to which the United States recognized Spanish sovereignty over territory that is now California, Arizona, New Mexico, and Texas in exchange for Spanish recognition of existing transcontinental boundaries. This Adams–de Onís Treaty (Tratado Transcontinental) resulted in recognition by a major European state of the United States as a continent-wide power (see Figure 1.2).

The Struggle for Texas

Relations between the United States and Mexico were formally initiated in February 1822 when Joel R. Poinsett of South Carolina was sent to Mexico as the first U.S. minister. This was followed a few months later by the appointment of José Manuel Zozaya as Mexico's minister to Washington. Poinsett had learned Spanish through earlier sojourns to Mexico and elsewhere in Latin America as a special agent of the secretary of state and amateur plant collector. (Our familiar Christmas plant, the poinsettia, is named after him.)

Poinsett understood early that the most grave difficulty between the two young nations was the disposition of the unruly territory of Texas, which was already being settled by a few slaveholding

Figure 1.2 Significant Changes in the U.S.-Mexico Border

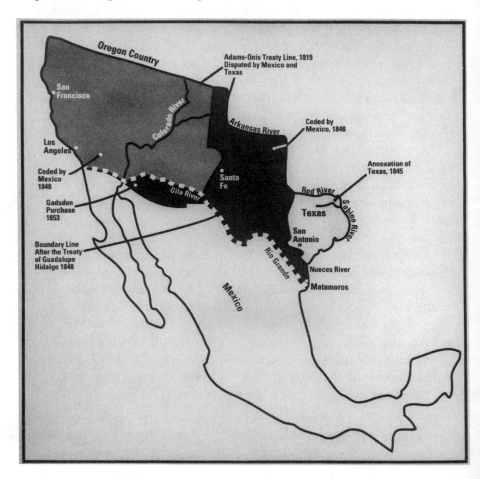

emigrants from the southern United States. These settlers seemed unlikely to live contentedly under Mexican laws, which required among other things an obligatory conversion to Catholicism and use of the Spanish language in the conduct of all official business.

Poinsett was also shrewd enough to see the Mexican Empire of Agustín I as ephemeral in the face of republican sentiments and "imperial" inefficiency and greed. The then-current Washington policy of encouraging New World colonies to declare their independence from Europe resulted in the premature recognition of the Mexican Empire on January 27, 1823, just two months before Iturbide abdicated and the Mexican Empire became a short-lived memory.

This same sentiment was manifested more dramatically several months later. On December 2, 1823, U.S. president James Monroe proclaimed what came to be known as the Monroe Doctrine, warning the European powers that further colonization—or, indeed, any form of intervention in the Americas—would be unacceptable to the United States. This policy remained effective during the following forty years, lapsing only when the United States became immersed in its civil war.

Though brilliant, the Spanish-speaking Poinsett soon found himself more involved than he should have been in Mexico's internal affairs, and was accused by Mexicans of meddling. He was notably critical, in private at least, of Emperor Iturbide. The latter, a military strongman, was unpopular with his people, but there was still resentment when the criticism came from an American diplomat.

Meddling aside, Poinsett was clearly a more competent diplomat than his successor, Anthony Butler, who arrived on the scene early in 1830. Butler, a rude and sometimes violent man, was the antithesis of the courtly Poinsett. He early attempted to pressure Mexico to change the border to the United States's advantage. (For example, it was proposed to move the border from the 42nd to the 37th parallel in the vicinity of the West Coast so as to include in U.S. territory the port city of San Francisco.) In exchange, Mexico was to receive a sum of money to be negotiated. Butler was also given instructions to inquire into a purchase price for Texas.

From 1825 until 1830 the situation in the northeast of the Mexican state of Tejas-Coahuila, now part of Texas, grew ever more volatile. The heavy inflow of American colonists—led by Robert Leftwich with 200 families, Hayden Edwards with 800 families,

Green Dewitt with 300 families, and others—overwhelmed the Mexican settlers and the feeble Mexican military garrisons spread thinly throughout the immense and almost totally undeveloped area. All this was exacerbated by the slavery issue, one that a generation later was to play an important role in the American Civil War.

In any event, unrest was rampant in the Tejas of the 1820s, and a strong local leadership was emerging. It was to the advantage of neither the emerging Texan leadership nor the beleaguered Mexican authorities when, in 1826, the maverick Hayden Edwards proclaimed from Nacogdoches the birth of the "Republic of Fredonia." Prompt joint action by a leading settler, Stephen Austin, and the local Mexican authorities soon put this rebellion down, and relations between the Mexican government and the Texans actually improved for a while. This changed dramatically on September 15, 1829, when slavery was abolished throughout all the territory of Mexico, including, of course, Texas. Colonists' resentment and restiveness caused the Mexican government to offer a carrot: All existing slaves could be maintained, but their children were free and no other slaves were to be allowed into Mexico in the future. To evade this policy, the colonists brought in black slaves by means of phony work contracts. In response to this widespread tactic, the Mexican government, in April 1830, banned all further immigration from the United States. (Mexico continued to welcome European immigrants during this time.)

In response, Stephen Austin, who had supported the Mexican authorities in the Fredonia incident, organized a series of regional political conventions in 1831–1832 that culminated in a decision to send Austin to Mexico City to petition for the establishment of Texas as a separate *estado* (state) within the Republic of Mexico. This would free the Texans from control by the neighboring state of Coahuila, whose governor had been given authority over them, and whose absentee rule (there is no record of a visit to Texas by a governor of Tejas-Coahuila), the Texans felt, had been capricious. The mission to the Mexican capital failed, and Austin was imprisoned for more than a year when a confidential report he was sending back to Texas was intercepted.

By the time he was released, Austin had come to believe that further accommodation with the ever-changing governance in Mexico City was impossible. (During this period the average tenure for a Mexican president was less than a year.) Accordingly, he began the discreet purchase of arms in preparation for the next fateful step: a fight for independence. While it is not surprising that the Anglo settlers in Texas proved eager to join his enterprise, it is remarkable that even many settlers who had their origins in Mexico favored independence from what they saw as the weak and vacillating government in Mexico City.

It was not long before the battles for Texas independence were being fought under such leaders as William B. Travis, who seized Anáhuac (now Galveston) on June 30, 1835. This was followed in December by the surrender of San Antonio Bejar (now San Antonio). A formal declaration of independence was signed on March 1, 1836. There were setbacks, such as Mexican general Antonio López de Santa Anna's capture of San Antonio's Alamo, and his summary execution of its defenders, including Davy Crockett and Jim Bowie. But the war for Texan independence ground inexorably on and was capped by the victory, at San Jacinto, of Texan troops led by Sam Houston over the Mexican army led by Santa Anna. The Mexican general (who was also serving one of his many presidential terms at the time) later recounted his surprise at not being executed after his surrender at San Jacinto, but Houston had other plans for him.

Under the duress of the moment, Santa Anna signed two agreements pledging him to withdraw his troops and to accept Texan independence and its boundary at the Rio Grande (to Mexicans, el Río Bravo y Grande del Norte) (see Figure 1.3), and, even more controversially, to attempt to persuade his government to abide by these accords. The treaty was repudiated by his government, and Santa Anna's capitulation brought him into temporary disrepute in Mexico, but he was later to rise again and again as a war hero and several-time president. Although Mexican government officials talked of reconquering Texas, internal weakness and lack of federal funds precluded any major military action.

Mexicans were highly resentful of the loss of Texas and blamed the United States for the disaster, claiming that without the arms and other supplies pouring in from the United States, the Texans could not have prosecuted the war for independence so successfully. Furthermore, in December 1845 the U.S. Congress formally annexed Texas, making it the twenty-eighth state in the Union. The actions leading to annexation prompted Mexico to sever diplomatic relations with the United States for a period.

Figure 1.3   The U.S.-Texas Border Dispute

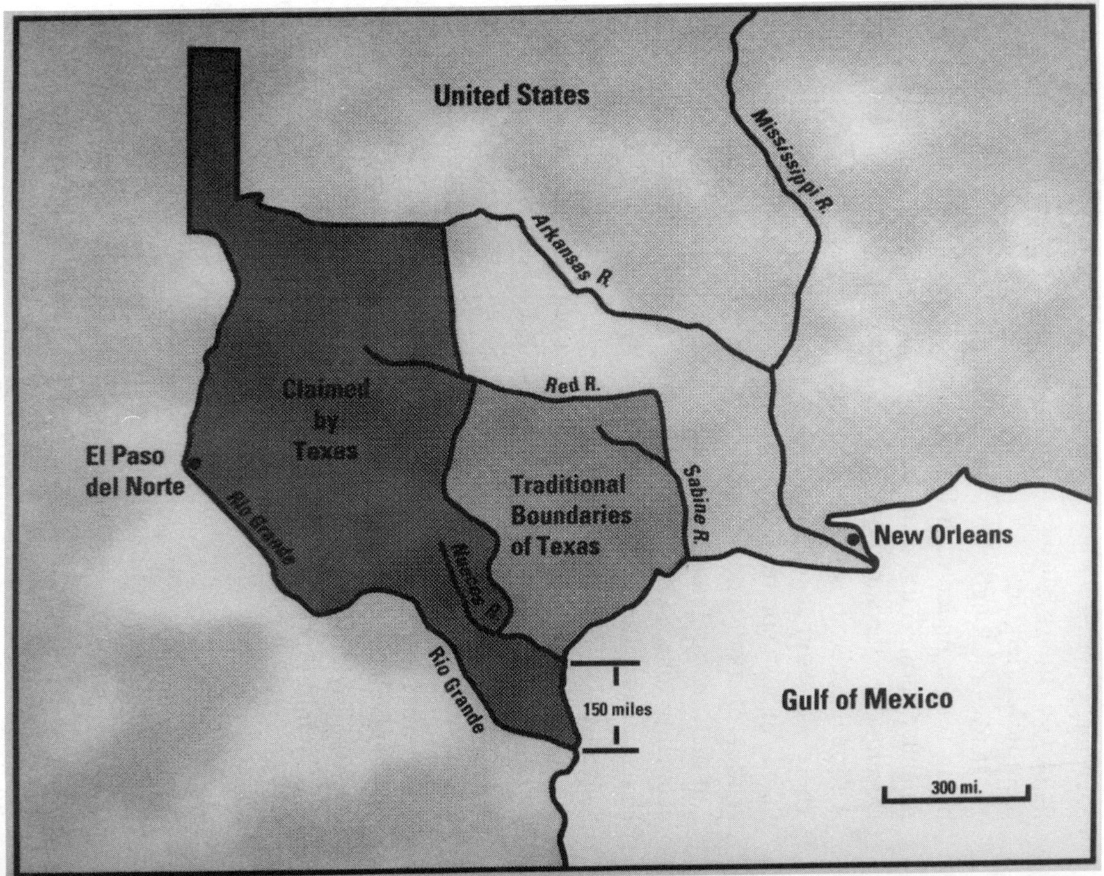

The War of the North American Invasion

In the view of many Mexican historians, the secession of Texas from Mexico and its subsequent annexation by the United States was only the first of a series of calculated steps that led in 1846 to what Mexicans call the "War of the North American Invasion" and Americans call the "Mexican War." This war had its roots in what the American journalist John L. O'Sullivan, in the December 1845 issue of the *Democratic Review,* called "the right of our Manifest Destiny to overspread and to possess the whole continent, which Providence has given us for the development of the great experiment of Liberty." The war was not long in coming.

It is clear in retrospect that by the autumn of 1845, when American president James Polk sent a special envoy, John Slidell, to Mexico, Polk was already prepared to initiate hostilities. Polk must have anticipated that Slidell's offer to purchase what is now western Texas, New Mexico, Arizona, and California for $30 million would be seen as totally unacceptable to the Mexicans. Indeed, the Mexicans had rejected many times in the past the sale of Mexican territory at any price. In any case, internal problems in Mexico, including yet another coup d'état, would have prevented any formal response to Slidell's offer at the time it was presented. On January 13, 1846, at a time when a new and inexperienced Mexican government refused to meet with Slidell and claimed that Mexican territory included all of Texas, President Polk issued orders to General Zachary Taylor to establish a military presence along the Rio Grande.

By mid-April the construction of Fort Brown, across the river from the Mexican city of Matamoros, had been undertaken. The U.S. presence was burgeoning. The "War of the North American Invasion" began on April 25, 1846, when a Mexican cavalry unit crossed the river and fired on a patrol of U.S. soldiers on the banks of the Río Bravo. Eleven Yankees were killed, six wounded, and sixty-three taken prisoner. General Taylor promptly announced that "hostilities may now be considered as commenced," and, with a U.S. cavalry force soon augmented by several regiments of Texan and Louisianan volunteers, moved slowly and deliberately south to capture Monterrey, the regional capital of the state of Nuevo León.

Meanwhile, a battle plan executed by General Winfield Scott, the commander in chief of U.S. forces, was under way on several fronts.

General Stephen Kearny's forces in Missouri marched on Santa Fe, captured it, proceeded through Arizona, and engaged Mexican forces defending California. The U.S. Pacific fleet under Commodore John D. Sloat was ordered to seize San Francisco and Monterey. These operations were successfully completed and California was secured in January 1847. In the Gulf of Mexico, U.S. Navy units under Commodore David Conner successfully blockaded Mexican ports.

Not surprisingly, the multifront attack by well-equipped and trained U.S. forces caused great dismay and political unrest in the Mexican capital. General Santa Anna, once again called to serve as president and commander in chief, found himself faced with substantial American armies in the north and south, his ports blockaded, and a much-divided Mexican body politic. An ill-advised effort by Santa Anna's predecessors to finance the war by seizing Church property and possessions caused a massive reaction on the part of many conservative, influential Mexicans, to say nothing of the powerful clergy. Even though the government soon gave up this tactic, much resentment remained, and the longstanding division between the clergy and landowners on the one hand and reformist liberals on the other was exacerbated.

As the war progressed with a series of U.S. victories, Santa Anna was wise and courageous enough to realize that further resistance to the American forces would only cause greater suffering for his people. Thus, his government leaders entered into negotiations with Nicholas P. Trist, a personal representative sent by President Polk. These negotiations were soon stalemated, in part by the intransigence of Mexicans who did not share Santa Anna's views, and the campaign began anew. After a bloody struggle, General Scott captured Mexico City on September 14, 1847, effectively bringing the Mexican War to a conclusion. Although many brave young soldiers on both sides were lost in the fighting, the campaign for Mexico City is best remembered by Mexicans today for the heroic defense of historic Chapultepec Castle, located on a strategic high point with a commanding view of the city. The castle was defended by nine hundred soldiers and forty-seven heroic cadets of the military college located there. Four of the teenaged cadets were wounded, thirty-seven were taken prisoner, and six died in the battle. Annual ceremonies still mark the event in Chapultepec Park, where a monument to *los niños héroes* has been erected.

Following General Scott's victory in Mexico City, several months of arduous negotiations between the two countries led to the signing, on February 2, 1848, of the Treaty of Guadalupe Hidalgo. It was ratified by both governments at the end of May 1848. Under the terms of the treaty, Mexico gave up all claims to Texas and ceded New Mexico, Arizona, Nevada, California, and parts of Colorado— virtually all its territory north of the Rio Grande—to the United States. In return for the cession of more than half its territory, Mexico received a cash payment of $15 million and relief from all outstanding claims by U.S. citizens, such claims to be considered and paid by the U.S. government.

But Scott's victory brought more than huge territorial gains to the United States. The siege of Chapultepec and the death of *los niños héroes,* which have epitomized the "War of the North American Invasion" to generations of Mexicans, created in Mexico a degree of hatred, humiliation, and xenophobia—particularly anti-Americanism—that remained strong for generations and has never fully dissipated. The failure of Americans today to understand the legacy of the Mexican War—indeed, most Americans seem unacquainted even with its broad outlines—stands as a barrier to the awareness of Mexican sensitivities so vital to a healthy relationship between the neighboring countries.

The sad end of the affair did not play out until 1853, when Santa Anna, serving as Mexico's president for the eleventh time in his long and stormy career, and much in need of ready cash, agreed to the Gadsden Purchase. He thus raised $10 million by the sale of 30,000 square miles of territory in what is now southern New Mexico and southeastern Arizona. This so sickened the Mexican people that they rose against Santa Anna, who went into his final exile, never to reappear on the scene.

The Presidency of Benito Juárez: A New Era of Liberal Reform Begins

A group of liberal thinkers that emerged after Santa Anna's downfall proclaimed the Revolution of Ayutla late in 1853. Headed by an old rebel leader, Juan Alvarez, as the provisional president succeeding Santa Anna, the group called for a constitutional convention to establish a liberal, democratic government, and the beginning of a new era of governance in Mexico. In the summer of 1855, President Alvarez embarked on a period of government restructuring called La Reforma. Among other things, La Reforma abolished *fueros,* an old privilege of Spanish origin that had long exempted members of the military and the clergy from trial by civilian courts. Up to now, neither military courts-martial nor clerical hearings often resulted in justice being done in the cases of military men or members of the clergy accused of common crimes. According to La Reforma, however, they were henceforth to be tried by civilian courts.

The liberal movement that gave birth to La Reforma significantly redirected the course of Mexican history. In the aftermath of the humiliation of the lost war with the United States, Mexico was fortunate to be able to turn for leadership to one of her finest historical figures—Benito Juárez, a full-blooded Zapotec Indian who rose from humble beginnings to serve as a liberal governor of Oaxaca in 1848. By 1855, Juárez, who had been exiled to New Orleans by Santa Anna, was back as private secretary to the provisional president, Juan Alvarez, and was one of a new triumvirate of liberal leaders of the country, along with Melchor Ocampo, the liberal governor of Michoacán and a philosopher with European leanings, and Santos Degollado, a general in the revolt that overthrew Santa Anna for the last time, and later governor of Jalisco.

The principal institutional base of La Reforma was the Constitution of 1857, which had been drafted by the liberal, anticlerical leadership. The leadership of the Catholic Church opposed the new constitution, which had failed to make the Church the official state religion and had established a free, nonsectarian educational system. Conservatives and a part of the Mexican army agreed, and subsequent tensions resulted in the War of the Reform (1858–1860). When the revolt began, Juárez was arrested by the army but subsequently escaped. In the ensuing chaos caused by the resignation of the constitutional president, he legally assumed the power of the presidency. After a long and bitter struggle, the liberals prevailed.

President Juárez was then faced with myriad problems caused by the War of the Reform: inflation, abrasive social frictions, widespread destruction of infrastructure, and a steep drop in agricultural and industrial production. In an effort to ameliorate these pressing problems, Juárez suspended all payments on Mexico's foreign debt.

This action, misunderstood to some extent, unfortunately met with a powerful, immediate, and negative reaction from the European powers, who quickly condemned the Mexican president. Much to their later chagrin, England and Spain joined with France in organizing a jointly manned fleet with troops on board and orders to capture Mexican ports and to exact payment of the foreign debt.

While England and Spain wished only to seize customs payments and to pressure Juárez into working out a debt payment plan, France, under Emperor Napoleon III, had something more sinister in mind: a new conquest of Mexico, an end to the liberal government by the leaders of La Reforma, and Mexico's rule by a European "emperor" of Napoleon III's choosing. Despite the protestations of the governments of Queen Victoria and Queen Isabella II, the French emperor persisted, eventually precipitating the withdrawal of English and Spanish troops. This left the French free to carry out their dramatic and far-reaching plan of armed intervention.

Early Mexican Victory at Puebla: The "Cinco de Mayo"

Shortly thereafter, some 6,500 French troops under the veteran general Charles Ferdinand Latrille de Lorencz marched from the port of Veracruz to take the old colonial city of Puebla, thought to be filled with conservative sympathizers. But President Juárez had other plans. He sent a capable Mexican general, Ignacio Zaragoza, and some 2,000 veteran troops to defend the city. The Mexicans acquitted themselves well. On May 5, 1862, a frenzied French attack ordered by General Lorencz was beaten off. Having sustained heavy casualties, the invaders retreated to Orizaba, leaving the Mexicans with a day still celebrated wherever they may gather—Cinco de Mayo.

Alas, this famous victory proved to be ephemeral. Napoleon III, hearing of the humiliating defeat, ordered 30,000 reinforcements to sail immediately to Mexico and to overwhelm the Juárez government, still weak from the devastation of the War of the Reform and under attack from within by conservative clergy, the landed gentry, and pro-French monarchists. The French force, several times larger in size than before, surrounded Puebla and bombarded it into submission,

meanwhile sending special forces to interdict the Mexico City–
Puebla railways and prevent Juárez from sending supplies to his beleaguered city. Once Puebla fell, in May 1863, the French army en-
countered little resistance on its march to Mexico City.

Initially determined to defend Mexico City, Juárez was convinced by his military advisors that it would be wiser to abandon the
city to the French army and set up a new capital in remote and more
easily defended San Luís Potosí. The French army entered Mexico
City on June 10, 1863, to the cheers of the conservatives, and a Te
Deum was offered in their honor in Mexico City's magnificent
cathedral.

The Short, Unhappy Reign of Emperor Maximilian

Shortly thereafter, Napoleon III and his conservative Mexican allies
called on the young archduke Ferdinand Maximilian of Hapsburg to
serve as emperor of Mexico. The Mexicans who paid the Austrian
archduke a visit in his Adriatic palace assured him that there was a
groundswell of popular fervor in Mexico for him to become emperor, and he agreed to do so. It was not long before he and his
young wife Charlotte (Carlota, to the Mexicans) were sailing for
Mexico.

Mexican Church leaders and other conservatives were delighted
at the arrival of the new rulers. They fully anticipated that Maximilian would move quickly in their support, for example to annul the
laws of La Reforma and to return Church property confiscated by
previous liberal governments. But the new emperor had other
thoughts. Himself a member of the Masonic order, and hoping to
gain favor with the liberals, he did not think it wise to permit the
archconservative Church to regain its old property and perquisites.
Not only did he spurn the entreaties of a papal nuncio recently arrived from Rome, he actually called on the Church for some emergency loans to help meet the expenses of his new government.

The fact that the emperor was holding the Church and its allies
at arm's length, however, did little to mollify the liberals, who had
been driven from Mexico City by French troops. Juárez, whose Republican government had been recognized de jure by U.S. president
Abraham Lincoln, moved his capital north from San Luís Potosí to

Chihuahua and, finally, to El Paso del Norte (Ciudad Juárez today) as pressures from French troops grew.

Lincoln's support of Juárez was necessarily tempered by the exigencies of the American Civil War. For one thing, military assistance for Juárez and his beleaguered Republican army was impractical at a time when Union forces were stretched thin. For another, Lincoln—who might otherwise have overtly supported the Mexican Republicans—did not want to risk an angry Napoleon III intervening on the side of the Confederacy. Thus, during the 1861–1864 period America's hands were more or less tied.

The year 1865 was to prove fateful for Maximilian. On the domestic front, lulled by his army's apparent successes against the Republicans and acting on a false rumor that Juárez had fled to the United States, he signed on October 3 the infamous Decreto de la Bandera Negra (Black Flag Decree), which called for the summary execution within twenty-four hours of anyone caught bearing arms and opposing his regime, including "all persons belonging to armed bands or corps, not legally authorized." Thousands of Mexican soldiers captured while fighting honorably for the Republic were executed under the terms of this terrible imperial decree, which, not surprisingly, resulted in a deep surge of opposition to the French-imposed emperor and a renewed dedication to his overthrow.

The Union victory in the American Civil War in 1865 was another blow to Maximilian. No longer concerned about French reaction, and influenced by Secretary of State William Seward and General Ulysses S. Grant, the U.S. administration felt free to encourage Juárez and to support the Republican cause more openly. Thousands of tons of surplus war materiel, purchased on credit by Juárez, were soon finding their way through circuitous routes to the Republican army. Accustomed to battle and lured by good salaries, about three thousand Union veterans of the American Civil War joined the Republican army and fought side by side with the troops of Benito Juárez against Emperor Maximilian. The emperor, in turn, recruited some two thousand veterans of the American Confederacy to fight on his side.

Meanwhile, Empress Carlota, sensing that the tide was turning against her husband's government and burdened with news that French support was weakening, returned to Europe to plead her husband's cause with Napoleon III and the pope. Not only did both the

French court and the Vatican ignore her pleas (the pope wondered aloud why Maximilian had not returned Church lands and properties), but a group of courtiers and papal advisors decided that she was suffering from a mental illness. Thus Empress Marie Charlotte Amelie, daughter of the king and queen of Belgium and cousin of Queen Victoria, was confined to a Belgian home where, judged to be insane, she lived on for sixty long and tragic years.

Nothing went well for Maximilian after Carlota's departure. Spurred on by a new flow of U.S. support and by the vacillating policies of Napoleon III, the implacable man who had sworn to overcome Maximilian—Benito Juárez—resumed the offensive early in 1866. By the year's end, Republican generals had captured such strategic sites as Monterrey, Tampico, Guaymas, Guadalajara, and Juárez's birthplace, Oaxaca.

The Mexican emperor, heartsick about the French perfidy (Napoleon III was withdrawing his troops and urging Maximilian's abdication, to which the proud Hapsburg would not agree) and Carlota's confinement in Belgium, courageously made a final and clandestine journey to the north to take personal command of the last contingent of the Imperial army, which was holding out in the city of Querétaro. Shortly after his arrival there, the Imperial garrison was completely encircled by a much larger force of Republican troops. The emperor was faced with the choice of either surrendering or attempting to flee alone through enemy lines and deserting his remaining troops. On May 15, 1867, Maximilian turned over his sword to the Republican general Mariano Escobedo.

Despite worldwide appeals that Maximilian be spared, the military tribunal convened to hear his case convicted him of capital crimes, including the issuance of the infamous Black Flag Decree. The death sentence, reviewed and approved by President Juárez, was carried out by firing squad on June 19, 1867.

Mexico Enters the Modern Age

On July 15, 1867, in stark and deliberate contrast to his predecessor, whose entourage was marked by gilded carriages and pomp, Benito Juárez arrived in Mexico City in the simple black carriage that had carried him through years of struggle against the French intervention.[2]

Figure 1.4 Historic Cities of Mexico

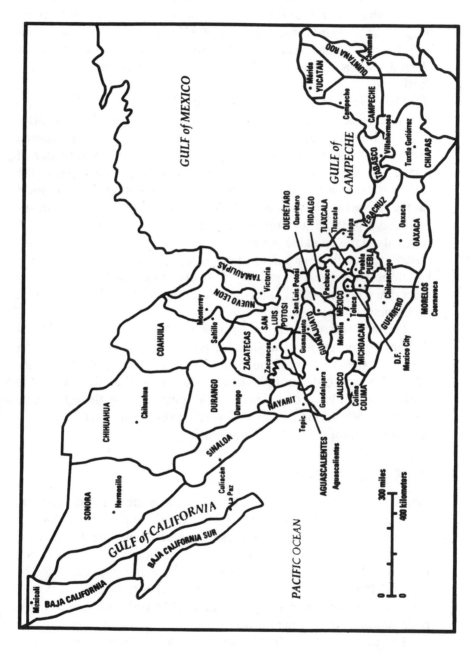

Juárez wasted little time on the triumphal ceremonies greeting the restoration of the Republic. He soon announced his candidacy for an unprecedented third term as president. (His first two terms had been largely spent in the struggle against the French.) He was easily re-elected and, on December 1, 1867, was sworn in as president for the third time.

The government of the newly restored Republic was faced with an immense economic and social challenge. The rebuilding job after years of French intervention and war was enormous. Juárez named Matías Romero to the most important cabinet position, minister of finance. As Juárez's official representative in Washington during the early 1860s, Romero had been instrumental in gaining U.S. support for the liberation of Mexico. A skilled economic planner, he soon announced a program to improve Mexican infrastructure (highways, railroads, dams, potable water projects) and the development of industry, agriculture, and natural resources—particularly mining, to which he gave a special priority. Romero sought and obtained considerable foreign credits and began to look for foreign private direct investment for these projects.

Private investors were nervous about the stability and safety of their proposed projects in Mexico, particularly in the countryside. However, the creation of the *rurales* (federal rural police who enforced law and order in the countryside), as well as the credibility of Romero and his economic team, did much to allay these fears; by the late 1860s foreign investors were traveling all over Mexico in search of mining and other opportunities.

The Porfiriato: 1876–1910

Mexico was desolate in mid-July 1872, when the popular President Juárez died suddenly of a heart attack. His successor, Sebastián Lerdo de Tejada, who was subsequently elected president in his own right in October 1872, continued Juárez's policies. However, he was less effective and more vulnerable to the growing opposition led by General Porfirio Díaz, a war hero who had served brilliantly as a cavalry commander at the Battle of Puebla and had subsequently risen rapidly through the officer corps.

President Lerdo de Tejada, though widely admired, did not have the popular support to counter the military strength of General Díaz.

Consequently, when Díaz launched a revolt in mid-1876, he had little difficulty in prevailing against the forces of Lerdo de Tejada. Díaz occupied Mexico City on November 21, allowing his adversary safe conduct to Veracruz and a steamship waiting to carry him into exile in the United States.

Porfirio Díaz began his thirty-four-year (direct and indirect) reign by drawing heavily on plans for economic stability and social development undertaken successfully by his two predecessors, Juárez and Lerdo de Tejada. The years of La Reforma had laid a solid base for economic growth and development. Díaz, wishing for a dramatic increase in foreign investment and American goodwill in general, quickly came to an agreement on some longstanding claims by U.S. citizens and paid off more than $4 million during 1877 alone. As conditions began to stabilize in Mexico, Díaz called for elections, easily winning a four-year presidential term.

Following his election, Díaz continued to work to improve U.S.-Mexico relations. One of his first moves was to hold a series of meetings with American officials on such border problems as marauding *bandidos* who would attack settlements and steal cattle on the U.S. side of the border. He also established a mechanism for inviting U.S. traders and investors to Mexico, and had new legislation passed that improved the investment climate. He also opened three new Mexican consulates along the border (at El Paso, Laredo, and Eagle Pass) to stimulate trade and investment.

Favorably impressed by the new regime, American president Rutherford B. Hayes recognized the Díaz government in the spring of 1877. Investment and trade slowly began to build, and U.S. and European investment soon emerged as a principal engine of growth in the Mexican economy, for example, in mining, petroleum, agriculture, and industry.

Mexico's leader was faced with a political dilemma in 1880. He had scored his initial triumph in part on the basis of the slogan of *no-reelección* (literally, "no reelection"—but interpreted by Díaz as meaning no *consecutive* reelection). Thus, to honor his commitment, he needed, and soon discovered, a suitable stand-in to run for the presidency while Díaz managed affairs from behind the scenes. His candidate was General Manuel González, who served nominally as president from 1880 to 1884, in a term marked by petty scandals. Needless to say, Don Porfirio had no difficulty in presenting himself for the presidency in 1884, and, as El Indispensable, easily winning back the office.

Díaz is often misunderstood as a sycophant playing for the favor of U.S. and other foreign governments and investors. In fact—an interesting paradox—he saw the opening of the Mexican economy to international trade and investment as a way to strengthen the country against undue foreign influence. Under the positivist rubric of *orden y progreso* ("order and progress"), Díaz began the immense task of building modern Mexico. Indeed, despite all the criticism that has been leveled at his regime, Díaz's first decades in office were marked by extensive economic development. He took on a huge array of tasks within the period of a few years. Thousands of new factories were built, creating substantial employment. Mail service was greatly improved, and the mining industry was modernized. Modern agricultural methods were introduced; the railway system was extended and upgraded; telegraph lines and dock facilities were built; public education and health care were expanded and modernized.

Díaz also played his political hand well. While a convinced liberal, he was able to come to a satisfactory accommodation with the Church, in part by allowing it to hold on to and even modestly expand its properties, including the establishment of new convents and seminaries. As soon as he felt more secure politically, he had the *no-reelección* provisions of the law rescinded, so that he no longer had to rely on straw men in his exercise of power.

The Mexican economy began to boom under Díaz, who was able to pay off the foreign debt by 1890 and to balance the federal budget by 1894, even generating a slight surplus. U.S. and British oil companies established a profitable oil industry that paid taxes into the Mexican government coffers. By 1908 a vast railway system crisscrossed Mexico, and Mexican reserves had risen to what was in those days the huge sum of 70 million gold pesos. More than 3,000 mines—840 of them foreign, mostly American—were producing silver, gold, copper, zinc, iron, and lead, making Mexico one of the world's top producers. Electrical plants were built; electric lights and streetcars became common in Mexico's major cities.

This economic growth was highly asymmetrical, though. Urban dwellers and the middle and upper classes were the principal recipients, while the rural population outside the modern agricultural sector was virtually unaffected by the progress. Nevertheless, by 1910 Mexico represented a respectable, emerging economy.

Notes

1. The United States purchased Louisiana from France, which had acquired the territory from Spain by the treaty of October 1, 1800. The vagueness of the boundaries of Louisiana covered by the purchase resulted in a serious dispute.

2. This carriage may now be seen in a place of honor at Chapultepec Castle.

2

Emerging Mexico: 1910–1970

Debate continues in Mexico to this day about the role of Porfirio Díaz in Mexico's development. Was he a helpful force in Mexico's modernization, acting in the best interests of his country? Or was he, as held by some historians, a simple doormat for foreign capitalists? In the judgment of Daniel Cosío Villegas, one of Mexico's foremost historians, Don Porfirio for all his faults was no lackey; he acted in what he believed to be the need for his country to enter the twentieth century as a modern, industrial nation.

During the boom period of the *porfiriato* (1876–1910), an astounding $2 billion in foreign private direct investment, half of it American, was attracted to Mexico. These investments, involving thousands of U.S. and Mexican firms and individuals, from the widest range of commercial interests, were an important factor in the growth of economic and social interdependence between the United States and Mexico.

By 1909, when William Howard Taft became the first U.S. president to visit Mexico, this billion-dollar U.S. investment in Mexican enterprises had spread from oil and gas, railroads, mines, and textiles to service industries such as insurance companies and banks. Similar investments had flowed in from Europe, chiefly Great Britain, Germany, and France. The Mexican economy had grown robust and was internationally respected.

Díaz inherited a country with only 640 kilometers of railway track and left it with 20,000 kilometers extending throughout the country—although, as critics remarked, rail lines were planned by foreign engineers and tended to join industrial and mining centers and ignore the needs of the countryside. To limit the rapidly growing influence of British and U.S. interests in the transportation industry,

José I. Limantour, a brilliant treasury secretary, created the Ferro-carriles Nacionales de México, the national railroad company, and, by an adroit combination of persuasion and veiled warnings, obtained for Mexico a part interest in foreign investments in the railway sector. During the *porfiriato,* huge strides in mining production also made Mexico a leading world exporter of silver, copper, and other metals and minerals.

There was a dark side to the *porfiriato,* which contributed heavily to the unrest that led to its downfall. Díaz and his followers adopted the positivist philosophy of Auguste Comte, which called for "order and progress." Of these two objectives, Díaz, a career military officer and a hero of the Battle of Puebla, stressed "order." He used the iron hand of his military and the dreaded *rurales,* or paramilitary national police, to keep peace in factories and in the countryside. These forces could be counted on to side with landowners and industrialists threatened with labor dissent, which was kept to a minimum during the long years of the *porfiriato.* The *rurales* and the military were the backbone of Díaz's "generation of peace."

In the rural Mexico of Porfirio Díaz, some eight hundred estate owners (*hacendados*) controlled more than 90 percent of arable land and exploited some 5 million landless peasants on their vast farms and ranches. Taking into account the complex payment arrangements for the *peones*—and the custom of deducting food and other "expenses" from their pay before they received it—it has been estimated that their actual salary was about 30¢ per day.

Conditions were not much better in Mexico's rapidly expanding industrial sector. Factory workers typically were employed for six 12-hour shifts per week, for which they earned about $7. Safety conditions were poor, and industrial accidents and deaths were common.

Even so, the wage differential between the rural and urban industrial sectors was enough to create a steady flow of migration from the land to the cities that would continue, though at a decreasing rate, until the present time, providing Mexican industry over the decades with an excess supply of workers. This has permitted rapid industrial growth while keeping wages down to a historical level of about one-tenth of equivalent U.S. wages.

Nevertheless, one-half of Mexico's population, including indigenous peoples in remote areas, lived throughout the *porfiriato* very much as they had for a thousand years, largely unaffected by the economic boom of 1880–1910. For those privileged to enjoy it, the *porfiriato* was a time of cultural growth in literature, poetry, and the arts. The architecture of the period was typically eclectic, with liberal borrowings from French and Italian styles. When the Palacio de Bellas Artes was built in the early years of the new century, its mammoth stage was adorned by a 20-ton glass curtain designed in the United States by Louis Tiffany, along with an elaborate steel mechanism to open and close it.[1]

To foreign investors, Díaz was a godsend: He paid off the national debt in full, created a national bank that could deal efficiently with foreign investors and traders, and offered internal order to foreign businessmen interested in Mexican investment and trade opportunities.

The Mexican Revolution

A narrow few at the top of Mexico's elite—including the Catholic Church, which profited immensely from its privileged position during the *porfiriato*—enjoyed great economic success. In stark contrast stood a growing number of intellectuals, workers, and peasants, led by such revolutionary heroes as the Flores Magón brothers, who hated the regime. Even after their organization of strikes and demonstrations in Mexico led to their exile to the United States, the Flores Magón brothers continued to publish their radical workers' newspaper *Regeneración*. For this, at the insistence of the Mexican government they were charged and convicted of violation of U.S. neutrality laws and imprisoned for three years in Arizona.

As early as 1906, the activities of the Flores Magón group and a critical number of other labor organizers and agitators were starting to weaken the industrial base of the *porfiriato*. More than four hundred strikes and other labor actions in Mexican industries and mines between 1906 and 1910 heralded the beginning of the end for the old regime. The situation was exacerbated by an ill-advised interview Díaz gave to an American journalist, James Creelman. In the interview, the aging dictator indicated that, after thirty-four years on the stage or in the wings of power, he would not seek reelection in the 1910 presidential race. This "announcement," which Díaz later tried unsuccessfully to retract, stirred up the opposition at a time when unrest in the urban industrial and rural areas was peaking. A greatly respected Mexican aristocrat from the north was quick to take advantage of the uncertain situation.

Francisco I. Madero, a wealthy landowner of pronounced liberal political views, captured great popular attention and support all over the country with a series of statements on the Mexican presidential succession of 1910. Although Madero did not explicitly call for Díaz's overthrow (he suggested that Díaz, as an elder statesman and patriot, should see the advantages of voluntary retirement), through his writings and speeches Madero was converted into a national hero. In 1910 Madero was chosen as the presidential candidate of a number of opposition parties, including one calling for a single presidential term with no possibility of reelection for the lifetime of the incumbent.

Madero's meteoric rise to popularity—he toured Mexico in his election campaign train, speaking to audiences measured in the tens of thousands—did not go unnoticed by the Díaz authorities. They had him arrested in June 1910 and imprisoned on trumped-up charges of "fomenting rebellion and insulting the President of the Republic." In subsequent weeks several thousand of Madero's party workers also were imprisoned, and hundreds of thousands of supporters were discouraged by intimidation from appearing on election day.

Madero was released on bail and ordered to remain in San Luís Potosí. In late September, however, he jumped bail and escaped to Laredo, Texas. After the election, officials declared that Porfirio Díaz had been almost unanimously reelected president, with Madero allegedly receiving only 196 votes. This was neither the first nor the last time that election figures have been juggled in Mexico, but it is certainly the most laughable. As the dapper Madero himself put it when informed of the results, "Why, I have more relatives than that who voted for me."

A combination of flagrant electoral fraud, labor unrest centered in the mining and textile industries, and the eighty-year-old Díaz's clear determination to stay in power indefinitely finally overcame Madero's reservations about leading a movement for the overthrow—by force if necessary—of the senescent and, by this time, embarrassing, Don Porfirio. Working closely with collaborators around the country from his self-imposed exile in the United States, Madero declared that "the violent and illegal system [of Porfirio Díaz] can no longer exist" and designated 6 P.M. on November 20, 1910, as the precise moment for "all the towns in the Republic to rise in arms." The response to Madero's call was in some cases ill-timed, causing a number of early rebels to be massacred by federal troops. Nevertheless, the uprising soon became nationwide and inexorable. The rebellion's first success, in the northern border state of Chihuahua, was followed by victories in a number of other states throughout Mexico. The capture of Ciudad Juárez (in the state of Chihuahua, across the Rio Grande from El Paso, Texas), a key center for U.S.-Mexico trade, contributed greatly to the rebels' domination of northern Mexico. High-spirited American supporters of the revolution lined the banks of the river to follow the action and greet the defeat of the federal forces with cheers.

The success in Chihuahua was due in significant part to the "Anti-Reelectionist" group headed by Abraham González, a U.S.-educated intellectual activist who soon after Madero's call to arms had assembled a number of capable chieftains from along Mexico's northern border. Among these was Pascual Orozco, Jr., from Chihuahua, the first rebel to be awarded a general's rank by a grateful Madero. The most famous, though, is undoubtedly Doroteo Arango, who as a teenager had allegedly shot a *hacendado* who had assaulted his sister, and had to flee to the mountains to lead the precarious life of a *bandido*. This young man early exhibited great leadership qualities and came to be known in the region by his nom de guerre, Pancho Villa. Urged on by González, Villa quickly assembled a large and effective band of revolutionaries, and, along with Orozco and others, played a critical role in the early successes of the northern campaign, including the capture of Ciudad Juárez.

As President Díaz quickly and decisively lost control of northern Mexico to the insurgents, he came to the realization that the long era of the *porfiriato* was coming to an end. On May 21, 1911, his representatives met secretly with Madero in Ciudad Juárez and agreed that Díaz would leave office within thirty days. In fact, before that month had passed, the old dictator boarded a waiting ship and sailed off to France for a golden exile. One of his final remarks was a telling one: "Madero has unleashed a tiger, now let us see if he can control it!"

Francisco I. Madero: A Troubled Term Cut Short

With Díaz's departure, Madero made a triumphant journey from Chihuahua to Mexico City, where he was greeted by multitudes of admirers, including his ally from the south, the charismatic Emiliano Zapata. Zapata's admiration, though, soon turned to hatred when Madero proved unable or unwilling to meet Zapata's demands for the immediate distribution of land to his peasant supporters. When federal forces subsequently fired on *zapatistas* who had disarmed at Madero's request, this hostility became irreversible.

The vastly different ideologies of these two heroes, Madero and Zapata, symbolize the tragedy of the revolution. Madero, a political liberal but economic conservative from the north, believed in bringing democratic government to a nation that respected private-property rights. Zapata, an indigenous leader of the south, believed in a revolution that would eliminate large landholdings and redistribute land to the peasants.

The conflict between Madero and Zapata was only one of innumerable problems that soon caused the major leaders of the Mexican Revolution to be at each other's throats at one time or another throughout the course of the next decade (1910–1920). While between one and two million Mexicans were dying on the battlefields, internecine warfare among revolutionary factions wreaked havoc on the Mexican economy and ripped the social fabric to shreds.

On a number of occasions during the tragic military phase of the revolution, it looked as if peace was at hand. The first of these was when the popular Madero and José María Pino Suarez were sworn in as president and vice president, respectively, of Mexico early in November 1911. It soon became apparent to everyone, however, that Madero was more interested in political than economic reform. Indeed, his family and friends, all *hacendados* in northern Mexico, had no intention of turning their lands over to the peasants. But for many rebels, *¡pan y tierra!*—"bread and land!"—was the rallying cry. Led by Zapata, a number of leaders, including the northern hero Pancho Villa, an enemy since his earliest years of the *hacendados* and their tight grip on land and the administration of justice, were soon in arms against the Madero regime.

It was not the rebels in the field, however, but internal treachery that cost Madero his presidential sash and his life. When a revolt was organized within the army, Madero unwisely named General Victoriano Huerta to put it down. For decades, Huerta had been a loyal follower of Porfirio Díaz.

For ten days in February 1913 (la Decena Trágica), artillery fire
and military sorties inflicted great damage and uncounted civilian
casualties throughout Mexico City. Contemporaneous accounts tell
of thousands of bloated bodies rotting in the streets, with people too
fearful of the deadly cross fire to attempt to collect them. The treach-
erous General Huerta took advantage of the confusion and terror to
come to an agreement with the military officers opposing Madero
and stage a coup of his own. He ordered Madero arrested. Within
days the former president and his closest associates were reported
by Huerta to have been "shot while trying to escape," a story no one
believed.

The U.S. ambassador to Mexico at the time, Henry Lane Wilson,
bears at least some moral responsibility for this outrage, and few
Mexicans have forgotten this, creating a burden for American diplomats in Mexico that proved to be long-lasting. During the course of
a meeting at the U.S. embassy arranged by Ambassador Wilson,
General Huerta and the counterrevolutionary leader Félix Díaz (a
nephew of the exiled Don Porfirio) jointly agreed to the overthrow of
the legitimate government of President Madero and its replacement
by a government to be headed by Huerta. While there is no convincing evidence that Wilson specifically condoned Madero's death, neither is there any doubt that he wanted Madero replaced with someone
more amenable to foreign interests. In any case, Madero's murder
was a violent act that, alas, was a prototype of the myriad tragedies
that marked the next dark years of Mexico's history.

The Huerta Regime
and President Woodrow Wilson

Once installed as president, Huerta began a reign of terror: assassination of political opponents, involuntary conscription into a federal
army that was quintupled in size, and accommodation of former
military and civilian followers of the exiled Porfirio Díaz, many of
them Huerta's longtime personal friends.

Huerta was soon involved in full-scale battles against a range of
opponents whose names are still famous in Mexico: Villa, Zapata,
Venustiano Carranza, Alvaro Obregón, and many others who saw

Huerta as a betrayer of the ideals of the revolution. Fortunately for Huerta, these insurgent leaders were often fighting one another as well.

Huerta was most anxious to gain for his regime of questionable legitimacy the formal recognition of the U.S. government. Despite the U.S. ambassador's recommendations, President Taft, in his waning days in office, decided to defer a decision on recognition to his successor. The idealistic new president, Woodrow Wilson, was like many Americans who had been shocked by the news of Madero's assassination and thousands of reported casualties. He refused to consider recognition unless Huerta agreed to a general cease-fire and to free elections in which Huerta would not be a candidate. Needless to say, Huerta refused these terms. The civil war in Mexico continued, leaving the newly inaugurated President Wilson and his secretary of state, William Jennings Bryan, to devise new policies for dealing with insurgent Mexico. Shortly afterward Ambassador Wilson (no relation to the new U.S. president) was recalled under a cloud. The Wilson administration's opposition to the Huerta regime was growing clear.

Initially, demonstrations of U.S. unhappiness with Huerta were confined to sending military equipment and other supplies to the northern insurgents, including Carranza and Villa. When that had no immediate result, President Wilson decided upon a course of direct military intervention. Early in 1914 the U.S. naval and marine forces in the Gulf of Mexico were substantially reinforced. Shortly thereafter an "incident" occurred that precipitated the direct U.S. action President Wilson had anticipated.

The Dolphin *Incident*

In April 1914, crew members of the USS *Dolphin,* sent to the port city of Tampico, Mexico, to seek needed motor fuel for the ship's boats, were arrested by Huerta's coast guard when they arrived at a "restricted" fueling dock. Though the sailors were soon released, tempers had so flared on both sides that when, a few days later, the U.S. consul in Veracruz reported that a German ship bearing arms for Huerta's forces would soon arrive at that major port, the atmosphere was right for a sharp U.S. reaction.

President Wilson immediately ordered the occupation of Veracruz by U.S. Marines, which was easily accomplished by the substantial

U.S. forces in the area. The cost was high: a number of Mexican military and civilian casualties, and considerable outcry throughout Mexico. The American consulate general in Monterrey was attacked, and the flag burned. Reports reached Washington that in Mexico City, a U.S. flag had been tied to the tail of a donkey and used to clean the streets.

The impact of these reports upon Washington can well be imagined. The U.S. marine and navy contingent in Veracruz was strengthened; rumors that U.S. military forces would soon march on Mexico City were not denied (though such a move was never part of U.S. strategic planning). Huerta thus found himself compelled to withdraw considerable forces from the battles being waged against Carranza, Obregón, and Villa, and assign the forces to defend the capital. Meanwhile, Wilson's generous supply of military and other materiel to the Mexican insurgents was beginning to take its toll on Huerta's depleted forces, resulting notably in Villa's capture of Zacatecas in northern Mexico and further actions by an emboldened Zapata in the south.

Huerta soon recognized that his situation was due in no small part to the actions of the man he called "el puritano en la Casa Blanca" (the puritan in the White House). It is true that President Wilson quite deliberately tried to orchestrate Huerta's downfall. But many other factors, including Huerta's growing unpopularity and the strength of the internal opposition to his brutal dictatorship, played their part in bringing about his fall from power. After announcing his resignation on July 8, 1914, he quietly arranged his orderly and profitable departure to Spain.

Carranza and the Constitution of 1917

Huerta's departure offered the insurgent leaders the opportunity to set Mexico on a new course. Sandly, they were unable to settle their internal disputes. Early steps toward reconciliation—for example, a convention called in Aguascalientes, which was to have resulted in unanimous backing for Venustiano Carranza as president—collapsed in the face of the fierce rivalry between Carranza and Pancho Villa. In the end, a Villa candidate, Eulalio Gutiérrez, was named provisional president and, with support from Villa's army and Zapata, took office in Mexico City. Gutiérrez's tenure was short, however, as he was soon run out of Mexico City by the advancing army of Alvaro Obregón. Carranza, thwarted in his presidential ambitions, moved to Veracruz, where a sympathetic American government evacuated its military forces just in time to allow him to establish a provisional capital. Pancho Villa, declaring himself the true leader of the nation, established his headquarters in Chihuahua.

Meanwhile, President Wilson, understandably wary of this warring pantheon of revolutionary leaders, slowly came to the decision to continue to support the "Constitutionalist" government of Carranza, which he recognized as the true successor to Madero in October 1915. This move enraged the previously rather pro-American Pancho Villa, who had recently been severely trounced by Carranza in the Battle of Celaya. Villa first took his revenge on a party of U.S. mining company employees who were traveling by train from El Paso, Texas, to the Cusihuiriachic mine in Chihuahua. At the village of Santa Isabel, the railroad right-of-way was barricaded, and all fifteen Americans were removed from the train by Villa's troops and murdered in cold blood.

Villa followed this savage act by another: the invasion by some 500 *villistas* of the sleeping American town of Columbus, New Mexico, on the dawn of March 9, 1916. Before being driven off later in the day by a nearby U.S. Cavalry unit, they had murdered eighteen Americans, wounded many times that number, and burned several buildings in the town to the ground.[2]

There followed an unsuccessful effort by the U.S. Cavalry, led by General John J. Pershing (shortly thereafter to command U.S. forces in Europe in World War I) to track down and capture Villa. The wily rebel, though, was at home in the difficult countryside, and eluded capture. In the end Carranza, facing domestic criticism for allowing U.S. forces to operate in Mexico, ordered units of the Mexican army to march northward, and demanded that General Pershing's expeditionary force be withdrawn. This was done in January 1917, ending the direct U.S. military intervention in the affairs of its southern neighbor. General Pershing's so-called "punitive expeditions" against Mexican villagers thought to be sheltering Villa added to the legacy of anti-Americanism in the Mexican psyche.

Carranza then turned his attention to the long-promised drafting of a new Mexican constitution. (The resulting Mexican Constitution of 1917, though much amended, is still Mexico's governing document.)

Carranza carefully chose the participants for a constitutional convention. Nevertheless, the delegates who met in Querétaro turned out to be more radical than Carranza anticipated. They incorporated into the document measures such as land reform, limits to the powers of the Church, and restrictions on the foreign ownership of property. In the end, the constitution was adopted. Carranza was elected president and took office on May 1, 1917.

Carranza soon found himself embroiled in the international events of World War I. As the United States entered the war, he faced a great dilemma: Should Mexico join many other Latin American countries in breaking diplomatic relations with Germany and siding with the United States and the Allies? Germany's foreign minister, Arthur Zimmerman, had another idea. In a famous telegram to Carranza in February 1917, he promised that, if Mexico were to side with the Central Powers, all of Mexico's territories lost in the Mexican War would be restored. Carranza wisely rejected the offer, although, rather than join the Allies, he declared Mexico's strict neutrality. Another earlier German plan, hatched in 1915, also failed. It called for smuggling the exiled Huerta back to Mexico to lead a counterrevolution—which, by involving U.S. troops in the defense of Carranza's forces, would keep the Yanks from going to Europe should the United States enter the war. British intelligence uncovered the plot, enabling U.S. authorities to arrest Huerta on his way to Mexico through Texas. He remained in U.S. custody until his death from cirrhosis of the liver on January 13, 1916.

Carranza then devoted himself to consolidating his position within Mexico. A campaign against the insurgent Zapata, resulting in thousands of casualties on both sides, was inconclusive. A frustrated Carranza successfully arranged for Zapata to be tricked into a meeting in April 1919 with a local military commander, where Zapata was assassinated. But Carranza's success was to be short-lived: Months later, he himself was shot to death, perhaps by one of his own guards, while on his way to exile after losing a power struggle with Obregón. The motive for the slaying has never been fully established, though many felt that Obregón or one of his followers wanted to make sure that a potent opponent was permanently silenced.

The assassinations of Zapata and Carranza were but fleeting scenes in the tragic decade of 1910 through 1920, when about a million citizens out of a population of 15 million lost their lives as a result of the violent conflict. The economic and social costs were terrible as well, ranging from the loss of many professionals and skilled workers who emigrated to the U.S. to neglected farms, destroyed industries and mines, and demolished public schools and hospitals.

Alvaro Obregón and the Beginnings of Peace

The election of Alvaro Obregón in Mexico City in 1920 ushered in a relatively peaceful era. The political situation was simplified by the deaths of Zapata and Carranza, and the co-optation of Villa, who lived on a large *hacienda* in Canutillo, Chihuahua, until his assassination in 1923. Mexico's economy began a slow recovery (though not to reach Porfirian levels until World War II) led by oil production, which reached 200 million barrels in 1922. This made the country a world leader in oil and gas exports and provided a tax base for modest social progress.

While Obregón was slow in applying the more radical measures in the Constitution of 1917, such as agrarian reform or the national patrimony of oil and gas, he did make substantial headway in the fields of education and culture. He appointed a distinguished intellectual, José Vasconcelos, to the new cabinet position of secretary of public education. It was Vasconcelos who brought public education to Mexico's rural sectors. He recruited thousands of bright university students to leave the major cities and go off—often on muleback—to remote villages in the countryside, carrying with them boxes containing school supplies and perhaps fifty carefully selected books for teaching reading, writing, mathematics, and Mexican history.

Vasconcelos's philosophy was based not on the later, popular notion of preserving indigenous cultures but rather on the desirability of incorporating all the peoples of Mexico into one economic and political unit: the Mexican nation. This nation was to consist, in Vasconcelos's vision, of a cosmic race (*la raza cósmica*) that would prove a unique force in securing Mexico's future greatness. In any case, more than a thousand schools were built during the first four years of Vasconcelos's term. Several thousand other communities were served by temporary schoolhouses located in modest village buildings.

Recognizing that the population was only 50 percent literate, Vasconcelos called on leading artists to tell Mexico's unique story to its citizens. He commissioned three great muralists (*los tres grandes*)—Diego Rivera, husband of the artist Frida Kahlo; José Clemente Orozco, an introspective painter from Guadalajara; and the fiery Stalinist, David Alfaro Siqueiros—to cover the walls of government buildings all over Mexico with pictorial histories of famous events. These muralists, and many others who are lesser known, depicted the great civilizations of the Mayans and Aztecs, the coming of the Spaniards, the struggles for independence, and the Mexican Revolution in a way that made history memorable for the masses. Many of their great works—for example, the murals of Rivera in the National Palace on Mexico City's main plaza (El Zócalo)—are still frequently visited by Mexicans and foreigners alike. In total, they represent one of the most important contributions to popular art of the twentieth century.

Relations with the United States Under Obregón

President Obregón soon found himself in the difficult position of dealing with one of America's most corrupt political regimes. Warren G. Harding's administration, dominated by the influence of such oil barons as Harry F. Sinclair and Edward L. Doheny, became enmeshed in the infamous Teapot Dome scandal. The oil and mining interests that had found scant support during the presidency of Woodrow Wilson were in their element with the pliable Harding and his corrupt secretary of the interior, Albert B. Fall. This influence, along with Obregón's refusal to abrogate the terms of the Mexican Constitution regarding oil ownership, caused the United States to withhold its recognition of the Obregón government from 1920 until 1923. Faced with growing internal security problems, Obregón finally negotiated an agreement satisfactory to U.S. oil interests, and Mexico was granted formal diplomatic recognition.

Recognition, and Obregón's consequent ability to gain credits for the import of needed military supplies and other material, came just in time. A military revolt from the north—this time led by Adolfo de la Huerta, of Sonora—had to be put down. This turned out to be the last serious effort at a violent change of government.

Obregón was able, in 1924, to pass the presidential sash peacefully to his elected successor, Plutarco Elías Calles. Though much criticized by radical intellectuals, Obregón had successfully performed the delicate task of stabilizing his country and dealing with its difficult northern neighbor. A new era for Mexico had begun.

Mexico Grows and Develops: 1924–1968

The history of Mexico after the violent stage of the revolution (some Mexicans consider that the revolution itself continues to this day) was written to a significant degree by President Plutarco Elías Calles, a liberal leader from Mexico's northern province of Sonora. During the decade 1924–1934, Calles built a solid political base for governance in Mexico, which is all the more a remarkable achievement when one considers the violent era that preceded it. Calles was able to enlist the support of a broad cross section of the Mexican people—agrarian reformers; the labor movement, headed by Luis Morones and his Confederación Regional Obrera Mexicana (CROM), the regional confederation of Mexican workers; and the business and industrial sectors.

However, Calles faced a difficult period of relations with U.S. government officials during his early years. Neither the U.S. ambassador to Mexico, a businessman named James Sheffield, nor the secretary of state, Frank R. Kellogg, showed any understanding of Mexico or its problems. Sheffield believed that Anglo-Saxons had a duty to guide the natives of nonwhite countries (such as Mexico) to understand their interests and obligations. Kellogg was little better, announcing at one point that "Mexico is now on trial before the world. . . . We cannot countenance violation of her obligations and failure to protect U.S. citizens."

Calles saw the American overtures as a threat to Mexico's sovereignty. He reacted by strengthening Mexico's laws on national ownership of untapped oil and gas reserves. (Those being exploited at the time by foreign companies were on the basis of a fifty-year lease that, during the period of the leasehold, for all practical purposes amounted to outright ownership.) He also worked, with success, to obtain the departure of Sheffield with a minimum of fuss.

Fortunately, the new U.S. ambassador to Mexico was one of the best ever sent to that country. Dwight Morrow, though a senior partner at J.P. Morgan, soon proved his independence from the U.S. business and financial communities, and his desire to improve U.S.-Mexico relations. The Morrows chose to live in a Mexican-style residence and traveled extensively throughout Mexico, learning its language and culture. In contrast to his predecessors, Morrow called publicly for dignity and mutual respect in the relationship between the two countries.[3]

Morrow early sought and achieved an easy, informal relationship with the sometimes prickly President Calles. The pair began a regular schedule of breakfasts together, capitalizing on these occasions to resolve many issues without the encumbrances of staff and formal negotiations. Morrow also used his influence at the White House to tone down the Washington rhetoric and to elicit key statements reaffirming U.S. recognition of Mexico's sovereignty.

During this period, Calles's greatest difficulties were with the right wing of the Church and its Cristeros, armed bands centered in Jalisco and nearby areas who attacked public schools and murdered schoolteachers with the cry ¡Viva Cristo Rey! (Long live Christ the King!). Calles responded with sanctions against the Church, deported foreign priests and nuns, and closed Church schools. Government troops entered the scene and committed atrocities of their own against suspected Cristeros. The result was a tragic standoff. Although the government had far greater force on its side, the conflict remained unresolved when Calles left the presidency in 1928. His elected successor, Obregón, was murdered by a Cristero fanatic, and the presidency went to one of Calles's protégés, Emilio Portes Gil.

This instability in Mexico concerned Ambassador Morrow, who persuaded U.S. clerics with Vatican connections to act as informal mediators. Thus, Portes Gil and the archbishop of Mexico were eventually able to come to an agreement effectively ending the Cristero insurgency.

While a series of Calles loyalists (Portes Gil, Ortiz Rubio, and General Abelardo Rodríguez) were serving as president, Calles was busily building the political institution that has governed Mexico for more than sixty years. In 1929, Calles organized the Partido Nacional Revolucionario (PNR) in a successful effort to reduce the power of local *caciques* (political bosses), and to institutionalize the revolution in a single national party dedicated to its goals. The present name of the party, the Partido Revolucionario Institucional (PRI), reflects this objective.

By 1930, the political stability that Mexico had long sought was at hand. The Church was under control; the military, labor, and business leaders had been co-opted into the PNR party mechanism; and the stage was set for the election of one of Mexico's most famous reformers, Lázaro Cárdenas, to the presidency.

Cárdenas, Roosevelt, and the Oil Crisis

Cárdenas, who first became known as a military leader during the revolution, was actually a quiet man of deep personal commitment to social change. As governor of his native Michoacán (1928–1932) he opened new schools and invited peasants and industrial workers to organize and work within the political system. He improved conditions in Michoacán even as a worldwide depression was hitting the Mexican economy.

This success called him to the attention of the PNR and its leader. Calles invited Cárdenas to run for the presidency, which he easily won in 1934. However, a disappointed Calles soon discovered that this new president was not another puppet. Far from it. When Calles began publicly to criticize the new regime, he suddenly found himself being flown off to the United States and permanent exile, never again to be a force on the Mexican political scene.

The balance of the Cárdenas term (1934–1940) saw educational reform and the building of thousands of schools throughout the country; the growth of the Mexican labor movement; and land reform, whereby many giant *haciendas* were broken up and the land given to *ejidos,* or peasant communities. But Cárdenas remains best known throughout the world for successfully taking on the United States and the powerful foreign oil companies that had been allowed to exploit Mexican oil fields for decades without even minimal government control, or a fair share of the profits for Mexicans.

The election of Franklin D. Roosevelt to the American presidency in 1933 began the era of the Good Neighbor policy toward Mexico and Latin America. During FDR's first year in office, U.S. military forces were withdrawn from Nicaragua and Haiti and a policy of nonintervention in Latin American countries was adopted. The new president's first ambassador to Mexico, Josephus Daniels, an old friend and mentor, was a staunch supporter of the emerging inter-American system. Daniels established a personal friendship with Cárdenas, whose social programs Daniels enthusiastically likened to the New Deal. Though Daniels did voice concern about the need for prompt compensation for U.S. landowners suffering from Cárdenas's agrarian reform measures, relations in general between the two men, and the two countries, were good.

Thus it came as a shock when, on March 18, 1939, President Cárdenas signed an edict seizing the holdings of more than a dozen U.S. and all other foreign oil companies. Ambassador Daniels described the seizure as "a thunderbolt out of a blue sky." But Cárdenas believed there was ample justification for the action. The oil companies had for some months taken illegal measures to stave off oil workers' demands for wage increases, and had refused to obey a Mexican Supreme Court edict upholding pay hikes recommended by a government commission. Cárdenas, calling this intransigence a defiance of Mexico's national sovereignty, declared that his action was sanctioned by the Mexican Constitution of 1917.

Though, as international legal experts argued, Cárdenas's initial action on March 18 was tantamount to confiscation (under international law, wrongful seizure without immediate and adequate payment), he soon showed a willingness to negotiate his action as an expropriation. (Expropriation is sanctioned by international law because it involves prompt and fair payment.) These negotiations were onerous and protracted, but the process itself relieved some pressure.

Meanwhile, Petróleos Mexicanos (PEMEX, the state oil agency) was created and—facing an Anglo-American boycott—began to sell oil to Germany, which was building up its reserves in anticipation of World War II. Ambassador Daniels and President Roosevelt were concerned about the intransigence of the oil companies, which they considered to be shortsighted in view of the crumbling world situation, and encouraged an early resolution of the issue. But it was not until November 19, 1941, virtually on the eve of America's entry into the war, that a final agreement was signed giving foreign companies a total of $40 million in compensation for their oil concessions. The companies were undoubtedly unhappy at this conclusion,

but at last the agreement, the efforts of Ambassador Daniels—who
from the first had counseled both sides in the direction of modera-
tion—and the world crisis all combined to bring the matter to a
close.

World War II

The atmosphere for a peaceful resolution of the oil company take-
overs was improved by the Roosevelt administration's desire to get
Mexico and Latin America "on board" as allies in what was clearly
the coming war in Europe—a goal with which Cárdenas, an ardent
anti-Fascist, was in sympathy. By the time Cárdenas left office in
1940, relations between the two countries were on a relatively even
keel.

The charismatic Lázaro Cárdenas, still remembered by many as
Mexico's greatest social reformer, was succeeded by the more conservative General Manuel Avila Camacho. After hearing for years
American complaints about the "Reds" running Mexico, that country's citizens found it quite humorous that the U.S. representative at-
tending Avila Camacho's inauguration, Vice President Henry Wal-
lace, was in fact well to the left of Mexico's new president on the
political spectrum.

This conservative reputation had actually helped Avila Camacho
in his electoral campaign. Nominated by the government party at the
behest of Cárdenas, Avila was opposed by the extremely conservative Juan Andrés Almazán of the Partido de Acción Nacional
(PAN)—then, as now, Mexico's major conservative party, representing industrialists, landowners, the Church, and the growing upper-
middle class, especially in northern Mexico. The PAN leadership had
expected to run against Francisco Múgica, a fiery radical, and would
probably have captured a broad range of moderate and conservative
votes. But the contrast between Almazán and Avila Camacho was
not dramatic enough to have much popular impact, and the better-
organized PNR won an easy victory.

During his term in office (1940–1946), Avila Camacho was preoccupied by World War II and its impact on his foreign and domestic policies. His policy of friendship with the United States and the
Allies gained him the enmity of the Mexican left—at least until the
summer of 1941, when Hitler's attack on the Soviet Union changed

some leftists' minds. Avila Camacho broke relations with Germany, Japan, and Italy on December 8, 1941, the day after Pearl Harbor. On May 24, 1942, after two Mexican oil tankers had been torpedoed by U-boats, he declared war on the Axis powers. Mexico's contributions to the war effort included sending a courageous fighter squadron to the Far East under General MacArthur's command; the export of vast quantities of strategic metals and minerals to the United States; and the dispatching of some 300,000 Mexican workers (*braceros*) to the United States to replace American farm and industrial workers who had joined the military services.

By 1946 the PNR, having changed its name to the Partido Revolucionario Institutional (PRI), was ready to embark on a new era (roughly 1946–1982) in which it would base its popularity and strength on Mexico's continuing economic growth and development. World War II had encouraged a rapid industrial expansion led by young, often U.S.-trained Mexican engineers and entrepreneurs. Expansion activities were centered in Monterrey, Guadalajara, and Mexico City. A state development bank, the Nacional Financiera, was created, and the country's financial and planning infrastructures were markedly improved. Mexico's economic renaissance set the stage for three decades of almost unbroken real economic growth, averaging more than 5 percent a year, with real GNP doubling during the years 1946–1958.

The Postwar Years

Mexican historians have made an important point about U.S. foreign policy in the years following World War II, from which the United States emerged as the most powerful nation in the world. They observe that the United States focused its attentions in the international economic arena on war-shattered Europe. On the other hand, the U.S. chose to frame its relations with Latin America, including Mexico, in an international-security context. There was no counterpart to the Marshall Plan in the developing countries of Latin America.

Even without the economic assistance that would have been provided by a Latin American Marshall Plan, though, the Mexican economy continued to grow robustly under the leadership of a new, private-sector-oriented president, Miguel Alemán Valdés (1946–1952). Alemán, the first civilian in decades to be elected president of

Mexico, also received the first visit by an American president to Mexico City when Harry Truman arrived in March 1947.

Recognizing that rapid industrialization could not take place without an adequate infrastructure, Alemán embarked early in his administration on a series of massive public-works projects including dams, power stations, electrification, telecommunications networks, and highways. PEMEX doubled its production during the Alemán years and provided subsidized oil and gas to industrial users. The huge new campus of the Universidad Nacional Autónoma de México (UNAM, the national university) was built at the edge of rapidly growing Mexico City.

Despite the economic growth and development that marked the Alemán administration, his successor, Adolfo Ruiz Cortines, came to office facing a number of serious challenges. Ruiz Cortines focused the first months of his administration on pressing social issues. One of these was the full enfranchisement of women into the political and electoral process, and this was accomplished. During his term in office (1952–1958), he also vastly expanded the Mexican version of Social Security. Despite his careful administration, though, social problems grew in intensity, exacerbated by Mexico's rapid population increases and stagnant real wages for workers. Salary increases for workers were obliterated by the inflation that was creeping into the economy as massive public-spending projects were paid for by an overactive printing press during Ruiz Cortines's last years in office. The crowning blow to his administration was a protracted series of strikes by railroad and other transportation workers, all put down with considerable police and paramilitary violence.

Ruiz Cortines's relations with the United States, in general friendly and uneventful, were dramatically marred in June 1954 by the U.S. intervention in Guatemala to overthrow the reformist president Jacobo Arbenz. A leftist democrat determined to pursue a land reform program that threatened the considerable landholdings of the wealthy *hacendados* (and of the United Fruit Company), Arbenz was overthrown in a CIA-supported coup by Colonel Carlos Castillo Armas. Thousands of Mexicans demonstrated on the streets against the action. The CIA's support was widely denounced in Mexico as being all too typical of past *yanqui* interventions.

In 1958, Mexicans elected one of their youngest and most charismatic presidents, Adolfo López Mateos, to succeed Ruiz Cortines. Sometimes compared to John F. Kennedy, who was elected in 1960,

López Mateos was forty-seven years old, energetic, and very popular, his service as secretary of labor having gained him a reputation for concern for the welfare of workers and farmers.

López Mateos, Cuba, and Chamizal

López Mateos (1958–1964) found his principal challenges in the arena of foreign policy. One of the first of these was the Cuban Revolution of 1959, when Fidel Castro came to power after overthrowing the right-wing dictatorship of Fulgencio Batista. Castro was seen initially throughout the Western Hemisphere, including the United States, as a heroic figure who had brought freedom to a people long suffering under the yoke of a tyrant. But it soon became obvious that Castro, with the strong support of the Soviet Union, was in fact intent on establishing in Latin America a communist dictatorship of the Eastern European variety.

Soon most of the Western Hemisphere's constituent countries were taking firm multilateral measures—breaking relations and imposing economic sanctions, for example—to curb the Castro regime's efforts to consolidate its hold on Cuba and export the communist revolution to other countries in the area. Despite the urging of the United States and other Latin American neighbors, Mexico, bound by its historic policy of nonintervention and its own revolutionary tradition, did not vote for several Organization of American States measures condemning Cuba and expelling it from this regional body. Within a short time, Mexico found itself the only Latin American country maintaining diplomatic relations or even regular air links with Cuba.

Surprisingly, the Mexican approach to the Cuban situation did not prove to be a serious problem in the U.S.-Mexico relationship. In fact, the period of the López Mateos regime, during which several Cuban crises (such as the abortive Bay of Pigs invasion and the Cuban missile crisis of October 1963) unfolded, was a very successful one vis-à-vis the United States. Certainly, the most dramatic and enduring success was the resolution of a boundary dispute that had festered for more than a century. In 1864, due to a shift in the course of the Rio Grande (Río Bravo) near the border towns of El Paso, Texas, and Ciudad Juárez, Mexico, 440 acres of what had been Mexican territory (known as El Chamizal) became part of the United States.

Numerous commissions, convened from time to time over the ensuing hundred years, had been unable to reach agreement on a new boundary. Talks undertaken between López Mateos and the new U.S. president, John F. Kennedy, during a Kennedy state visit to Mexico City in 1962, led to an agreement between Mexico's Secretariat of Foreign Relations and the U.S. State Department. The agreement, which called for a permanent channeling of the river through the disputed area, the construction of an international park, and a new international bridge connecting El Paso and Ciudad Juárez, was approved by both countries' legislatures. In November 1963 President Kennedy was assassinated; the final pact was actually signed by López Mateos and Kennedy's successor, Lyndon B. Johnson, in September 1964.

On the domestic scene, too, López Mateos moved very adroitly. Responding to critics' charges of PRI dominance in the legislative branch, he had Mexico's electoral procedures modified to permit the participation of such opposition parties as the conservative PAN and the socialist Partido Popular Socialista (PPS). While these and other moves in the direction of electoral reform did demonstrate some sensitivity on López Mateos's part to the need for reform, they did little to diminish the power of the PRI at the presidential level.

President Díaz Ordaz and the Tlatelolco Massacre

López Mateos led Mexico skillfully for six years, handling the Cuban crises well and developing good relations with a series of U.S. presidents—Eisenhower, Kennedy, and Johnson. He left the presidential office in the hands of his secretary of the interior, Gustavo Díaz Ordaz, a dour, unimaginative conservative who soon found himself in a sensitive political situation beyond his capacity to manage. The results were tragic. Perhaps because Díaz Ordaz's tenure (1964–1970) was in most ways undistinguished, he will be best remembered for his responsibility for the horror of Tlatelolco.

Mexico was proud to be chosen as the host for the 1968 Olympic Games, and Díaz Ordaz was determined that nothing should interfere with their complete success. Yet on the eve of the games, numerous large groups of Mexican high-school and university students attempted antigovernment demonstrations around Mexico City. Díaz Ordaz ordered immediate and severe police and military actions against the students; thousands were arrested and beaten. The government's action, of course, served only to heat up the situation. Within days, tens of thousands of National University students, professors, and even parents were demonstrating against the Díaz Ordaz regime.

In response, Díaz Ordaz ordered the Mexican army to occupy the university and sent thousands of members of his security forces to cover possible sites of further demonstrations. Inevitably, tragedy struck. On the night of October 2, 1968, security police stationed at Plaza de las Tres Culturas, in Tlatelolco—an old area of downtown Mexico City where the Secretariat of Foreign Relations is located—opened fire on students and their supporters with automatic weapons. To this date, there is considerable debate on how many were massacred that night, though responsible estimates are in the range of two to four hundred, with more than two thousand arrested. Whatever the real figure, the trauma of Tlatelolco is still not fully behind the Mexican people, just as Americans have not entirely forgotten the similar tragedy of Kent State, which, though with far fewer casualties, was symbolic of the era.

Notes

1. This curtain is still in daily use and has been seen by millions of American and other tourists who have visited the Palace of Fine Arts to see the famous Ballet Folklorico.

2. The author's grandfather, Dr. G.W.R. Smith, a physician and surgeon in nearby Mesilla Park, New Mexico, alerted by a railway telegrapher to the tragedy, drove immediately to the scene with several boxes of medical supplies and treated the wounded from both sides.

3. Morrow's invitation of Charles Lindbergh on a goodwill visit resulted, as it happened, in Lindbergh's marriage to the ambassador's daughter Anne.

3

Decades of Dramatic Change: 1970–1994

The Echeverría Years

Luis Echeverría Alvarez, who as secretary of the interior in the Díaz Ordaz administration also bore considerable responsibility for the Tlatelolco tragedy, was nominated by the Partido Revolucionario Institucional (PRI) in 1970 to succeed Díaz Ordaz. Echeverría was faced with the huge task of regaining credibility for the party—and the government—after Tlatelolco. Though running against very weak opposition from the left and right, he traversed the country, visiting more than eight hundred cities and towns and touring thousands of rural areas during the campaign. Up to that point Echeverría had been considered quite conservative. During the campaign the rhetoric of his speeches, later echoed throughout his first year in office, began to take on a nationalistic, leftist hue—what he called "revolutionary nationalism." Rural development became a major theme; innumerable promises were made along the campaign trail to bring roads, electricity, water, and schools to impoverished parts of the country.

To his great credit, Echeverría made a startling turnaround in the vitally important field of family planning. Long an opponent of birth control, he now gave it his endorsement, undertaking a joint public- and private-sector campaign that has continued through successive administrations. As a result, the net annual population growth rate has declined from 3.3 percent in 1970 to 2.1 percent in 1997. Without Echeverría's initiative, there is no doubt that Mexico's population explosion, serious enough as it is, would now be considerably worse.

Despite Echeverría's calls for domestic social reforms, the aftermath of Tlatelolco continued to be felt. Terrorist groups perpetrated a number of kidnappings, including those of U.S. Consul General Terrance Leonhardy in Guadalajara, and the PRI senator from Guerrero, Rubén Figueroa. Eugenio Garza Sada, Mexico's leading industrialist, was shot to death in a botched kidnapping attempt in Monterrey. A terrorist group organized by former university student leaders and led by Lucio Cabañas was responsible for several bank robberies and kidnappings. In the end, it took Echeverría more than a year and the assignment of more than 10,000 army troops to neutralize Cabañas's group. Cabañas himself was killed in a clash with army special forces.

Despite—or more likely, because of—the troubles and mistrust that plagued his administration on the domestic front, Echeverría made an extraordinary effort to propel himself and Mexico onto the world scene. Speaking as much for internal effect as international, Echeverría told a startled nation and world that Mexico was "following a path between capitalism and socialism." His bid for leadership in the Third World involved him in whirlwind travels to Africa, the Far East, and elsewhere. He promoted a "Charter of Economic Rights and Duties of States" that was passed by the UN General Assembly but had little practical effect. As one critic noted, it gave the developing countries all the rights and the developed countries all the duties, without suggesting any effective means of collaboration for mutual benefit.

In the end, Echeverría's international campaign, including an unsuccessful bid to be elected secretary general of the United Nations, had little global impact, and did not restore confidence in him as a national leader. One of his actions was particularly disastrous. Perhaps in a desire to win Arab support, he lent Mexico's voice to a 1975 UN General Assembly resolution equating Zionism with racism. The resulting massive boycott of Mexican tourist resorts by American Jews and many others should not have surprised anyone. Dozens of Mexican resort hotels stood near-empty at the height of the tourist season, resulting in considerable economic loss.

During his last years in office, Echeverría resorted to public-spending policies, including public works, social welfare, and subsidies, that soon plagued the country with growing inflation—more than 20 percent a year at one point—and a trade deficit in 1975 of $3.5 billion. A 1973 law restricting foreign private investment had a chilling effect on the business climate both at home and abroad. His final acts in office—for example, an ex post facto approval of illegal land seizures by peasants in Sonora; orchestrating the removal of a principal press critic, Julio Scherer, editor of the respected Mexico City daily newspaper *Excélsior;* and a too-long-deferred devaluation of the peso—did nothing to redeem his administration.

Thus, in his last weeks, Echeverría faced a rapid decay in confidence and the flight of several billions of dollars by concerned Mexican businessmen and investors sick of being excoriated by Echeverría as betrayers of the national patrimony. The troubled regime, which had begun in the shadow of the Tlatelolco massacre and never did gain the trust of students and intellectuals, ended with a crisis of confidence on the part of the middle-class business and professional communities.

José López Portillo: Oil, Debt, and Corruption

José López Portillo, an aristocratic intellectual who served as finance minister in the latter part of the Echeverría administration, took office on December 1, 1976. Though he inherited a mismanaged economy (for which he bore some responsibility), he soon found himself in what appeared to be a most fortunate position.

At a time when the Arab oil producers and the Organization of Petroleum Exporting Countries (OPEC) were driving up the price of oil to historic highs, and Americans were waiting in long lines at gas stations, Mexico found itself sitting on proven reserves of oil estimated at more than 60 billion barrels—this compared with only 42 billion barrels in the United States and 228 billion in incredibly oil-rich Saudi Arabia. Mexico's economic problems seemed to be resolved forever. The country, López Portillo believed, had only to pump out the requisite amount of oil and sell it abroad to bring wealth into his treasury. Oil production rose from 800,000 barrels a day in 1976 to 2.3 million barrels a day in 1980. Mexico's trade surpluses in this era of rapidly rising oil prices were the envy of the non-oil-producing world. "The world is now divided into two camps; nations that produce oil, and nations that do not. Mexico is a nation that does!" declared López Portillo.

In the brief but heady days of Mexico's oil supremacy, López Portillo exercised what he perceived as a new position of power on the international stage. He ignored the U.S.-led boycott of the Moscow Olympic Games in 1980 after the USSR's invasion of Afghanistan. He used President Carter's state visit to Mexico to needle the visiting U.S. leader about America's "past deceits" and to warn him against such actions in the future. López Portillo also officially recognized the legitimacy of the insurgents in El Salvador and made state visits to Cuba, the Soviet Union, Bulgaria, and the People's Republic of China.

Even early on in the López Portillo administration (1976–1982), however, knowledgeable observers found the economic situation disturbing. Though oil exports were up dramatically, so was unemployment. Mexico's resources were flowing to capital-intensive petroleum exploitation, while slower growth in more labor-intensive manufacturing and other sectors failed to provide enough jobs for the 800,000 young Mexicans entering the job force each year.

López Portillo's response was to embark on myriad government spending programs of unparalleled magnitude, driving Mexico—able to borrow because of the oil boom and its petroleum and gas reserves—deeply into foreign debt. This borrowing and spending spree gave a brief illusion of economic dynamism, with real GNP growth of more than 8 percent in 1981 and 1982. With the world oil bust of the early 1980s though, Mexico was left desperate and virtually bankrupt. In August 1982, Mexican negotiators had to fly to Washington to arrange an international bailout.

On the morning of August 12, 1982, newly appointed finance minister Jesús Silva Herzog, who was much respected in world financial institutions, called U.S. treasury secretary Donald Regan, Federal Reserve Board chairman Paul Volcker, and Jacques de Larosière, managing director of the International Monetary Fund (IMF), with a compelling message. Mexico had run out of reserves and could not meet its international financial obligations, including interest payments on its $80 billion foreign debt, after Friday, August 13. He received an urgent invitation to Washington.

Though perhaps tempted by López Portillo's earlier posturing to let him stew in the economic disaster he had created, U.S. and world financial leaders acted quickly to arrange a resolution to the crisis. Mexico's crisis was unprecedented in size and, if not resolved, could have a severe impact on the world's financial markets.

The U.S. government, led by U.S. ambassador to Mexico John Gavin (a personal friend of President Reagan), Regan, and Volcker, along with private bank lenders represented by William Rhodes, a senior officer at Citibank, launched an extraordinary effort, over several weeks, to negotiate a set of measures with the Mexicans. Terms included advance purchase of Mexican oil for the U.S. Strategic Petroleum Reserve; establishment of Treasury and Federal Reserve lines of support; restructuring of the commercial bank debt; negotiation of an IMF standby agreement (which López Portillo at first opposed because, under the agreement, the IMF funds would be made available only if Mexico undertook needed internal economic restructuring); and import credits for grains and basic foodstuffs. The package met Mexico's $20 billion need, and the crisis was averted.

The decline in the Mexican economy was exacerbated by widespread corruption, which reached high levels of the López Portillo administration. Indeed, Mexicans were distressed, if not surprised, to hear that in his last year in office the president had constructed four large mansions for himself and his family in an elegant part of Mexico City. This was symbolic of the corruption during his administration, and just the tip of the iceberg.

Even more seriously, the regime's borrow-and-spend binge left Mexico in the worst economic shape of its modern history. During López Portillo's last year in office, profligate government spending, financed by borrowing against Mexico's oil reserves, so affected the business climate that Mexican and foreign businessmen scrambled to ship billions of dollars out of the country. López Portillo responded by attempting a series of financial controls that resulted in a huge devaluation of the peso (from 26 to the dollar to 100 in a year's time). But he saved the greatest disaster for the end of his regime. In September 1982 López Portillo, in a tearful address to the country, nationalized the banking system, fired the respected head of the central bank, and embarked on a series of draconian exchange control regulations that were, given the porous nature of the U.S.-Mexico border, utterly ineffective.

De la Madrid: A Period of Patient Rebuilding

Miguel de la Madrid Hurtado, while not a seasoned politician, was an economist and public-policy specialist with degrees from the National University of Mexico and Harvard. He was well qualified to take over the governance of Mexico late in 1982. Casting aside advice to repudiate Mexico's foreign debt, which had grown to a staggering $90 billion during López Portillo's administration, De la Madrid elected instead to negotiate the foreign debt payment. He also embarked on a domestic austerity program designed to bring Mexico slowly back to stability and a resumption of real economic growth.

The new Mexican president instituted drastic reductions in the public-sector budget, cutting 50,000 government jobs in the first year of his administration, reducing federal subsidies on most foodstuffs, and selling off a number of money-losing state enterprises. Abandoning the attempts of López Portillo to introduce exchange controls, he adopted a policy that, by means of small daily corrections, kept the peso at a reasonable rate of exchange with the dollar. He assembled a world-class economic team, headed by finance minister Silva Herzog and Banco de México (central bank) director Miguel Mancera, to ensure the success of his international-finance efforts.

In a dramatic opening of the Mexican economy, the De la Madrid administration eschewed the protectionist, closed policies of the past and brought Mexico into the General Agreement on Tariffs and Trade (the GATT), an international body dedicated to lowering trade barriers. Mexico adopted a much more open policy regarding foreign ownership of Mexican enterprises and began to encourage, on a case-by-case basis, foreign investments that would bring needed new technology and jobs to Mexico.

Perhaps recognizing that economic reform alone could not rebuild the public confidence shattered over the previous two administrations, De la Madrid moved to confront the corruption of the past. This led to the arrest and conviction of several leading figures of previous administrations, including the former director of PEMEX. For reasons of tradition—and perhaps political reality—De la Madrid did not seek to indict a previous president. Nevertheless, he made a convincing case for the need to reduce the rampant corruption of the past.

President de la Madrid was also faced with a crisis of the old political order. Before 1982, the apparently robust Mexican economy, with its sustained annual growth rates of 6 percent or better per year and an expanding middle class to which many could aspire, had muted all criticism of the autocratic nature of the PRI leadership. The economic crisis changed this dramatically. De la Madrid was faced with the challenge of instituting political reform at a time when doing so was made more difficult by a bad economic situation. Such reforms, long urged by the leadership of the conservative PAN as well as by the splinter parties of the left, were clearly overdue.

De la Madrid's first effort at political reform came early in his administration and proceeded along three fronts: a call for free and fair elections across the nation and at all levels; a restraining arm on local political *caciques* traditionally loyal to the PRI; and improved access of opposition candidates to the media. These moves resulted in a number of victories for the PAN's mayoral candidates in Mexico's northern cities. The strong showing by the PAN stimulated the PRI apparatus to select better-qualified candidates capable of winning a free election. De la Madrid also instituted important reforms in the congressional election process that served to increase the number of opposition party representatives in the Mexican Congress.

On balance, and despite a disastrous earthquake in the autumn of 1985 that rocked Mexico City in the midst of his presidential term (1982–1988), De la Madrid did manage to bring stability to the Mexican economy and to set the stage for the real growth that was to come under his successor, Carlos Salinas de Gortari. A cabinet secretary, Salinas pronounced himself dedicated to building on De la Madrid's progress in opening the Mexican economy, restoring economic growth, and permitting greater pluralism in the Mexican political system.

No sooner had Salinas won the PRI nomination though, than a powerful element within the PRI central apparatus, opposed to the continuation of De la Madrid's international and domestic economic policies, elected to leave the party. One of this group's leaders was Cuauhtémoc Cárdenas, the charismatic son of former president Lázaro Cárdenas. The young Cárdenas and his fellow members of what they called the *corriente democrática* ("democratic current") formed a leftist coalition party, which later became the Partido de la Revolución Democrática (PRD). In the presidential elections of 1988, Cárdenas ran in a three-way race against Salinas and a strong and popular figure from PAN, Manuel Clouthier, for the Mexican presidency.

The results surprised many seasoned observers of the Mexican political scene. After some mysterious whirring and clicking, the official government computers gave Salinas 50 percent of the vote, with 33 percent going to Cárdenas and 16 percent to Clouthier. Although some questioned whether Salinas actually obtained a majority of the vote, most objective analysts believe that he obtained at least the close plurality needed to make him the legitimate victor in the election. (This is, however, still hotly disputed by the opposition.)

Another notable aspect of the 1988 elections was the victory by the PRD in two senatorial elections, both in the Federal District. The seats went to two members of the *corriente democrática*, the group that had left the PRI along with Cuauhtémoc Cárdenas. In total, 240 of the 500 seats in Mexico's Chamber of Deputies went to opposition parties (mostly to the PRD and the PAN), leaving the PRI with 260 seats—its slimmest majority in history.

And that was not all. In July 1989 the governorship of Baja California Norte went to the PAN candidate, Ernesto Ruffo Appel. This was the first time the PRI had lost a gubernatorial election since its founding in the aftermath of the revolution. On November 1, 1989, after giving his Informe (State of the Union message) in Mexico City, President Salinas flew to Baja California to attend Governor Ruffo Appel's inauguration—an unprecedented occurrence in Mexican political history. (Annoyed by this display of a political opening between the PRI and the PAN, the *cardenistas* quickly claimed that, in contrast, the PRI had stolen the gubernatorial election from the PRD candidate in Cárdenas's home state of Michoacán.)

It is far too simple to label Cárdenas as a leftist reformer and Salinas as the inheritor of the tradition of the Revolutionary Family, an expanding group originally formed by military leaders of the revolution, later to include their descendants, and emerging civilian leaders of the PRI. In fact, as we have seen, it was Cárdenas's father, Lázaro, who was one of the most important members of the Revolutionary Family. It can be argued that the Cárdenas candidacy in 1988 more nearly represented a continuation of traditional Mexican politics, with its base in economic nationalism, state controls, and a suspicion of the outside world in general and of its often irksome northern neighbor in particular. Certainly an important underlying theme of the Cárdenas campaign was that the PRI—the party of the revolution—had been captured from the top by a group of highly educated *técnicos* enamored of free-market economics, and was being led off in a dangerous direction. By inference, a vote for Cárdenas was a vote for the traditions his revered father espoused. This campaign strategy gained him considerable support in the countryside, which was often controlled by an older generation of rural politicians loyal to Lázaro Cárdenas and the old order, and among members of the industrial unions, notably the petroleum workers, whose special privileges inherited from the Lázaro Cárdenas era were seen to be at risk. Under this scenario, it was the Salinas group within the PRI that represented the changing direction of the parties and the modernization of Mexican economic and political structures along the path first taken by De la Madrid in the mid-1980s.

Carlos Salinas de Gortari:
From Promise to Disaster

When President Salinas took his oath of office, two major clouds were still hanging over the recent Mexican past: the Tlatelolco tragedy of 1968, with its political fallout; and the debt crisis of 1982, with its legacy of austerity and decline in living standards. The former marked the end of an era of political stability that had extended over four decades; the latter revealed the bankruptcy of the economic policies that had paid for economic growth with a deficit-spending spree that brought Mexico to its knees on the international financial stage. The new president was fortunate in being insulated to some degree from these epochal events—by the passage of time in the Tlatelolco case, and by the shrewd austerity program of his predecessor, Miguel de la Madrid, in the case of the debt crisis.

Salinas wasted no time in expanding the economic programs that had marked De la Madrid's term in office. His steps to continue the modernization of the Mexican economy included rapid privatization of the state telephone monopoly, major steel mills and mining complexes, and the national airline. In a reversal of López Portillo's nationalization of the banking industry, a somewhat controversial return of banks and other financial institutions to private control was initiated. This measure alone resulted in an estimated $10 billion in capital returning to Mexico during 1990–1991, a sure sign of a revival in investor confidence since the dark days of the López Portillo regime, when at least three times that amount fled abroad. Salinas also liberalized import restrictions and encouraged the flow of foreign private direct investment from the United States and abroad. He instituted tax reforms and cut the public-sector deficit dramatically.

Much structural change in the Mexican economy was still required, however, perhaps most significantly in the agricultural sector. In 1990, the net agricultural deficit on Mexico's balance of trade was about $4 billion. The *ejido* system of the Mexican Revolution, designed to break up large landholdings and distribute them to campesinos, had remained largely untouched. It stood as a bar to internationally competitive agro-industry since the *minifundia,* or small communal landholding system, does not permit the development of a modern agricultural economy.

On the other hand, as Salinas knew well, it would be politically difficult for a Mexican president to turn his back on the reforms of the revolution that broke up large landholdings in the early decades of the century. He began by permitting a few joint ventures between *ejidos* and private Mexican investors in some agricultural zones— particularly in northern Mexico, where the atmosphere is more conducive to such arrangements, but also in the more sensitive (and impoverished) southern state of Chiapas. These activities actually continued in Chiapas even after the Zapatista uprising of January 1, 1994, in an attempt to mitigate land tenure and poverty problems.

Renegotiating the Foreign Debt

One of Salinas's most important actions was the successful renegotiation of Mexico's foreign debt, whereby more than five hundred creditors agreed to a series of measures that effectively reduced Mexico's obligations by more than 10 percent. The expected surge of foreign investment that was expected following this historic agreement failed to materialize, due in part to competition from the newly privatizing formerly communist countries of Eastern Europe. Nevertheless, the debt-payment reduction and new foreign private direct investment were welcome developments.

Salinas also instituted a massive economic-development program with an annual budget that grew from $2 billion in 1992 to $4 billion in 1994, the Programa Nacional de Solidaridad, or PRONASOL. Directed at the poorest economic regions, PRONASOL announced that it actively encouraged the emergence of community leaders who could decide for themselves what a town or village's greatest needs were. The leaders then received government support, through PRONASOL's representatives, to accomplish these goals—whether they be potable water, schools and playgrounds, roads, medical centers, or even sports facilities. There is no doubt that this program had a dramatic effect on many communities. From a political point of view, of course, there is much to be gained by the recruitment of authentic community leaders into projects that associate them with the government representatives of PRONASOL: some observers believe the program explains the PRI victories in some August 1991 local elections. But even with such successes, Salinas and his supporters of reform within the PRI, notably Luis Donaldo Colosio, PRONASOL's leader, still faced considerable obstructionism from the entrenched elements within the party structure.

President Salinas moved forward, although not as fast as many critics wished, in the area of political liberalization. In July 1989 the PRI, the PAN, and some smaller parties in the Mexican Congress (the PRD was notable by its absence) jointly created a federal code of electoral procedures and set up a nongovernmental electoral commission. Subsequently, measures to improve electoral fairness, such as a modernized process of voter registration and identification, poll watching, and vote counting, were instituted. While these steps in themselves did not wipe out voter fraud, they certainly made it more difficult.

In an extraordinary session in September 1990, party members approved a dramatic series of changes within the PRI itself: providing secret ballots for internal elections; making PRI membership voluntary rather than compulsory for members of party-affiliated unions and rural workers' organizations; and increasing grassroots influence in naming party candidates more attractive locally. These moves were a clear victory for reformers interested in modernizing the PRI, but they left many old-timers disgruntled. A few of these resigned and joined the growing ranks of the PRD.

The Elections of August 1991

President Salinas was broadly criticized during 1991–1993 for the slow pace of political reform. The president invited some of this by giving first priority to economic reform, with political changes, however necessary in the long term, coming second. One critic, Nobel Laureate Octavio Paz, warned the president that if reforms did not come soon, the PRI would remain an obstacle to democratization and modernization of the Mexican society.

The August 1991 elections provided some evidence that change was possible. The PRI, which had greatly improved its local campaign organizations and won back a more robust majority in the Congress, ceded the governorships of three contested states—Guanajuato, San Luís Potosí, and Tabasco; "results" showed narrow PRI victories. Observers saw a direct presidential hand in these decisions, which addressed domestic and international sensitivity to the issue of political openness. Local election results in late 1991 and early 1992 also reflected a growing pluralism, with gains by the PRD in such states as Michoacán and by the PAN mainly in the north. In short, though Mexico remained some distance away from the long-promised "transparent" electoral process, it seemed headed in that direction.

Salinas, Bush, and Free Trade

Salinas was determined from the beginning to improve Mexico's relations with the United States. As president-elect, he held a historically unprecedented meeting in Houston, Texas, with president-elect George Bush and a broad range of senior aides from both sides. The two men hit it off almost immediately, and their mutual confidence from 1988 through 1992 had a dramatic and favorable, if in the end evanescent, effect on relations between the two countries.

By far the most dramatic move in U.S.-Mexico relations during that period occurred on June 11, 1990, when Presidents Bush and Salinas jointly announced a schedule for the successful completion of a U.S.-Mexico Free Trade Agreement (FTA). After six months of intensive activity on the part of both U.S. and Mexican trade negotiators, the two presidents met again in November 1990 to confirm their commitment to achieving an agreement at the earliest appropriate time. During the November summit it was also announced that Mexico was being granted a $1 billion credit with the Export-Import Bank of the United States (Ex-Im Bank) for petroleum exploration and exploitation.

Expansion activity by PEMEX, with consequent greater production capacity, relieved the tensions caused by regional crises such as that in the Persian Gulf, where U.S. oil imports were threatened. This was true for two reasons. First, it permitted the Mexicans, if they wished, to increase production for sales on the U.S. market or to the U.S. Strategic Petroleum Reserve. Second, by increasing potential production capacity (called surge capacity), it allowed Mexico to react in an international oil emergency by immediately increasing production to meet Western Hemisphere needs.

The decision on Mexico's part to seek financing from the Ex-Im Bank for the oil industry was controversial in Mexico. Critics feared it was the first step toward *yanquis* getting back into a business Lázaro Cárdenas had driven them out of. Other Mexicans saw it as a way not only of increasing Mexico's export potential, but also of ensuring that Mexico would have the oil and gas to meet the growing needs of its own improving economy. The debate continues to this day.

The North American Free Trade Agreement: Origins and Negotiations

In a quantum leap from the traditional piecemeal style of bilateral negotiations, in October 1989 Presidents Salinas and Bush signed three critical trade and investment accords: a timetable for negotiations on specific product areas; the establishment of a system for bilateral negotiations on trade and investment facilitation; and the establishment of a Joint Committee on Investment and Trade to identify and promote business opportunities in both countries.

Government officials cautioned at that time that the two countries "did not contemplate a free trade area." The Mexican delegation preferred to emphasize a sectoral approach, with Salinas stating that his long-term intention was to achieve "the elimination, sector by sector, of non-tariff barriers to trade between Mexico and the United States." Elected only one year earlier, Salinas was reluctant to propose a free-trade agreement. Out of deference to Mexican political sensitivities, the report of the blue-ribbon committee, the Bilateral Commission on the Future of United States–Mexico Relations, did not go so far as to recommend the formation of a free-trade area in its report, though trade experts on both sides believed that such a move would be mutually beneficial (Bilateral Commission, 1989).

By the spring of 1990 President Salinas was ready to propose a U.S.-Mexico free-trade agreement to President Bush. The Mexicans felt that such an agreement was necessary for two important reasons. The first related to the importance of long-term investment to the new Mexican investment model. There was a feeling that a free-trade agreement, even negotiations toward such an agreement, would have a positive effect on perceptions of investment risk in Mexico, and hence result in substantial new foreign private investment there. Indeed, the negotiations for a free-trade agreement (soon with Canadian interest to be a North American Free Trade Agreement, or NAFTA) had a deliberate focus on the agreement's potential to spur private-sector investors in Mexico. The second reason for Mexico's high priority on NAFTA negotiations was the realization that Europe and Japan had their own problems and agendas, and had not shown, during extended foreign visits by President Salinas, any overwhelming desire to embark on substantial foreign investment in Mexico, or to establish special new trade relationships.

The Canadian Dimension in the Trade Negotiations

By June 1991, following a personal visit to President Bush from Canadian prime minister Brian Mulroney, Canada joined the United States and Mexico in negotiating NAFTA. The Canadian road to such negotiations was long and intense. It included the U.S.-Canadian Automotive Agreement of 1965, which had "North Americanized" automobile production, and, of course, the U.S.-Canada Free Trade Agreement of 1989, previously the most important benchmark in U.S.-Canadian trade relations.

The road to the 1989 U.S.-Canada FTA, however, provides important clues about traditional Canadian diffidence in the area of trade and other relations with its powerful southern neighbor. Canadians were happy during the first decades of this century to rely on high tariffs and nontariff barriers to keep the southern giant at bay, even though this meant higher prices to Canadian consumers.

The automobile agreement in 1965 began to change that attitude. It was clear to many Canadians that this agreement had greatly increased the efficiency and economies of scale in the U.S. and Canadian automobile industries. It resulted in the rationalization of production on a continental basis (special agreements with Mexico provided for this) and resulted in dramatic improvements in Canadian productivity and wages, as well as a greatly increased share of the North American automobile market for Canada.

Another consideration that led Canada to join the NAFTA negotiations was the fear that with a series of bilateral free-trade agreements, the United States would be the sole beneficiary of privileged access to all markets. This would also make the United States the most favored investment location for any company desiring duty-free access to all countries with which the United States had a free-trade agreement. With the trilateral NAFTA, all three countries of the continent would benefit equally in terms of trade and investment decisions.

In joining NAFTA, then, Canadian investors and exporters gained equal access to a large and growing Mexican market and the ability to participate in the creation of the largest free-trade area in the world. NAFTA would elimiate the great discrepancy between Canadian and Mexican tariffs—before NAFTA, Mexican tariffs were triple the Canadian average.

The Selling of NAFTA: Side Agreements and the NADBank

The final NAFTA agreement was signed by the executive branches of the three countries, in a December 1992 ceremony witnessed by Presidents Salinas and Bush and Prime Minister Mulroney. The task of "selling" NAFTA then fell to a new administration in Washington, following the November 1992 election of Bill Clinton. (It should be noted in this regard that given the vagaries of the Canadian parliamentary system and the composition in 1992–1993 of the Mexican Congress, ratification by Canada and Mexico was not really in doubt. The real struggle if NAFTA were to take effect in January 1994 was in and around Washington, D.C.)

Taking office in January 1993, President Clinton did not have a clear agenda on NAFTA, nor did his young and generally inexperienced White House staff. The newly designated special trade representative, Mickey Kantor, a Hollywood lawyer who had been of great help during the campaign, was innocent of trade negotiation experience or expertise. It is not surprising, especially given the way unexpected agenda items were thrust on the new president by his overzealous staff and others—the issue of homosexuals in the military, the "nannygate problem" that plagued a number of his proposed cabinet- and subcabinet-level appointments, the Medicare fiasco, and a host of other issues—that scant attention was given in the early months of the Clinton presidency to the serious challenge of getting NAFTA approved.

But this delay in focusing on the NAFTA issue provided a field day for NAFTA opponents, including such traditional Democratic Party supporters as the AFL-CIO and some environmental groups. While the White House dithered, these forces gathered unexpected strength among congressional Democrats and some Republicans, and by the time the administration got moving, it was almost too late.

One of the issues Clinton had raised as a presidential candidate was the need for "side agreements" involving Mexico, the United States, and Canada on the environment and labor. Soon negotiators for the three countries began to meet on these accords. The provisions for environmental and labor side accords became key to the completion of the selling of NAFTA to the U.S. Congress. During the summer of 1993 such issues arose as how labor and environmental standards should be enforced in the three countries and how violators should be penalized. One particularly difficult issue, the penalty provisions for enforcing labor and environmental safeguards, held up progress (and hence full-scale Clinton support for NAFTA in Congress) on the negotiations.

Mexico rejected as a violation of Mexican sovereignty any moves by the United States and Canada to include the possibility of legal action against the government in Mexican courts. This was based on the Mexican principle that sovereignty does not allow for the Mexican government to be brought before Mexican courts by foreign entities for rulings that might be against the government.

The U.S. argued for unilateral trade sanctions in case of violations of the side agreements. Both Canada and Mexico strongly objected, due to their fear that "environmental" or "labor" issues might mask protectionism in the United States. Canada maintained that the U.S. approach was too adversarial and too prosecutorial. Both Canadian and Mexican negotiators suggested the use of fines instead of trade sanctions, as a way to break the stalemate.

Thus a possible impasse in the NAFTA negotiations was avoided, and substantial progress was made on the issue of trade sanctions. On August 13, 1993, the three nations came to an agreement that labor and environmental commissions would not have supranational powers and would not have the authority to apply trade sanctions. Agreement was reached shortly after President Salinas offered to take action to raise Mexico's minimum wage.

The new trinational commissions on labor and the environment were empowered only to make recommendations and to monitor countries for violations of labor and environmental standards. Two secretariats were established—one in Canada to handle environmental complaints, and the other in Washington, D.C., to handle labor

cases. The agreements on side issues did not require the three countries to enact new legislation, but only to enforce those laws already
existing. Fines of up to $20 million could be levied on national gov-
ernments, and limited trade sanctions could be imposed on countries
that allowed their companies to gain unfair competitive advantage by
breaking domestic environmental or labor laws. The final approval of
the agreements set the stage for the ratification process in Washington.

The agreements on the side accords appeared to fall between positions taken by Republicans and business leaders, who feared the
additional regulation and the unnecessary additional bureaucracies,
and the trade pact's opponents, who argued that the side agreements
did not go nearly far enough in protecting workers and the environment. Many Republicans and business groups, however, fell in line
to support the agreements because they represented one more step
toward NAFTA ratification. Many of the Democratic Party's most
loyal constituencies, as noted earlier, argued that the side agreements
would not prevent American jobs from being lost to low-wage Mexican workers, and several Democratic leaders in the House of Representatives announced their opposition to NAFTA. It is likely that
these Democrats were emboldened to take this anti–White House
stance because of the lack of strong and clear signals from the president prior to the August 13, 1993, signing of the side agreements.

Clinton kept a low profile on NAFTA, preoccupied with budget
and other battles, and fearful of offending anti-NAFTA Democrats.
This permitted anti-NAFTA campaigners to gain a momentum that
was on the verge of being fatal to NAFTA's passage. Anti-NAFTA
forces, including trade unionists, some environmentalists, and Ross
Perot, were allowed to attack the trade agreement through the long
summer of 1993 without much organized defense on the part of the
Clinton administration. Support for NAFTA in Congress diminished
dangerously. As on other matters, the president was seen as wavering,
and possibly unwilling in the end to make a strong pro-NAFTA effort.

To overcome this perception of wavering or indifference, Clinton
finally began a public campaign to prove his commitment to
NAFTA. At a September 14, 1993, ceremony at the White House,
flanked by former presidents George Bush, Jimmy Carter, and Ger-
ald Ford, all of whom supported NAFTA, Clinton clearly pledged his
support for free trade. He maintained that, "Mexican citizens spend
more money on American products than Germans, Japanese, or even

Canadians." He urged Americans to "create the jobs of tomorrow" rather than trying to preserve "the economic structures of yesterday."

The appearance of the former presidents was meant to signal that NAFTA was considered an issue of national interest that would require bipartisan support to achieve. Given the opposition of many Democrats to the agreement, Clinton understood the necessity of gaining Republican support. The four presidents—two Democrats and two Republicans—set out to counter opposition claims about NAFTA by offering the arguments that NAFTA would create jobs for Americans, not eliminate them; that NAFTA would stem illegal immigration by creating more jobs for Mexicans in Mexico; and that NAFTA would enhance the process of democratization in Mexico and provide more stability.

The September 14 ceremony marked the beginning of a hard and eventually successful campaign by the White House to get NAFTA through Congress. President Clinton himself became increasingly active in promoting the agreement, traveling around the country to promote the virtues of NAFTA and making daily phone calls to undecided House members. California was a particularly important state for the Clinton administration to target, as many of the state's fifty-two House members remained undecided in the weeks before the vote. Clinton argued that NAFTA was the best way for Californians to boost export sales and to lower immigration levels.

Vice President Gore, perhaps the strongest environmentalist in the administration, also played an important role in promoting NAFTA. He maintained that NAFTA would have tremendous benefits for the environment through the endorsement of environmental standards written into the trade agreement itself and the establishment of a fund for environmental cleanup along the U.S.-Mexico border. Gore also debated Ross Perot, a NAFTA opponent, on television, and was deemed to have emerged as the clear victor in that debate.

The Clinton administration continued with the NAFTA campaign through the very day of the House vote on November 17, 1993. A week before, it appeared that the administration was perilously close to losing the NAFTA vote, with a divided House and many members still undecided. Up to the last hours before the vote, Clinton made a number of explicit deals with House members, including support for a North American Development Bank (NADBank), and special consideration for the makers of textiles, apparel, glass products, and even brooms. Deals were made in the agricultural sector as well, involving wheat, citrus, sugar, beef, vegetables, and peanut butter. After a tough day of debate, NAFTA finally was approved by the House by a vote of 234 to 200 and shortly thereafter was easily approved by the Senate. The Canadian and Mexican legislatures followed suit and NAFTA, as previously envisioned, came into effect on January 1, 1994.

Mexico in 1994: A Year of Turbulence

There was every reason for President Salinas to celebrate New Year's Eve on December 31, 1993, with a feeling of satisfaction and a sense of accomplishment. It must have seemed to Salinas that 1994 would be a year of enjoying the benefits of the successful transformation of the Mexican economy which had begun under President de la Madrid (1982–1988) and seemed to be coming to fruition under Salinas's leadership. It was logical to expect on easy election for his party's presidential candidate and, possibly, his own election to the presidency of the new World Trade Organization, the successor to the GATT, in January 1995. A series of cataclysmic events destroyed any such expectations.

First, in the early morning hours of January 1, 1994, the day NAFTA came into force, some thousand members of Mexico's Zapatista Army of National Liberation (EZLN) took control of four towns in the southern state of Chiapas. This uprising was Mexico's largest since the religious rebellion of the Cristeros in 1926–1927, and was also Latin America's first guerrilla movement in the post–Cold War age. The rebels' sophistication surprised many observers, as EZLN representatives quickly called a press conference and faxed carefully crafted press releases in both English and Spanish. It was clear early on that the Zapatista movement was not a spontaneous revolt, given their centralized command, substantial communications and logistics capability, and sophisticated sense of public relations. Nevertheless, most of the rebels were quickly driven back into the countryside after four days by about 12,000 Mexican army troops, leaving some 150 dead and about twice that number wounded.

The roots of the Chiapas uprising can be found in the history of poverty and discontent in this southernmost state, an area plagued by decades of unresolved land disputes, unfulfilled promises by the government, and economic exploitation. Many observers believed that conditions for a revolt had been brewing since the 1981 economic crisis as socioeconomic problems, long a part of the history of southern Mexico, became even more acute. The population in Chiapas is made up mostly of rural Indians who live in the harshest conditions; 80 percent of the population earns less than $8 per day. According to the National Statistics Institute, the average salary in the states of Chiapas, Oaxaca, Guerrero, Hidalgo, and Veracruz, home to large numbers of indigenous people, lies below the poverty line.

Aside from the poverty and discrimination that face the indigenous peoples of Chiapas, there also have been political causes for the current rebellion, rooted in archaic political structures that have long governed not only Chiapas, but many areas in rural southern Mexico. Article 27 of the Constitution of 1917 addresses the land question, and directs the government to preserve an "equitable distribution of the public wealth" through such measures as the breaking up of large landholdings and ensuring that all communities, particularly small farmers, are entitled to their lands and waters. Succeeding Mexican presidents after the revolution maintained the support of the peasantry by issuing land titles to rural communities.

José Patrocinio González, the governor of Chiapas from 1988 to 1994, was unpopular with the poor and indigenous. Human-rights groups accused him of violating the spirit of the Mexican Constitution by using violence to silence peaceful Indian protests. He and his administration were also linked to numerous human-rights abuses. Particularly critical of Patrocinio González was Bishop Samuel Ruiz of San Cristóbal de las Casas, Chiapas, who spent thirty years of his life promoting indigenous rights in the area. It was unfortunate, therefore, that Patrocinio González was subsequently named secretary of government, the department that oversees internal affairs in Mexico. Shortly after the Chiapas rebellion began, he was replaced by Jorge Carpizo, a prominent figure in Mexico's human-rights arena. President Salinas also named then–foreign secretary Manuel Camacho, a popular ex-mayor of Mexico City, to assume the task of negotiating with the Zapatistas. The first of what was to prove to be a number of agreements during these protracted and continuing negotiations was signed on March 2, 1994, only to be rejected by the Zapatistas a few weeks later.

The timing of the Chiapas rebellion to coincide with the ratification of the NAFTA treaty on January 1 was not an accident. It reflected the viewpoint of many indigenous peoples in Mexico that their interests were not considered in economic reforms, and that they did not stand to benefit from NAFTA. Most of the rebels interviewed by journalists since the Chiapas rebellion have echoed the same sentiment—that they have no future in the "new" Mexico. In the state of Chiapas, approximately one-third of the population are Indians, many of whom work corn patches and were seriously affected by cutbacks in agricultural subsidies and credits throughout the De la Madrid and Salinas economic reforms.

The Chiapas uprising further signaled that more political reforms were needed in Mexico, reflected the longstanding neglect of indigenous peoples in Latin America, and illustrated the social costs of economic reform that fails to take all sectors of the populace into account. Politically, Mexico faced a difficult year of political turmoil after the Chiapas uprising, in which the social costs of inequitable structural reforms and the lack of a complete democracy became prominent.

Luis Donaldo Colosio

After the January rebellion in Chiapas, Mexico faced another serious crisis two months later. On Wednesday, March 23, while campaigning in Tijuana, PRI presidential candidate Luis Donaldo Colosio was fatally shot by twenty-three-year-old Mario Aburto Martínez. The assassination was the first of a major political figure since 1928, when president-elect Alvaro Obregón was killed. Although political violence on the local level is not uncommon in Mexico, assassination of a national political figure is something Mexicans had never considered a part of their political process. The Colosio assassination was a traumatic event in Mexico, and was compared by Mexicans to the assassination of President John F. Kennedy.

Colosio had been supported by President Salinas as the next PRI presidential candidate, and widely regarded as a Salinas protégé likely to continue his economic and social programs. Colosio, a forty-three-year-old social development secretary, was virtually assured of the presidency. In his acceptance speech in November 1993, Colosio pledged to stay on course with the Salinas reforms and reaffirmed his support of NAFTA. Although Colosio was predicted to continue the economic policies that Salinas had begun, many also considered him a staunch social reformer. He claimed that he would work to change Mexico's image abroad as a nation that neglects its poor, and wanted to demonstrate honest, democratic elections. Colosio also saw Mexico's primary challenges in the future as arising in the domestic arena as opposed to the international, after a decade of resolving the debt crisis and entry into NAFTA. His staunch opposition to illegal narcotics trafficking is seen by some as the key factor in his assassination.

The Colosio tragedy complicated Mexico's efforts to confront demands from the populace for political reforms. The unusually public dissension between members of the PRI over who should succeed Colosio indicated the renewed strength of the PRI "dinosaurs" unhappy with economic reforms and threatened by promises made to the Zapatistas on enacting political reforms and decreasing electoral fraud. So the successor to Colosio faced the difficulty of achieving political reforms and at the same time mediating between disgruntled factions of the PRI.

Ernesto Zedillo

One week after the assassination, Ernesto Zedillo Ponce de León was named as the PRI candidate for the presidency. Although Zedillo, the personal choice of President Salinas, was the immediate favorite of the party at large, the decision by President Salinas was made amidst the unusually open objections by certain members of the PRI who considered the forty-two-year-old economist to be a technocrat unappealing to workers and peasants. PRI president Fernando Ortiz Arana was the favorite of the hard-liner faction. Salinas's entire cabinet was ineligible, including Pedro Aspe, the well-respected minister of finance, due to the law barring any officeholder as of February 21 of an election year from running for president. Zedillo, however, had given up his position as education minister in December to run the Colosio campaign.

Zedillo was born into a lower-middle-class family in Mexicali, and earned scholarships to attend the National University of Mexico; later he went on to earn a doctorate in economics from Yale and rose quickly through the ranks of Mexico's central bank. In 1988 he became Salinas's budget and planning minister, and helped to engineer the Pacto de Solidaridad Económica, an influential and successful plan to control inflation in the wake of the debt crisis. He was characterized as "austere, rigorous, and highly intelligent." In 1992 he was appointed minister of education, partly because of Salinas's desire to allow Zedillo to sharpen his political skills. He soon found himself in the midst of a national brouhaha over the distribution of new school textbooks with a more balanced view of Mexican history, the first, for example, to acknowledge the 1968 Tlatelolco tragedy.

In his acceptance speech, Zedillo emphasized that his was not a new campaign but a continuation of Colosio's. However, he initially lacked the public support that Colosio had enjoyed. Zedillo was not the charismatic campaigner that Colosio had been, and furthermore faced the difficult task of balancing political and economic reforms and appeasing hard-line elements in the party.

The 1994 Elections

In November 1993 the government had made several changes to make elections more credible, particularly after widespread charges that Cuauhtémoc Cárdenas actually had won the presidential elections in 1988. However, these changes, along with another round of reforms in January 1994, did not quell criticism that the reforms only tinkered with the electoral system. Amidst demands by the Zapatistas for greater democratization and more credible elections, the Mexican government agreed in principle to another round of changes. These included a more independent electoral institute, more intense scrutiny of voter registration lists, and greater access by opposition candidates to television time. The government also acknowledged that it would be willing to accept international observers.

The United States was forceful in advocating to Mexican officials that the 1994 elections be free and fair, or the U.S.-Mexico relationship could be harmed. In May, Secretary of State Warren Christopher, Attorney General Janet Reno, and other top U.S. officials conducted a two-day mission to Mexico to deliver the message that the United States supported democratic reforms, and that electoral fraud would prove disastrous. Christopher publicly praised the electoral reforms and hinted at the importance of clean elections. In private conversations with Mexican officials, he was reportedly much more direct. Christopher voiced his concerns over the implementation of the electoral reforms, emphasizing that their success would be dependent upon how they were put into effect. In particular, U.S. officials pressed for Mexico to accept and support foreign election observers to increase the legitimacy of election results. This more hard-line stance by the United States clearly represented a shift in U.S. policy toward Mexico after such events as the Chiapas uprising and the Colosio assassination.

In May 1994, Mexicans witnessed the first televised debate between presidential candidates. Zedillo agreed to debate his two main opponents, Cuauhtémoc Cárdenas and Diego Fernández de Cevallos, on national television. The candidates debated for ninety minutes, although they did not field questions from the audience. The most obvious beneficiary of the debate was PAN candidate Diego Fernández de Cevallos, who shot from a distant third in polls before the debate to a close second to Zedillo. Fernández suddenly appeared to the public as charismatic, compared with a somber Cárdenas and a stiff Zedillo.

During the balance of the campaign, Zedillo successfully played on voters' concerns about stability and security, running on a "law and order" ticket, and stressing continuity with the stable past, the experience and competence of his team, and the need for further economic, political, and social reforms. Cárdenas's main appeal to the voters in 1988 had been as a "new broom" bent on sweeping away the austerity programs of De la Madrid, but, by 1994, he was endorsing NAFTA, and seemed unable to present a coherent, differentiated economic policy of his own. Fernández de Cevallos saw his early boomlet, based on the debate, fade away as he conducted a generally desultory campaign based on "God, the family, and the fatherland," which had decreasing appeal as the campaign wore on. By early June, independent polls put Zedillo's support at 50 percent, Fernández de Cevallos's at 32 percent, and Cárdenas's at 13 percent. The final election results gave Zedillo 48.8 percent, Fernández de Cevallos 25.9 percent, and Cárdenas 16.6 percent. The balance went to minor parties or were annulled. Although some election irregularities were reported by the well-respected human rights group Civic Alliance and others, the clear consensus among independent observers and analysts was that Zedillo emerged the legitimate victor in the 1994 elections.

Inauguration of a New President

A brief period of great optimism surrounded the ceremonial farewell to outgoing President Salinas in late November and, on December 1, the inauguration of President Zedillo. Hundreds of dignitaries from the world's financial powers, political leaders and others attended the cermonies. The new president impressed Mexicans and foreigners alike with his apparent openness and simplicity, and his determination to ensure an improved legal system, more fair elections, and continued economic progress. His new cabinet included as secretary of finance Jaime Serra Puche, whose work as secretary of trade and industry in the NAFTA negotiations had earned him a favorable reputation in international trade and financial circles.

The first days of the Zedillo presidency were almost euphoric in nature, with the promise of early institutional reforms and the December 8 prediction by Serra that in the coming year Mexico would enjoy low inflation and real GDP growth of 4 percent. Questions about the wisdom of Mexico's international financial policies were dismissed, and the door was closed on any question of a possible devaluation. Serra explained that a narrow "flotation band" would give the financial authorities ample margin to confront transitory problems.

The Mexican Peso Crisis

These "transitory problems" very quickly proved to be anything but transitory. They were far more pervasive and severe than the new Mexican economic team had imagined, and only twelve days later— December 20, 1994—Mexico was forced to act, initially by attempting to expand the "flotation band" by 15 percent, which was seen by the investing public as tantamount to a 15 percent devaluation. The controversial management of this emerging crisis exacerbated investor fears and shortly thereafter resulted in a further, uncontrolled fall in the peso after Serra announced that the peso would be allowed to trade freely against the dollar. "The financial authorities," he explained, "have decided that supply and demand will freely determine the rate of exchange until the currency markets show conditions of stability" (Reuters, December 24, 1994).

The finance minister's much-publicized trip to New York to present Mexico's case did little to reassure foreign investors, and the promised prompt unveiling of an emergency plan to confront the economic crisis was slow in coming. By early January 1995 the crisis had reached its peak. Events had led the Mexican government and its new cabinet into an almost unbelievable series of policy and procedural errors that cost Mexico most of its remaining cash reserves, a meltdown of the peso-dollar exchange rate, and a severe cabinet shakeup. When the abortive announcement was made, first privately to Mexican investors and businessmen and then to the world, of the planned de facto 15 percent devaluation of the peso, the instant demand for dollars was ruinous. It was then that the peso was allowed to float as the Bank of Mexico's cash reserves were fast disappearing, interest rates soared, and the peso lost half its value. A few days later, Guillermo Ortiz, a former undersecretary of finance who was then serving as secretary of telecommunications, replaced Serra as finance minister, and the long, painful process of recovery of confidence in the peso began. Essentially, the Mexican authorities sharply limited public-sector spending and retrenched to deal with rising inflation. The 1995 plan worked, but the price was excruciatingly high, particularly for middle-class Mexicans. GDP fell by 7 percent; unemployment and underemployment rose dramatically; real wages fell by some 20 percent; bankruptcies increased; and bank credit almost totally dried up. In the end, these draconian austerity measures succeeded, and well into 1996 real GDP growth was observed and the peso had steadied.

Washington's Uncertain Trumpet

The beginning weeks of the Zedillo government were marked by muddled economic leadership. This confusion was echoed in the early handling of the crisis by the Clinton administration in Washington. Conflicts between the administration and Congress led to a failed attempt in late January 1995 to push a $40 billion currency guarantee program through the Republican Congress, despite initial support offered by House Speaker Newt Gingrich and Senate leader Bob Dole. But President Clinton recovered his touch, and went around a reluctant Congress to arrange a loan package using $25 billion from the emergency Exchange Stabilization Fund (ESF), to round up support from international financial institutions and foreign central and commercial banks. A $50 billion total package was first announced on January 31. While the peso hit a low of 6.35 to the dollar on that day, it soon improved to the general 5.8 level, where it achieved some short-term stability.

There is little doubt that the financial crisis was greatly ameliorated by the efforts of the United States. The assistance package grounded in the ESF agreement was an essential element in giving the Mexican government the economic-policy space it needed to take other necessary measures (Roett, 1996). The difficulties both Mexico City and Washington had in addressing the crisis offer valuable lessons for efforts to identify viable new alternatives to resolution of international financial crises. These lessons are discussed in detail in Part 2 (Chapter 4), which concerns Mexico and the global economy.

The Relationship Today: Contemporary Issues

4

Mexico and the Global Economy

In the 1990s notions about international relations that had been formed during the post–World War II period continued to crumble. During the late 1980s, one after the other, communist regimes in Eastern Europe fell. The essential internal weakness of the Soviet Union became increasingly apparent, culminating with its total disintegration in 1992.

The attention of the United States was thus shifted from the international security issues of the bipolar nuclear world of the 1950s through the 1980s to pressing global and regional economic issues. This change of focus has had favorable implications for U.S.-Mexico economic relations, for trade negotiations involving North America, and, prospectively, for a Free Trade Area of the Americas (FTAA).

At the same time that world events, as well as growing trade deficits, were turning America's attention to regional economic issues (such as the negotiation of the U.S.-Canada Free Trade Agreement of January 1988), Mexico likewise was paying greater attention to economic matters. Under the leadership of Presidents Miguel de la Madrid and Carlos Salinas, Mexico was contemplating the economic-policy reforms needed to launch the country successfully into the world economy.

The United States has played a persistent role in the course of Mexico's political economy, particularly since the time of the *porfiriato* (1876–1910). The economy, which suffered dramatically during the violent stages of the revolution (1910–1920), recovered only slowly afterward. The next twenty-five years were shaped by a world depression; the growing involvement of the state, exemplified by the nationalization of Mexico's oil industry in 1938; and World War II (1939–1945).

World War II catalyzed a considerable degree of economic cooperation between the United States and Mexico. The United States bought raw materials from Mexico for its war effort and used the *bracero* program to substitute Mexican laborers for American youth called to military service. This cooperation continued during the postwar era, when Mexican leaders saw that building by the state of a firm infrastructure and control of primary industries should be balanced by development of a viable private sector and an expansion of foreign trade.

Mexico fostered this private-sector growth by adopting a policy of import-substituting industrialization (ISI). The state erected stiff protectionist barriers to foreign imports in order to subsidize "infant" private industries. From 1950 until 1982, tariffs were increased whenever necessary to protect both private and state-controlled industries in what effectively became a closed Mexican economy. The resulting growth, while dramatic (output rose by an average of 6.5 percent annually during this period), proved unsustainable in the long run. While ISI may have seemed to make good sense in its earlier years, the Echeverría and López Portillo administrations did not design government policies to create an orderly transition to the open-market system. This was clearly required by the advancing globalization of the international economy.

Mexico's growing economic difficulties and difficulties in its relations with the United States were exacerbated by rising deficits and the inflammatory Third World rhetoric of the Echeverría administration (1970–1976), which culminated in rampant capital flight and the devaluation of the peso by 60 percent.

The Mexican economy underwent significant changes during both the Echeverría and the López Portillo (1976–1982) administrations. The economy continued to grow at an average rate of 5 percent during this period, but was marked by slower growth in the late 1970s and unsustainable buoyant growth in the early 1980s due to the world oil boom, new oil "discoveries" in Mexico, and resultant free-and-easy international credit. The external sector was very active through 1982, with total exports, led by oil sales, increasing at an average annual rate of 35 percent in 1977–1982.

The economy went into a recession, then recovered powerfully but briefly at the height of the oil boom (1979–1981). But the amassing of incredible new debt during that boom ended with the crash of 1982. During his final weeks in office, a troubled López Portillo nationalized the banking system, which was followed by the collapse of private-sector confidence in the Mexican political and economic situations.

The 1982 crisis was a clear reflection of the weakness of the Mexican economy caused by overdependence on the import-substitution development model, which created a closed, noncompetitive economy vulnerable to external shocks. The collapse of world oil prices and rising international interest rates wreaked havoc on Mexico's foreign debt, which had reached historic highs during the brief "oil boom" years.

The Mexican Debt Crisis

When President de la Madrid took office in 1982, Mexico's debt was, at $100 billion, the largest of any developing country in the world. Even worse, much of this debt had been negotiated when international interest rates were very high. This meant that during the De la Madrid administration, the payment of interest alone on Mexico's foreign debt amounted to a startling 6 percent of total GDP, exerting a crushing effect on the public expenditures and private-sector borrowing needed to get the economy moving again.

Working with foreign governments and international banks, both the De la Madrid and Salinas administrations renegotiated debt repayment down to a more manageable 2 percent of Mexican GDP. A single agreement, signed in February 1990, covered the $50 billion Mexico owed to foreign commercial banks. The agreement converted high floating interest rates to lower fixed rates, in the bargain giving Mexico needed protection from future rises in world interest rates. This freed up some $6 billion in funds for infrastructure and other investments to promote Mexico's economic growth.

Mexico was then considered by foreign financial experts to have resolved its series of debt crises, and from 1990 to 1994 was again eligible for new, development-oriented lending. This invigorated relationship with the international financial community triggered a rebound in confidence among Mexican investors, who during the 1990–1994 period returned several billion dollars in repatriated capital (which had left the country during the final year of the López Portillo administration) for new private-sector investments in Mexico's future.

De la Madrid Embarks on Economic and Political Reform

With the advent of Miguel de la Madrid to the presidency in late 1982, U.S.-Mexico economic relations began what was to be a decade of dramatic improvement. The six-year term of President De la Madrid (1982–1988) was divided almost evenly between internal economic adjustments and international economic-policy reform. During his first three years in office, De la Madrid reduced inflationary pressures, stabilized the exchange rate at a level where Mexican exports were more competitive, limited government expenditures, and cut traditional subsidies on basic foodstuffs.

Later, Mexico joined the General Agreement on Tariffs and Trade (the GATT); tariffs were sharply reduced to an average of only 7 percent, with a maximum tariff of 20 percent; the requirement that imports of foreign goods be subject to government licenses was all but eliminated; and an arrangement for resolving U.S.-Mexico trade disputes was created.

Mexico's accession to the GATT represented a watershed in Mexican foreign-trade policy, and reflected the change from the ISI development model to an export model of growth. Mexico's GATT accession also placed both Mexico and the United States within a multilateral framework of rules, established rights and obligations for both countries, and significantly reduced conflicts in the bilateral trading relationship. The GATT was created in 1947 to reduce tariffs and eliminate discriminatory practices in international trade. Originally signed by twenty-three countries, by the time Mexico joined the number had grown to almost one hundred. Mexico played a key role in GATT negotiations, which resulted in a new trade agreement that cut global tariffs overall by more than one-third, gave greater protection to intellectual-property rights, and opened trade in investments and services. The negotiations also created a successor entity to the GATT, the World Trade Organization (WTO).

The importance of this improvement in trade relations was underscored by the fact that by the early 1990s Mexico was the third most important export market for the United States (preceded by Canada and Japan), and 65 percent of Mexico's total exports were to the United States.

The decision to join the GATT was evidence of the De la Madrid administration's growing commitment to trade liberalization. This was followed by the U.S.-Mexico Bilateral Framework Agreement on Trade and Investment signed in November 1987 by Presidents Reagan and De la Madrid. The agreement provided a framework for bilateral trade negotiations and dispute settlement, and established an agenda for specific sectoral discussions.

The adjustments and reforms of the De la Madrid administration resulted in important new world-trade relationships. Ironically, these strides were facilitated by the failed policies of the López Portillo regime, as many informed Mexicans came to realize that years of ideological rhetoric, nationalizations, and protectionism had brought them to disaster. They were now ready to try the sometimes bitter remedies of austerity and stabilization.

Salinas Expands Internal Reform, U.S. Trade Relations

The steady progress of the De la Madrid years set the stage for the further opening of the Mexican economy during the Salinas administration (1988–1994). Internal economic reform accelerated, relations with President Bush's administration were close, and the foreign debt was restructured. Encouraged by a growing U.S. economy in the early 1980s and by improving trade relations, Mexican industry shifted to an export-driven strategy, which was rewarded by a significant improvement in the composition and level of U.S.-Mexico trade balances.

In fact, while much attention is paid to NAFTA, it should be remembered that considerable trade liberalization was taking place in Mexico well before January 1994. For example, Mexico's average tariffs fell from 27 percent in 1982 to 12 percent in 1993, and to 6 percent in 1996. Mexico's serious efforts at trade liberalization during the De la Madrid and Salinas administrations, still under way under Zedillo, have resulted in its ranking of fifteenth place in total exports among all exporting nations, as compared with twenty-eighth in 1982.

But, as elsewhere in U.S.-Mexico relations, asymmetries abounded in bilateral trade. In the years before NAFTA came into effect on January 1, 1994, the U.S. share of total Mexican trade (exports and imports) rose from 65 percent to 75 percent; exports to the United States accounted for 14 percent of Mexico's GDP. In comparison, Mexico's share of total U.S. trade rose from 5 percent to 7 percent, with exports to Mexico accounting for less than 1 percent of the huge American GDP. This steady growth in trade has been a great plus for the Mexican economy.

Moreover, the composition of trade changed substantially in the pre-NAFTA years. In the early 1980s, Mexican exports to the United States were dominated by petroleum, with crude-oil exports running strong until 1984, after which they began to decline. This decline, however, was accompanied by a significant increase in Mexico's exports of manufactured goods to the United States. Important Mexican exports included machinery and transportation equipment, automotive parts, cement, steel, iron pipes, tiles, glass products, minerals, agricultural products, apparel, and shoes.

As Mexico began to recover from the crisis of 1982, U.S. exports rose markedly, especially in the vital areas of capital goods, machinery and transportation equipment, and chemicals. Mexico's opening of its economy, accompanied by new private investment, created a growing demand for capital and intermediate goods. This demand greatly stimulated U.S. exports in 1987–1994.

U.S. economy and impact on Mexican trade relations. The U.S. economy during this period also experienced profound changes that affected its trading relationship with Mexico. In 1971 the United States abandoned the gold standard, contributing temporarily to international financial instability. The United States also experimented briefly with protectionist measures such as a 10 percent surcharge on imports. The dollar was devalued as the country faced a growing U.S. balance-of-payments deficit. In 1977 the current-account deficit totaled $15 billion, in contrast to positive balances with primary trading partners such as Japan and Germany. The decade was marked by stagnation, inflation, unemployment, and reduced investment. The recession of the early 1980s proved to be the deepest and most prolonged since the Great Depression, which, along with inflation, created a very difficult economic situation for the U.S. economy.

The evolution of U.S.-Mexican trade relations during this period was characterized by changes in both composition and volume of bilateral trade flows, and increasing conflicts over trade policies. The years 1970–1982 saw major changes in the importance of trade and investment for both the U.S. and Mexican economies, and in the composition of bilateral trade. The importance of trade to the U.S.

economy grew as deficits in the U.S. balance of payments continued to pose economic problems. Total U.S. trade as a share of GDP, historically low, grew from 8.8 percent in 1972 to 22 percent in 1987. This shift made foreign trade much more important than before to the American economy.

Changing patterns in Mexican trade. Mexico's trading situation also changed during this period, as a result of both oil exports during the oil boom of the late 1970s and the growth of non-oil exports after the oil bust and Mexico's resultant economic crisis. By 1986 Mexico for the first time recorded a surplus in nonpetroleum trade with the United States. By the mid-1980s, levels of bilateral trade in manufactured goods were at five times the level of the 1970s. This was matched by the growth of Mexico's in-bond and assembly industries. The number of *maquiladoras*—plants that assemble imported parts and reexport the final product—rose from 350 in 1972 to 1,100 in 1986.

Trade Performance After NAFTA

This strong growth in trade between the U.S. and Mexico continued after the implementation of NAFTA. Total bilateral trade—which amounted to only $53 billion in 1989—rose in anticipation of NAFTA to $81.5 billion in 1993, and $100.3 billion in 1994. And, despite the Mexican peso crisis, the increase in total bilateral trade has continued, reaching $108 billion in 1995, $131.1 billion in 1996, $157.3 billion in 1997, and some $174 billion in 1998 (see Figure 4.1). During 1993–1996 Mexico's trade with Canada increased modestly, but its trade with non-NAFTA countries increased by 27 percent, providing some healthy trade diversification.

Mexico is now ranked tenth among the world's largest trading countries, and ranks third in the Western Hemisphere, after the United States and Canada. Thus NAFTA includes the top three trading countries in the hemisphere. Mexico is the United States' third largest trading partner, and second most important market for U.S. exports, having surpassed Japan in 1997.

The bilateral trade balance was, of course, affected by the peso crisis and devaluation in late 1994 and early 1995. As shown in Figure 4.1, Mexican exports to the United States grew from $49.5

Figure 4.1   Mexico-U.S. Trade (in billions of dollars)

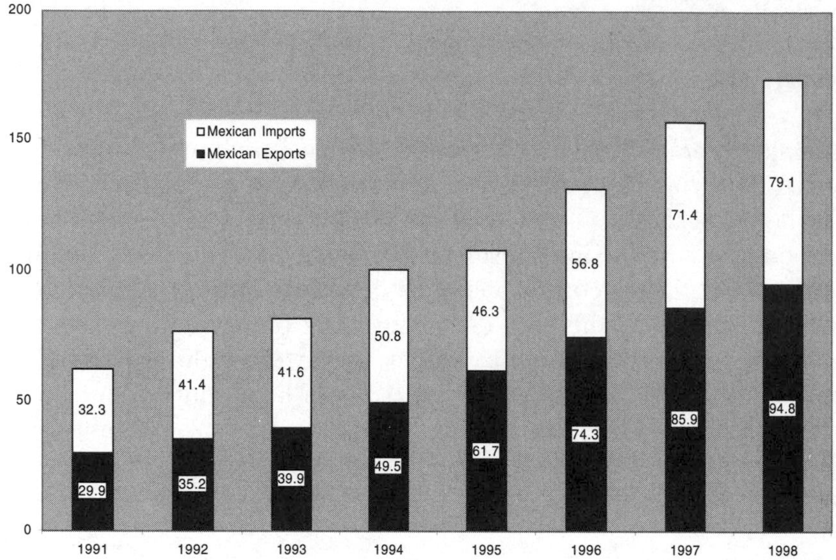

Source: U.S. Department of Commerce

billion in 1994 to $61.7 billion in 1995, and $74.3 billion in 1996, while imports from the United States fell slightly, from $50.8 billion in 1994 to $46.3 billion in 1995, recovering to $56.8 billion in 1996.

Mexican Foreign Investment

The climate for foreign private direct investment (FPDI) in Mexico has remained strong since NAFTA was enacted, even during the Asian, Russian, and Brazilian financial crises of the late 1990s. Factors such as progress toward democratization (see Chapter 5), some recovery in consumer buying power, and the Mexican government's positive attitudes toward attracting FPDI seem to have lessened the impact of global turbulence outside Mexico's borders. FPDI in Mexico averaged $4 billion in the 1990–1993 period, grew to a dramatic $11 billion in 1994, tapered off a bit to $9.5 billion in 1995, and then, despite the severe peso crisis of 1994–1995, continued at $7.6 billion in 1996.

An upward trend in FPDI was noted in subsequent years, growing to $8.9 billion in 1997, $9.0 billion in 1998, and a projected $8.5

billion in 1999. The failure in 1998 to meet the government's $10 billion FPDI goal was attributed to international financial uncertainties, particularly in emerging markets. In general, more than half of Mexico's FPDI is from the United States, and much of that is from U.S. subsidiaries already operating in Mexico in the form of new or re-investments.

Prospects for foreign investment, both direct and indirect, in 2000 and beyond will depend in part on the ability of a multiparty system to compromise on the basic institutional changes needed for modernization and democratization in Mexico. A positive sign in this regard is the agreement by the PRI and PAN to reorganize the $61 billion Banking Fund for Savings Protection (FOBAPROA) bank bailout that was the subject of heavy debate in the Congress and the press throughout the whole of 1998. These debates culminated in early 1999 with agreement by the PRI and PAN leadership (unsurprisingly drawing the ire of the PRD) to request congressional approval to establish a new agency with power to issue government-backed bonds to raise capital in international financial markets, and to investigate bank loans originally granted under fraudulent circumstances.

It is worthy of note that the final banking plan also ended the restrictions limiting foreign ownership of Mexican banks, which is expected to give rise to a greater salience of foreign-owned banking operations in Mexico in 2000 and beyond. The banking agreement helped ease Mexico's prospects at a time when it was facing a global environment marked by weak oil prices and at least slightly reduced capital inflows.

Oil Remains a Sensitive Issue

Despite the recent opening of much of their economy, many Mexicans are still reluctant to surrender state control over oil and gas exploration and exploitation. Mexico's estimated reserves of some 48 billion barrels represent one of the largest undeveloped oil fields outside the Middle East and the former Soviet Union. Mexicans are proud of President Lázaro Cárdenas's nationalization of the oil industry in 1938, and there is little enthusiasm for returning to the days of foreign ownership and control. So, while the state-owned PEMEX is dealing cautiously to develop some relationships (drilling contracts, for example) with U.S. and other oil companies, it would be both dramatic and unexpected if President Zedillo's successor were at some future point to initiate the constitutional changes necessary to invite foreign companies to participate directly in the exploration and exploitation of Mexico's oil and gas resources. Furthermore, government economic policymakers are very aware that a significant portion of the federal government budget originates in oil revenues, and an outright privatization of the oil industry would threaten that important revenue source.

Meanwhile, the links between PEMEX and international financial institutions are growing. For example, PEMEX has obtained a $1.6 billion loan from the U.S. Export-Import Bank to finance U.S.-origin oil equipment and services needed to boost production. Apparently, Mexico's oil policy experts have concluded that Mexico needs to increase its surge capacity to profit from unexpected world situations like the Gulf crisis of 1990–1991. Petroleum exports are already important to the Mexican economy, bringing in $10 billion in earnings in 1997.

But Mexico's annual oil production of 3 million barrels per day, half of which is exported (with the U.S. as the biggest customer), could be much greater. With the Ex-Im Bank loan and other assistance, including a half-billion-dollar investment from Japan's Mitsui group, plans are under way to prepare Mexico for a more flexible strategy in times of sudden, unanticipated oil price increases. Mexico's effective crude oil reserves would increase dramatically if the current ban on direct foreign participation in exploration and extraction were lifted. As Mexico oil expert George Baker has noted, independent oil companies could exploit existing fields at lower lifting costs than PEMEX, and large multinational companies could access deep-water resources well beyond PEMEX's operating range (Baker, 1999). For clear political reasons, though, this is unlikely to happen soon.

Mexico's energy sector remains largely in the hands of PEMEX and the Federal Electricity Commission (CFE), though recent changes in laws and regulations allow private-sector electricity generation and establish a new commission to regulate public-private sector competition. Under NAFTA, U.S. and Canadian firms have an expanded access to Mexico's gas, petrochemical, and energy services and equipment markets. Scores of electricity generation permits for cogeneration, or for factories for self-generation of their own power, were awarded in the 1996–1998 period. Gas distribution and transport contracts were negotiated in 1998, and negotiations continued into 1999. Exploration and production of petroleum, however, remained firmly in government hands, though progress was made toward the privatization of the state-owned secondary petrochemical industry despite political crossfire from opposition parties and the strong petroleum workers' unions.

Privatization of electricity sector moves forward. President Zedillo's February 1999 proposal to privatize existing electrical-power plants and allow concessionaires to distribute electrical power in regional zones moved forward despite strong opposition from the electrical-workers unions and their supporters. The Zedillo plan also called for a private-sector contract to maintain a national power grid and create new markets for electrical power. Total FPDI in this sector could amount to $25 billion in the 1999–2005 period. The proposal was clearly designed to use FPDI to make it economically self-sustaining, rather than a drag on the federal government budget. It is sure to be hotly debated by the PRI, PRD, and PAN candidates during the course of the 2000 general elections in Mexico.

Mexico's Future Economic Strategies

By early 1999 Mexico had emerged once again from economic crisis and the subsequent stabilization and austerity programs that marked the economy in 1995–1996. Recovering from a loss of real GDP of more than 6 percent in 1995, GDP actually grew by 5 percent in 1996, and 7 percent in 1997. Though growth was more modest, around 5 percent in 1998, and perhaps half that is projected in 1999 (see Figure 4.2), the fact is that Mexico appears to have adopted most of the measures needed to continue real growth even in an unfavorable global economic situation. The growth of foreign investment and Mexican exports has helped.

Clearly, foreign investment and export growth must remain strong beyond 2000 if recovery is to continue. An ideal government policy would combine these needs by actively encouraging FPDI as well as domestic investment in the field of manufacturing for export,

Figure 4.2 Mexico: GDP Growth (% Change)

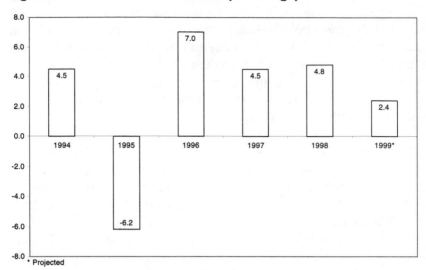

* Projected

Source: Banco de México

including the energy sector, e.g., gas, electricity, and petrochemicals. Both goals are also well served by maintaining a floating exchange rate policy rather than succumbing to the short-term controls that have had an unfortunate history in Mexico.

Will Budget Austerity Continue?

It will be interesting to observe to what degree Mexico eschews the sexennial temptation of what observers call "the Year of Hidalgo," after the Mexican hero whose face appears on Mexican currency. In 1999 Mexico approached the final year of the presidential *sexenio,* which is traditionally marked by dramatically increased government spending in support of the PRI's presidential candidate. Mexico's minister of finance José Angel Gurría cut public-sector spending three times in 1998, due in large part to declining world oil prices; presented an austere budget for 1999; and then proceeded to cut spending again. This represented a departure from the sexennial norm, and was greeted warmly by the international financial community.

These same austerity measures, however, had an adverse effect on social spending, and, as the peso depreciates, minimum wages in Mexico in 1999 were just about $4 per day, with one-third of all working Mexicans earning less than that. Mexico has responded by instituting a sharply focused program, called Progresa, to help the poorest of the poor. It offers the neediest families assistance to meet their nutritional, health, and basic educational needs. Often assistance is provided through contacts with women through schools and health clinics. But the positive results of the Progresa program will be difficult to measure before the early years of the next century.

5

Mexico's Political Transformation and Democratization

The End of the Old Order

The overriding need for internal stability in postrevolutionary Mexico resulted in the creation by Mexico's political and military leaders of a central government dominated by a single party, founded in the 1920s, and known since 1946 as the Partido Revolucionario Institucional, or PRI. For the decades stretching from Alvaro Obregón (1920–1924), the first postrevolutionary Mexican president to be able to hand power peacefully over to his elected successor, through the tumultuous years of ephemeral grandeur and economic disaster of José López Portillo (1976–1982), the old order in Mexico enjoyed a largely unchallenged six decades of authoritarian rule. Power was focused within a presidency that expressed its will most forcefully through the ruling political party, whose members held all the key positions within the government. The conventional wisdom in Mexico is that the old, authoritarian order in Mexico began its process of decay following the dramatic days of the Tlatelolco massacre of 1968. That may well be true, but the fact is that in general the Echeverría and López Portillo regimes were very much marked with the traditional, authoritarian stamp of their predecessors.

The administration of President Miguel de la Madrid (1982–1988), however, began a process of economic reform combined with careful moves toward more honest elections, and the beginning of the political transformation of Mexico. These first moves, made with commendable firmness by De la Madrid, helped to win the public confidence required for his austerity program to be palatable, and to succeed. His successor, Carlos Salinas (1988–1994), accelerated the transition of Mexico into a global economy and proceeded more

103

cautiously with important electoral reforms and greater political pluralism.

This transition proceeded dramatically, if sometimes erratically and unpredictably, with President Ernesto Zedillo (1994–2000). Zedillo from the very beginning of his administration sought openly to reduce the awesome power of the presidency, and to build up long-neglected institutions such as the national legislature, the judicial system, and state and regional governments. Zedillo announced early in his administration that he wanted to keep a *sana distancia*— a safe distance—from the PRI leadership, and called for a more democratic selection process to choose PRI candidates for elective national and state offices.

His own role, he suggested, was not to be the de facto head of the PRI, but rather to preside over the national process of democratization. This, of course, turned out to be an ideal not always realized. Now, as his term comes to a close, it is a good time to assess the successes and failures in the complex process of political transformation in Mexico, and to give some preliminary judgments on how far Mexico has come in the continuing struggle for greater democratization of the political and social systems.

Assessing Political and Social Transformation: 1995–2000

Given the broad scope of institutional change in Mexico over recent years, it is useful to pick up some specific strands of the process and to examine them in some detail. These include judicial reform, electoral reform and political pluralism, the changing dynamic of church and state, and the strengthening of civil society. We will assess how these strands intertwine and hazard a prediction about the prospects for progress along Mexico's path toward democratization.

The Reach of Judicial Reform

As detailed in many public statements by President Zedillo during his first year in office, his program of judicial reform was aimed at reducing corruption, providing Mexicans equal access to the law, and bringing even senior executive-branch officials under impartial judicial scrutiny. These goals required, among other programs, a thorough top-down reorganization of the Mexican judiciary. One of Zedillo's early actions was to dissolve the old supreme court, which consisted of twenty-six justices, some of whom were incompetent or corrupt, and all of whom were de facto subordinate to the interests of the ruling party or to high government officials.

In its place Zedillo created a new supreme court, consisting of eleven better-qualified justices, all of whom had to be confirmed by the Mexican Senate. The Supreme Court is now more independent and more powerful; for example, for the first time it can resolve conflicts arising between the legislative and executive branches of government. The court's power of judicial review of lower court rulings, familiar to those knowledgeable about the U.S. Supreme Court, was also greatly expanded.

However, many issues, including those focused on lower criminal and civil courts, were not addressed in the first wave of Zedillo's judicial reforms, leading millions of Mexicans to feel, and to complain publicly, that contemporary Mexican society was not enjoying the benefits of the rule of law. There is no doubt that a leading reason for such a reaction—among both Mexicans and foreigners—is the prevalence of corrupt practices within the law enforcement and legal systems. Zedillo's top-down reforms have had some small effect on this problem, but corruption, particularly at the lower levels of courts, and certainly in law enforcement, is still common, and discourages citizens from reporting crimes and otherwise participating in the process.

Public security and the rule of law. Regular visitors to Mexico are impressed with Mexicans' concerns about personal security. Their testimony strongly suggests that the risk of physical attack, robbery, kidnapping, and even death is real. The rudimentary statistics that can be gathered bear this out; for example, there were some 140 bank robberies committed in Mexico City in 1998. Car thefts and related crimes are pandemic, despite efforts to improve salaries and training of Mexico City's 27,000 policemen. All this suggests that while some progress is undoubtedly being made, much more needs to be done in the area of public security. Meanwhile, visitors to Mexico and Mexicans themselves are learning to take proper precautions, which have been shown to decrease markedly the chance of being the victim of a criminal act.

On a more fundamental level lurks the precarious nature of law and law enforcement in Mexico today. During the Zedillo administration, there were important changes at the top, for example, the restructuring of the Supreme Court. But despite Zedillo's reforms, the judicial system is still filled with instances of unqualified or dishonest judges, lack of funds for institutional upkeep and salaries, and the lack of modern communications systems to ensure that judicial warrants, arrest orders, and the like are being executed. Indeed, pitifully few are.

On the level of law-enforcement leadership and officers on the street, the situation is little better. Again, low salaries offer little incentive for honesty in the police forces. Indeed, there is a common perception that many crimes are actually committed by ex-policemen or others still on active duty. It is little wonder that Mexicans report in poll after poll that public security is a very important concern, especially in the face of recent statistics demonstrating that only four out of every hundred crimes result in the perpetrator being punished.

This crisis in the rule of law in Mexico has more than domestic implications, no matter how important these are. Foreign investors have proven to be just as sensitive as Mexican businessmen to the threat of kidnapping, extortion, payroll robbery, and theft of merchandise. Finally, Mexican commercial law leaves much to be desired, and trade disputes often end up in lengthy arbitration.

There is still a long way to go, then, in improving public security and establishing the rule of law in Mexico. But without a meaningful effort in these areas, economic, social, and electoral reform, however successful, will have been in vain.

Electoral Reform and the New Power of the Mexican Congress

A key element in President Zedillo's political plan was electoral reform. He worked hard at this during his first year in office, and he was successful in negotiating with the major opposition parties, the PAN and the PRD, the passage through the Congress in August 1996 of an important electoral reform law, which he announced would "mark a firm, irreversible, and definitive step to leave behind the controversies and dissatisfaction" that marked many previous elections. His reform package included a wholly independent Federal

Electoral Institute (IFE), a reliable voters' list, and at least the first step toward campaign finance reform.

July 1997 elections. The impact of electoral reform on the Mexican political process was not long in coming. By June 1997 almost half of Mexico's population was governed by opposition parties (either the PRD or the PAN). But the really dramatic example of growing pluralism in Mexico came with the important elections in July 1997, with six state governorships, all the Chamber of Deputies (lower house), one fourth of the Senate (upper house), and many local-government officials up for election. The dramatic results of these elections, accepted as being among the fairest in Mexican history, included the victory of the PRD war-horse and perennial presidential candidate, Cuauhtémoc Cárdenas, who became the first elected mayor of Mexico City. The other opposition party, the PAN, won two of the state governorships, in Nuevo León and Querétaro (giving them a total of six).

The PRI loses control of Congress. The most dramatic change occurred in the Chamber of Deputies elections in July 1997, where after six decades of rule the PRI lost control of the Chamber of Deputies (see Figure 5.1). While the PRI maintained a plurality of 239 seats (out of 500), the combined opposition could muster up to 261 votes on the odd occasions when they united. The breakdown was PAN, 121; PRD, 125; Green Party, 8; and Workers' Party, 7. In the Mexican Senate, only 32 of 128 seats (31 of which were PRI seats) were up for election, so it would not have been possible for the PRI with its 95 seats to lose control. However, the Senate became a more balanced house with the July elections, with the PRI winning 13 seats, the PAN 9, the PRD 8, and minor parties capturing 2.

Opposition parties in the Chamber of Deputies have established a mixed record of effectiveness. Key votes, such as the annual federal budget, are usually passed by a PRI-PAN coalition, much to the quiet relief of Mexico's global trade and financial partners, who look nervously at new uncertainties in the Mexican political process. Gone are the days, they have discovered, when the Mexican president enjoyed complete control over economic and political policymaking.

A case in point is the protracted brouhaha in and out of Congress concerning the government's request for the creation of a new Savings

Figure 5.1   Composition of the Chamber of Deputies (seats held by parties)

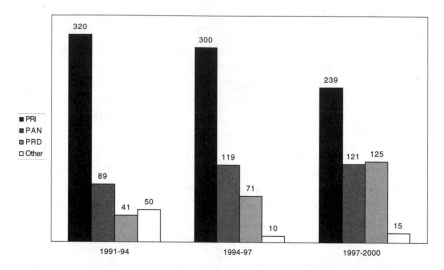

Source: Federal Electoral Institute

Protection Institute that would manage some $67 billion in bad bank debt accumulated principally during the Salinas administration. The new institute was proposed to replace the discredited Salinas-inspired FOBAPROA mechanism for bailing out ailing banks. The new institute would have the FOBAPROA books audited, and illegal debts, probably a small fraction of the $67 billion, would be thrown out. The institute was also designed to reduce home mortgage debt (the bane of the middle class), and farmers' debts as well. In this case, faced with a political hot potato (including frequent demonstrations by the debt-resisting El Barzón, a well-organized middle-class revolt against high interest rates and foreclosures, and general left-wing attacks), the leadership of the PAN and the PRI were able to work together with some independent congressmen to approve the Savings Protection Institute by a 325–159 vote on December 12, 1998. This was seen as one of the clearest demonstrations of a congressional leadership beginning to show some maturity and a willingness to cooperate on matters of keen national interest.

Certainly, many of the principal areas of international concern, including migration, drug trafficking, and environmental issues, will now include an analysis of the growing role to be played by the Mexican Congress. The expectation is that the Congress will learn to be an institution capable of rising above petty partisanship to become truly accountable to the people of Mexico, and that the executive branch will respond with such measures as making its economic policy goals and the federal budget agenda more transparent. That these goals are possible was demonstrated by the successful passage in late 1998 of Mexico's federal budget for 1999, and the approval of the Savings Protection Institute, a move generally believed to be important to strengthen Mexico's financial system in the face of global financial crises. Much more, including structural reforms within the Congress itself, needs to be done.

The electoral process continues: 1998–1999. Mexico's slow transformation toward elections that are more free and fair, and hence open to the occasional surprise, continued. In July 1998, the PRI, running as an opposition party in the PAN-controlled state of Chihuahua, elected a popular businessman to the governorship. This was the first time in this century that a governorship in Mexico was recaptured by any party. The election was seen as a major defeat for the PAN, which had controlled the key border state since 1992, and which sees a united northern Mexico as its best, if not only, hope for a victory in the presidential elections of 2000. It was also a personal defeat for the incumbent governor, Francisco Barrio. Barrio was once a rising star in the PAN, having been elected mayor of the northern border city of Ciudad Juárez (a *maquiladora*-filled city across the Rio Grande from El Paso, Texas) on his way to the governorship. He was one of the most viable alternatives to the seemingly implacable drive of the PAN governor in Guanajuato, Vicente Fox, for the PAN presidential nomination for the 2000 elections.

Results of other elections in July 1998 were mixed, with the PRI winning by a landslide in Durango, but losing to a PRI defector to the PRD in Zacatecas. Over the next two years the PRI struggled with how to select its candidates for major state offices. In cases such as Chihuahua, where the attractive entrepreneur Patricio Martínez García was chosen for the first time in a party primary, the PRI was victorious. In the case of Zacatecas, the most popular local candidate, Ricardo Monreal Avila, a lifelong member of the PRI, was passed over by the PRI dinosaurs in favor of a less attractive candidate. Refusing to admit defeat, young Monreal immediately joined the PRD, not normally an extremely popular party in Zacatecas, and led it to a gubernatorial victory. This puts him in a very independent position, and observers are closely watching his interactions with the PRD and PRI national leaderships.

The July 1998 elections in Chihuahua, Durango, and Zacatecas, with their different results, were generally conceded to have been conducted by the independent Federal Electoral Institute in an exemplary manner. The careful new procedures, which involve a positive identification of voters and scrupulous vote counting, were introduced in 1996, and were first utilized in a national election with the congressional, state, and local elections of 1997, which drove the PRI from its majority in the Chamber of Deputies. Thus the electoral process in Mexico appeared to be maturing in terms of fairness as the nation prepared for the critical presidential elections of 2000.

Welfare Reform: Problems and Prospects

As Mexico proceeds with the economic and political reforms needed to assure continuing economic growth and political development, it will become more and more important to focus on the often neglected problems of income inequality and poverty that affect the majority of all Mexicans. During the last years of the 1990s, even as Mexico's macroeconomic indicators showed signs of real growth, social indicators were suggesting that inequality, particularly in Mexico's rural sector, was becoming more pronounced. A myriad of government programs, stretching back over the three most recent administrations, and bearing a long list of acronyms, have failed to make significant progress in treating the problems of the poorest of Mexico's poor.

Clearly, it is necessary for the new Mexican administration, when it takes office in December 2000, to be ready with a comprehensive strategy to resolve these pressing social issues. It must ask how the rural and urban poor can be made to benefit from the anticipated economic gains enjoyed by the country as a whole. A more immediate question is how, until this happens, the social fabric of Mexico can be preserved through a national program of poverty alleviation and the effective delivery of adequate social and health services. This is a much broader question than the resolution of the

Chiapas situation, though of course Chiapas is a tip-of-the-iceberg signal of pervasive rural discontent.

As the Chiapas situation might suggest, the regional inequality in Mexico is marked, and becoming sharper. Poverty levels in Mexico vary from about 3 percent in northern Mexico to 10 percent in the south. While the northern states of Chihuahua and Nuevo León have long benefited from trade and investment links with the United States and abroad, the southern states of Guerrero and Chiapas have experienced few benefits, other than governmental transfer payments. (Since 1994, Chiapas has the number-one priority for Mexico's social programs.)

An obvious problem in Mexico's social welfare programs has been the very political way in which the presidential stamp was placed on the many discrete, discontinuous, and highly publicized initiatives in the past. Since the 1930s, the PRI has used social programs for political advantage and as a source of patronage. By the 1970s, this power became more sharply focused in Los Pinos, that is, in the Mexican president's office. President Salinas made welfare policy the most highly publicized vehicle to ensure the succession of his hand-picked candidate, Luis Donaldo Colosio, who was early on made head of the National Solidarity Program (PRONASOL) with a multibillion-dollar budget aimed at bypassing local leaders and encouraging a new grassroots constituency loyal to Salinas—and to Colosio. These plans were ruined by the assassination of Colosio, and the subsequent deterioration and fragmentation of the PRI leadership. By 1997, President Zedillo, moving away from the centralization of power, oversaw the dispersion of resources for welfare programs to the states, where their efficacy has yet to be measured.

Zedillo's remaining funds focused on the Integral Program to Overcome Extreme Poverty, with efforts to use the modest resources available to attack such problems as health and nutrition, education, and welfare. Perhaps because of sensitivity to improving church-state relations in Mexico, very little attention is being given to questions of women's reproductive health and family planning. In 1998, Zedillo also launched the Food, Health, and Education Program (Progresa) aimed at the poorest regions of Mexico, and other efforts targeted at short-term alleviation of unemployment. But, even at a time when poverty and income disparity are becoming more pronounced, a truly comprehensive welfare program will probably have to wait until a new president, from whichever political party, takes office at the end of 2000. Even then, such an effort will require national dedication, with the cooperation of the Congress and a strengthened civil society, if it is to succeed.

Church and State in Mexico

Mexico has a long history of conflict between the Catholic Church (to which more than 80 percent of Mexicans belong) and the federal government. Mexican independence from Spain and the establishment of a secular liberal government resulted in increasing tension with the conservative Church. The liberal Constitution of 1857, which restricted Church power, was met with violence. The Church supported the establishment of Maximilian as emperor, who was captured and executed by liberal forces in 1867.

The years of the *porfiriato* (1876–1910) saw the Church gaining some strength and influence under the benign rule of President Porfirio Díaz. It strongly supported Díaz in his losing cause, and paid the price under a series of revolutionary governments in the decades after 1910. An earlier chapter has described the Cristero rebellions in the 1920s and their aftermath. It took a long time, but by the 1970s church-state relations in Mexico had become very low key, and low profile.

The first papal visit to Mexico was by John Paul II in 1979 at the invitation of President José López Portillo (Mexican wags claimed that his mother made him do it). The second visit came during the administration of President de la Madrid, and the third, in 1993, under President Salinas, who had clearly embarked on a deliberate effort to woo the Church as an ally at a time when greater support was needed to confirm the legitimacy of his regime after the disputed elections of 1988, and for the approval of his dramatic economic reforms opening Mexico to the global economy.

This period was marked by increasingly friendly relations, the establishment of formal relations between Mexico and the Vatican, and changes in the Constitution in 1992 that gave the Church greater legal status and gave ordained priests and nuns for the first time since 1917 the right to vote. These changes strengthened the position of parochial schools, and allowed priests and nuns to appear in public in religious attire.

This pronounced change in atmosphere also emboldened Church leaders to take a more active role in offering political and economic views ex cathedra. Several of the more conservative Mexican bishops publicly condemned what they saw as growing corruption and violence in the country. A smaller number of priests, whose symbolic leader was Bishop Samuel Ruiz of Chiapas, have embraced liberation theology. They have strongly supported the cause of the native population of southern Mexico, including the actions of the Zapatistas. Ruiz was fond of identifying himself with the first bishop of Chiapas, Bartolomé de las Casas, who in the sixteenth century inveighed against his fellow Spaniards' subjugation of the Mayans (Krauze, 1997).

The Pope's visit in January 1999. In this new atmosphere, the pope's visit was awaited with an unusually high level of expectation. Advance planning by Church authorities, supported significantly by private-sector leaders, created an atmosphere that was to lead Mexicans to appear by the millions at a series of public events. Meanwhile, in Rome, the pope was determined to build on his three prior visits to bring a new message to these millions of faithful, and to the political and economic elite. The death of communism and a marked diminution of interest in liberation theology (*pace* Bishop Ruiz), led the Pope to declare his serious concerns about the danger of unbridled capitalism. He noted in a Vatican talk on January 19, that "international institutions, national governments, and the centers controlling the world economy must all undertake brave plans and projects to ensure a more just sharing of the goods of the world" (*New York Times*, January 22, 1999). The pope's spokesmen made a point of describing his trip, which included St. Louis, Missouri, as well as Mexico City, as being a visit to the Americas and providing an opportunity for encouraging greater hemispheric solidarity of the Catholic faithful.

In his many public addresses in Mexico, the pope called on his bishops to minister to all, poor and rich alike, and to use the power of faith to help all of society as it attempts to overcome "the corruption that permeates many institutions and many citizens . . . and to root out drug trafficking, based on the lack of values, on the lure of easy gain . . . and to put an end to the violence that divides brothers and social classes" (*New York Times,* January 26, 1999). In what was perhaps an unintended consequence of the papal visit, Bishop Ruiz in Chiapas publicly welcomed the pope's remarks as supporting his own long struggle there.

Mexico's Civil Society Gains Strength

One of the most remarkable phenomena in Mexico's development since the mid-1980s has been the creation and strengthening of the broadest range of nongovernmental organizations (NGOs). An early catalyst was the severe Mexico City earthquake of 1985, where civic groups organized in many neighborhoods to supplement, or in some cases to substitute for, government assistance. For the first time in their experience, millions of Mexicans began to participate actively and seriously in social and political activities through countless NGOs covering a vast sphere of activities, including the struggle for women's rights and environmental and sustainable development issues. This grassroots democratization has challenged the old hierarchies in a variety of ways, from public demonstrations in support of the indigenous peoples of Chiapas to protests of high interest rates on middle-class citizens' bank loans, e.g. the El Barzón movement. These activities have been reported in a mass media that is far less constrained than before. As civil society gains strength in Mexico, the prospects for positive social transformation and democratization improve accordingly. Nowhere is this more evident than in the labor sector, where the death in June 1997 of ninety-seven-year-old Fidel Velázquez, leader of the official labor movement in Mexico for sixty years, appears to have opened the door to the incremental development of grassroots free labor organizations springing in some cases from the spadework of civil associations. While a strong, free labor organization in Mexico is many years away, it appears that this process is at long last under way.

Steps Toward Democracy

Is Mexico experiencing a transformation from the authoritarianism of the 1970s toward a truly democratic regime early in the new millennium? The prospect seems promising. We have seen that voting reform affecting the composition of the Chamber of Deputies and the Senate, including proportional representation, began in the late

1970s, and continued through the 1980s (see Figure 5.2). Issues of campaign reform in the 1990s culminated with the establishment of the wholly independent supervision of the electoral process nation-wide by the Federal Electoral Institute (IFE). At a broader level, efforts have been made to improve the education system, and some progress is noted there. The mass media in Mexico have improved in quality, and as the 1990s came to an end, were increasingly able to inform the voting public on current issues of the day.

Figure 5.2   Composition of the Senate, 1994–1997 (number of seats)

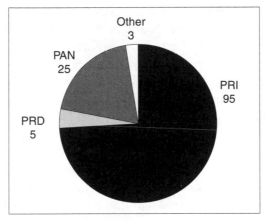

Composition of the Senate, 1997–2000 (number of seats)

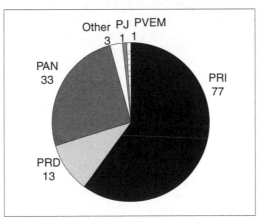

Source: Federal Electoral Institute

During the last decade of the twentieth century the old authoritarian system lost a significant amount of its influence. While there were efforts during this period to reimpose the old order, particularly in poorer states and outside of major urban areas, they became less effective in the late 1990s. Particularly during the Zedillo presidency the move toward a more democratic presidential regime became notable. At the same time, there was a growing sense of maturity on the part of the three principal political parties, the PRI, the PAN, and the PRD. While there are many policy differences and a sharp contrast in personal styles among the major political leadership in Mexico today, there is remarkable agreement on a number of key issues.

The parties seem to accept the concept of an open global economy for Mexico, with the encouragement of expanding trade agreements, and inviting foreign private direct investment. This suggests that the three parties are likely to choose presidential candidates for the 2000 campaign who are known quantities to voters, and are unlikely to take extreme positions on the right or left of the political spectrum. One positive result of this scenario is a diminution of the possibility of violent confrontation in an atmosphere that reflects the Mexican public's clear desire for stability and moderate change.

Finally, as Mexicans in the new millennium grow accustomed to more variety in political outcomes, the major parties themselves are becoming more sophisticated and more adept in their political campaigns. During the past few years elections have more and more been won by the political party that chose the most attractive candidates and mounted careful campaigns. This is a marked change from the past, when fraud and voter manipulation were far more common.

6

Mexican Migration and U.S. Policy

Historical Perspectives

Not only is the United States truly a nation of immigrants, but for the first century of its existence the country saw little need to control immigration. By and large, foreigners arrived on U.S. shores and entered into its economic life and civil society with a minimum of red tape. Others, including Mexican citizens who lived in the territories acquired by the United States with the Treaty of Guadalupe Hidalgo in 1848, following the Mexican War and the Gadsden Purchase in 1853, became U.S. citizens.

It was not until 1882, with the passage of the infamous Chinese Exclusion Act, that Congress made its first effort to limit the influx. This law not only deterred Chinese (and, subsequently, Japanese) immigration, but declared ex post facto that resident Asians could be stripped of their right to citizenship and deported.

That ominous harbinger was followed in 1921 by universally applicable immigration control legislation aimed primarily at immigrants from southern and eastern Europe. This was accomplished by restricting the number of entrants from each foreign nation according to the frequency with which that nation already figured into the ancestry of America's resident population, as alleged under the 1920 census—a method heavily favoring northern Europeans. During the first two decades of the twentieth century, immigration was much more substantial than it is today. At the peak of the wave, some 1.3 million immigrants were arriving yearly. This compares with the 800,000 legal immigrants who arrived in 1994. In 1913, America had thirteen immigrants per thousand residents, but only three per thousand in 1994. More recently, immigration legislation refined the control process to take into account such factors as family reunification, the U.S. economy's need for skilled laborers, and a recognition of the growing problem of political refugees.

The U.S.-Mexico Dimension

Mexican emigration to the United States has been a factor in the two nations' relations for more than a century. In fact, since the times of the Texas Secession and the Mexican War, there has been a net increase in the Mexican population of U.S. border states. In the 1890s, for example, increasing numbers of Mexicans emigrated to Texas and, to a lesser degree, to New Mexico, Arizona, and California in search of social stability, better education for their children, and improved economic opportunities.

This movement accelerated during the decade of the Mexican Revolution (1910–1920) as hundreds of thousands of Mexican citizens, many of them from the upper social classes, fled the violence of the times and sought refuge in the United States. Nor were their peregrinations confined to the border states; Mexican immigrant communities began to develop in several major industrial cities, especially Chicago.

These influxes, at least up to 1920, were seldom accompanied by significant social friction, and with few exceptions the Mexican immigrants tended to find jobs and acceptance in their communities. But gradually, conservative groups in the United States began to grumble about "losing control of our borders." As a result of such complaints from constituents, Congress created the U.S. Border Patrol in 1924, and organized efforts were undertaken for the first time to arrest and deport "illegal Mexicans," sometimes disparagingly called "wetbacks" (*mojados*, in Spanish) because some of them gained entry to the United States by wading or swimming across the Rio Grande.

When the Great Depression hit the United States (and the world) in 1930, there were an estimated one million undocumented Mexican men, women, and children living in the United States. Overreacting to the shrinking job market, the U.S. began a "voluntary repatriation" program that eventually sent some 300,000 Mexicans back to their country. Although its impact on combating the social effects of the U.S. Depression was small, this program succeeded in exacerbating economic problems in Mexico, adding to already serious unemployment and fueling anti-U.S. feelings there.

The outbreak of World War II changed the migrant picture dramatically. Far from discouraging Mexican workers, the U.S. government and Mexico negotiated in 1942 a *bracero* (laborer) agreement that brought more than a quarter-million farm and transportation industry workers to the United States with a guarantee of decent wages, health care, and working conditions.

The end of the first *bracero* program in 1947 (similar programs were initiated from time to time until 1964) ushered in a period of some two decades of benign neglect on the part of U.S. authorities. Border Patrol activities were predictable, enforcement was spotty, and millions of undocumented Mexican workers—usually unaccompanied young males—came and went, pushed by unfavorable economic conditions in their communities in Mexico and pulled by the greater job opportunities in a generally expanding U.S. economy.

The typical undocumented worker of those days left his family behind in a small village in central or southern Mexico, to which he returned regularly. After a few years in the United States, during which he acquired savings and a knowledge of the world outside rural Mexico, this worker found himself a well-respected and even revered member of his home community, and often bought property and settled down there after fifteen or twenty years' work in the United States.

This description of the undocumented worker has changed over the past twenty years. He or she (by 1991, almost half of all undocumented border crossings were by women) is better educated, almost certainly literate, and leaving a job in Mexico. This reflects changing internal migration patterns in Mexico. As *campesinos* leave the countryside and seek work in towns or cities, they are apt to replace workers who have acquired education and skills and only then emigrated to the United States. In time, after having acquired job skills and a better understanding of the dynamics of the emigration process, the former *campesinos* may themselves join the flow.

Alternatively, the *campesinos* who are more adventurous and perhaps even leaders in their rural communities may go directly to a "home" community in the United States, populated by friends and relatives from their particular region of rural Mexico. These networks of *gente de confianza*—people in whom they have confidence—take them to a friendly and welcoming neighborhood in, say, California, Texas, or Illinois where they are made to feel at home, given employment, and begin what is likely to become a permanent residence.

In any case, the skill and educational level of the typical Mexican worker coming to the United States rose markedly in the 1990s. In addition, more women and children join the immigration stream each year, suggesting that residence in the U.S. might be more permanent in nature. Both of these phenomena are believed to have been in part the result of the Mexican economic crises of 1982 and 1995.

While in the past there was an unspoken perception in Mexico that emigration to the United States was a safety valve releasing the social tensions of unemployment, many Mexicans now see unmanaged emigration as a net economic and social loss for their country. They are rightly, and increasingly, concerned about the loss of young, educated, skilled men and women to productive jobs in the United States, where they contribute to the U.S. rather than the Mexican economy.

It is estimated that more than 25 percent of the work force in California's high-tech Silicon Valley are undocumented Mexicans. They also, of course, play important roles in construction, agriculture, food processing, and service industries such as hotels and restaurants (see Chapter 9 for an extended treatment of Mexico-California economic and social relations). Mexicans hope that continued economic growth will enhance local industries and create employment through increased foreign and domestic private direct investment, thereby keeping workers at home.

For the United States, however, the benefits of Mexican immigration are immense and will increase in the new century. Demographic patterns of the United States indicate that we are entering an era of growing labor scarcity. The U.S. Census Bureau reports that a decreasing birthrate since the middle of the 1960s has produced a declining and increasingly "geriatric" U.S.-born work force. According to the bureau, annual growth of the U.S.-born work force has declined from 5 percent in the 1970s to an estimated 1.5 percent in the 1990s. U.S. economic growth and new job creation on into the next century can thus be supported only by external supplies of young entry-level workers.

Mexico, on the other hand, a "pediatric society," has an excess supply of workers, with an estimated one million young Mexicans coming into the job pool each year. These potential workers find only about two-thirds that number of new jobs open to them, even in a growing Mexican economy. In any case, a young and able Mexican worker can earn in an hour in the United States what a day's work at a similar job would bring him or her in Mexico. That 8-to-1 or greater wage differential exerts a powerful attraction on mobile, usually young, Mexicans. This is fortunate for the United States. Without this supply of youthful labor in the service, light-industrial, high-tech, and other sectors, many businesses in the United States would close—with a consequent loss of jobs for U.S.-born as well as foreign-born employees.

While no one disputes the sovereign right of the United States to bar illegal workers, these economic considerations suggest that a solution to the problem be sought that is based on our real best interests. For example, over the next twenty years, at least 30 million new jobs will be created in the United States—10 million in California alone—most of which will be at entry level in the service, information, and other sectors. Given our demographics, only a fraction of these jobs can be filled from domestic sources. Where will the new workers come from? The most reasonable response: from Mexico.

This will happen despite official U.S. law enforcement policies and misguided state initiatives such as California's Proposition 187 (see Chapter 9). Time and again, the U.S. government has spent substantial sums to build miles of fences or other barriers to Mexican emigration, only to have them skirted (or dug under) in a matter of hours or days. The sooner we conclude that these efforts are essentially a waste of the taxpayers' money, the better. It is highly unlikely that the American public would ever stand for a virtual militarization of the entire border, which would require thousands of troops and uncounted millions of dollars to noticeably affect the migration flow.

More disturbingly, as long as such border crossings are illegal, great suffering and even physical harm is visited upon undocumented workers by *coyotes*, criminals who prey on them while ostensibly offering them safe passage across the international border. Anyone who has seen the moving film *El Norte* (directed by Gregory Nava, 1983) is aware of this situation. But as long as jobs are opening up, in California or elsewhere in the United States, young Mexicans will be there to claim them. The real challenge for U.S. and Mexican policymakers is to work together and learn how to make migration work for the benefit of both countries.

The Numbers Game

The most frequent questions concerning Mexican immigration deal with the numbers of legal and illegal persons of Mexican origin now in the United States, and how many are added each year. While the questions are simple, they are hard to answer. When 1990 census data were analyzed they suggested that of the 16 million or so people of Mexican origin now living in the United States, perhaps 9 million are U.S.-born. Of the approximately 7 million Mexican-born residents, about half are legal immigrants and the remainder are undocumented, both transient and permanent. Analyses of census, Immunization and Naturalization Service (INS), and other government data indicate that an average of 200,000 new legal immigrants per year entered the United States from Mexico during the 1990s, and about 300,000 undocumented immigrants are added each year from Mexico on a net basis.

These numbers, tentative at best, fluctuate with the millions of border crossings that take place in both directions every year (which are, in turn, a function of prevailing economic conditions), the registration and subsequent legalization of previously undocumented workers under the amnesty provisions of the Immigration Reform and Control Act of 1986 (about 3 million by 1999, of whom some 2 million were Mexican), and numerous other factors.

One message that often gets lost in the shuffle, however, is that the vast majority of Mexican Americans are in the United States legally. The constant focus on illegal immigrants tends to cause us to lose sight of this important fact, and to fail to recognize the immense richness of the cultural diversity, creative imagination, and productivity that Mexican Americans are bringing to our shared society.

Of course, the question of Mexican immigration also needs to be seen in a larger context. The Hispanic population in the United States stands at some 30 million as the nation enters a new millennium and, according to the U.S. Census Bureau, will overtake the African-American population around 2005 (*New York Times*, August 7, 1998). The Census Bureau reported that the Hispanic-American population accounts for 11 percent of the total U.S. population, and is closing in on the African-American population percentage of 12.8 percent, given the higher birth rates of more recent immigrants. In fact, the report continued, the Hispanic population in the United States will have doubled in the period between 1980 and 2005. The

Mexican-American population amounts to about half of the total Hispanic population, and its growth rate closely matches that of the Hispanic population in general.

The U.S. Debate on Immigration Reform: 1970–1986

At least until recently, the greatest debate over illegal immigration from Mexico has taken place within the United States itself. But fallout from that debate frequently spills over the border, especially when some opponents of immigration make highly intemperate arguments that sound suspiciously like racism to the admittedly sensitive Mexican ear.

After the end of the last *bracero* program in 1964, the growing conflict between the need for workers and the desire to "protect the borders" forced U.S. lawmakers to take a new look at the broad field of immigration and American society. Following a decade of debate that failed to produce any congressional consensus on new legislation, President Carter appointed a Select Commission on Immigration in 1978 and named Father Theodore Hesburgh, then president of the University of Notre Dame and a well-respected national figure, to head it.

The commission's report, issued in 1981, set the broad outlines for immigration reform, including amnesty and the imposition of employer sanctions, but discarded certain controversial suggestions. A tamper-proof national identity card, which among other things would provide immediate validation of residence or citizenship status, was opposed by many civil libertarians—despite the fact that, as proponents of the card noted, many other major democracies around the world require such identification from their citizens and permanent residents, apparently without any staggering deprivation of their civil rights. In any case, the commission eventually abandoned the national identity card idea.

The Immigration Reform and Control Act of 1986

There followed a five-year struggle in the Congress to get immigration reform legislation passed. Over time, the bill took on the coloration of special interests: more enforcement for the Border Patrol, to satisfy conservatives; broader amnesty provisions, to make liberals happy; weakened rules for employers, to appeal to business and industry interests; special programs for agricultural workers, to appease agribusiness; and so on. Finally, in 1986, after intense debate and persistent efforts by Senator Alan Simpson (a fan of the Border Patrol) and Represenatatives Romano Mazzoli and Peter Rodino, a catch-all law was passed.

During the months preceding its passage, both supporters and detractors had declared the bill dead, but it was resurrected at the last moment—in part so that senators and congressmen could return to their constituencies in an election year with a claim to have done something about an immigration "problem" that (shades of the 1920s) was again said to be threatening the control of our borders. In signing the bill into law on November 6, 1986, President Reagan suggested that "future generations of Americans will be thankful for our efforts to humanely regain control of our borders. . . . In the past thirty-five years our nation has been increasingly affected by illegal immigration. . . . This legislation takes a major step toward meeting this challenge to our sovereignty" (White House, November 6, 1986). As we shall see, these remarks proved to be overly optimistic.

The law, known by its acronym IRCA (for Immigration Reform and Control Act), departed from all previous immigration legislation in at least two important respects. For one thing, it recognized that the border between the U.S. and Mexico was so porous that it was virtually impossible for law enforcement agencies alone to significantly reduce illegal immigration. The bill instead put the onus on employers by including a provision that made it illegal in most cases to knowingly hire an undocumented worker.

Until the passage of IRCA, a curious anomaly had existed: While it was illegal for undocumented immigrants to come to the United States for work, it was not illegal for employers to hire them. By requiring employers to verify the immigration status of new employees under pain of civil and criminal penalties, IRCA seemed initially to be eliminating this anomaly. But in practice, this provision has turned out to be almost impossible to enforce. Employers merely have to certify that they viewed the proof of legal residence presented by the worker when he or she was hired, and were satisfied that the credentials appeared genuine.

There is no requirement that the employer take any further steps to verify the authenticity of the documentation offered. And, of course, the employer cannot retain the documents. So when Immigration and Naturalization Service inspectors arrive at a job site, they see only a company record that claims: "Yes, Juan Gómez appeared on a certain date and showed documentation, which seemed genuine." Needless to say, such procedures constitute an invitation to evasion, ranging from a less-than-careful scrutiny of documents to the sharing of documents among illegal workers, forged documents (readily available in any major U.S. city for a modest price), etc. It is not surprising, then, that IRCA's "employer sanctions" provisions have proven ineffective.

A second major way in which IRCA differed from all previous immigration legislation was that it provided for amnesty, and eventual permanent residence, to illegal aliens residing continuously in the United States since January 1982. While there have been hitches—in some cases forged documents, in others the inability of some genuinely eligible candidates to prove their case—in general the amnesty program has been a success. By 1999 some 3 million previously undocumented immigrants had been able to regularize their status.

A third provision of IRCA—a reward to Senator Simpson—was not pathbreaking; it simply reinforced the Border Patrol budget—a trend that has continued throughout the 1990s, growing from $347 million in 1993 to $631 million in 1997. Still other provisions attempted to ensure the civil rights of resident aliens and U.S. citizens of Hispanic origin, and provided federal support for local welfare programs serving newly amnestied clients. Finally, as a reflection of the serious concerns of U.S. agribusiness, the bill gave special preference to seasonal agricultural workers from Mexico.

The legislative record illustrates that the passage of IRCA reflected an understandable desire on the part of the legislative and executive branches of the government to reassure the American electorate they were acting together to "regain control of our borders." Whatever good IRCA may have accomplished—for example, the humanitarian aspect of the amnesty provisions—it did not appear over time to have slowed the number of undocumented workers entering the United States from Mexico, although in the months immediately after the law's passage, a decline in attempted entries was noted. Illegal immigration dipped slightly in late 1986 and early 1987, but it did not take long for Mexican workers to discover that there were still jobs to be found north of the border, as well as easy ways to present "proof" of legal residence. By 1988 flows were back to pre-1986 levels.

While the northward flow does vary, it appears to do so independently of immigration laws and border-control procedures, and mainly in response to economic conditions. For example, during the Mexican economic "boom" of 1980–1982, which coincided with a recession in the United States, illegal immigration to the U.S. declined modestly, only to pick up again in the years 1982–1985 and 1995, which were marked by severe economic crises in Mexico and economic recovery in the United States.

U.S. Immigration Policies in the 1990s

During the 1990s, particularly as the decade came to an end, the policymaking process in Washington was remarkable for its cacophony. Debates about immigration policies were no exception. Anti-immigration efforts by special-interest groups raised such specters as environmental damage from "too many people," a resurgence of the image of the sinister "welfare mother" preying on the gullible taxpayer, and the introduction of drug trafficking and terrorist activities among the inflow of undocumented immigrants. The relatively more civilized debates of the past—the calm process of Father Ted Hesburgh's committee, for example—fell by the wayside in an increasingly petulant decade.

During its eight-year tenure (1992–2000), the Clinton administration generally considered it more politically expedient to attempt to adjust to, or even preempt, the strident criticism that the United States was losing control of its borders. The INS, meanwhile, basking in its vastly increased budget, vowed to "effectively regulate the border, deter illegal employment in the interior, combat and punish smuggling as well as other immigration-related crimes and remove expeditiously ever-greater numbers of criminal aliens and other deportable aliens" (U.S. Government, 1997).

Meanwhile, the Congress was passing the Illegal Immigration Reform and Immigrant Responsibility Act of 1996 (IIRIRA), an occasionally self-contradictory and sometimes unenforceable law that has bogged down in the courts and mired the INS administrative and enforcement process. One case in point is Section 110 of IIRIRA, which requires the attorney general to develop a system to collect a record of departure for every alien departing the United States. The next step is to match it against the records of entry and departure to identify those visitors to the United States who have overstayed their leave. It is left to the reader to imagine what would happen at U.S. ports of entry and departure, airports and land and sea crossing points, if even an army of federal bureaucrats attempted this maneuver, and the chaos that would reign as attempts were made to identify and search out those who had overstayed their visas. While some in the U.S. Senate are aware of the foolishness of these provisions, and have attempted to amend them, such hard-liners as Senator Dianne Feinstein (D-CA) have pledged to fight for them on the floor of the Senate.

The new immigration policies of the late 1990s, centered on IIRIRA and including more robust Border Patrol budgets, the adaptation of military technology, and the construction of new fences and barriers on the California-Mexico border, have resulted, a Mexican observer noted, in a macabre though unintended consequence. Mexico's consul general in San Diego reported "notably significant increases in the number of migrants who have died in attempts to gain unauthorized entry into the U.S.," adding that "85 Mexican migrants died in border crossing attempts in 1997 alone . . . [and] from January to October 1998, 120 have died under the same circumstances." "Such developments," he concluded, "must certainly have negative effects on U.S.-Mexican relations" (Herrera-Lasso, 1999).

The IIRIRA also has provisions for selecting aliens for deportation based on their political views and associations. These provisions were supported in a February 1999 decision by the U.S. Supreme Court in a 6–3 decision written by Justice Scalia. The aliens in this case resided in California and were supporters of the Palestinian cause, never charged with terrorist acts, whose deportation had been enjoined by the 9th U.S. Circuit Court of Appeals in San Francisco. While the issues under scrutiny by the courts narrowly concerned the idea of selective prosecution, nonetheless the Supreme Court's green light for deportation was an important ruling. It is certain that in the first years of the new century, courts all over the United States will continue to be untangling cases involving the administration of the IIRIRA.

Opposition to Mexican Immigration

Even if it is generally accepted that the overall impact of immigration on the U.S. economy is positive, there are areas of legitimate concern to stakeholders and policymakers considering the need for specific immigration reform. And there are many voices within the United States that are seeking relief from specific sectoral or geographic impacts of immigration flows. It is worthwhile to examine some of these views.

Displacement of U.S. workers. A common complaint of such organizations as the AFL-CIO and the Federation for American Immigration Reform (FAIR) is that U.S. workers are being displaced by immigrants, or that wages are being driven down as the supply of workers is increased by both legal and illegal immigrants.

One specific case involves the high-tech industry, centered in California's Silicon Valley but extending to many other states. High-tech entrepreneurs have for many years recruited engineers and computer scientists from a number of countries around the world, including India, Japan, China, and Mexico.

In 1997, the high-tech industry asked Congress to double the number of professional workers who could enter the country under the H-1(b) visa program, from 65,000 per year to 130,000 per year in 2001, an increase of 20 percent per year. High-tech firms claim that the United States is training many fewer engineers and scientists than are required to meet the challenges of global competition in this field.

Labor representatives contend that the H-1(b) program, ostensibly intended for temporary workers filling a special high-tech need, is in fact being used as a probationary employment program, and often leads to applications for permanent residence (to obtain a "green card") by high-tech professionals. Morton Bahr, president of the AFL-CIO Communications Workers of America, claimed that "there is no proven crisis regarding the demand for information-technology workers that justifies the drastic action of filling these jobs with foreign workers" (AFL-CIO's press release, March 18, 1998). The labor movement view on high-tech professionals is that the focus should be on education and training of American graduate students in universities, and retraining of current high-tech industry workers to meet future demand.

A second example of labor union apprehension about immigration policy occurs in the area of temporary agricultural workers who are issued visas (H-2A is the designation) to fill specific, identified needs in the agricultural sector of the U.S. economy. There are several concerns: ensuring that Americans have the first opportunity at the jobs; limiting the program to the actual number of Mexican workers needed on a seasonal basis in a given sector and ensuring their subsequent departure; and protecting the wage levels and health and living standards in temporary-worker housing provided by employers.

At a Senate hearing on the agricultural guest worker (H-2A) program, Cecilia Muñoz of the National Council of La Raza made it clear that her organization strongly opposes expansion of the H-2A program. She called instead for a review of the regularization process for the present large numbers of undocumented farm workers now permanently residing in the United States, who she claims are subjected to substandard wage and living conditions because of their undocumented status. Granting the agricultural industry access to more labor through the H-2A program, she asserted, would simply add to the supply of workers to the detriment of the existing work force (U.S. Senate, Hearing on Guest-Worker Programs, May 12, 1999).

Immigrants, education, and public health and welfare. There is also the fear that immigrants are overwhelming the school systems of some highly impacted receiving communities. Some statistics bear this out. In California, for example, immigrants, mostly Mexican and almost all with limited English, now account for 1.3 million enrollees in the public-school system. These limited-English students cost an additional $319 million per year in California's education budget over and above the average student cost. Some school districts are disproportionately affected. One solution is to identify and provide supplementary state or federal funding for these impacted districts, thus relieving the unfair impact on specific receiving communities. Similar support for impacted communities might be appropriate in such areas as public health (immigrants often have inadequate or no health insurance) and public welfare. Specific support of this sort might go a long way toward alleviating criticism of immigrants and increasing their acceptance in the community.

U.S.-Mexico Policy Implications

The implications for U.S.-Mexico policy and relations are pretty clear. It would be highly useful to change focus from immigration as primarily a law enforcement problem and recognize that long-term solutions can be found only in the context of the two countries' rapidly growing economic and social interdependence.

In the NAFTA context we have seen that labor and migration issues, while not directly free-trade concerns, are closely related. Discussions parallel to continuing trade talks and institution building (for example, on North American environmental issues—see Chapter 8) might be an ideal mechanism for discovering ways to change the emphasis from the criminalization of migration and consider more seriously the underlying economic and social forces instead. An optimum result would be a cooperative trinational program that deals effectively with North American labor flows.

Mexican immigration to the United States in the 1990s has assumed a combination of familiar and newly emerging patterns. While significant numbers of young males continue to work in the U.S. agricultural sector, returning to Mexico when the season ends, they are rapidly becoming outnumbered by immigrants who intend to stay permanently. In both cases, an increase in "pull factors" drawing new workers can be expected as the U.S. economy continues on a historic pattern of sustained growth, and labor demand in almost all sectors rises. Migration flows appear to be sensitive to economic conditions in both countries, but particularly to those in the United States, for while in theory the improvement in Mexico's economy achieved since 1995 (see Chapter 4) should have reduced "push" factors in Mexico, there is little evidence at present that the willingness of Mexican workers to emigrate has diminished very significantly.

Mexican and U.S. policymakers clearly should be working together to develop a joint migration policy that meets the needs of employers, workers, and consumers, as well as the economies of both countries. The United States should welcome a continuing dialogue with Mexico to identify ways to better manage migration issues. Such ideas include placing migration concerns on a formal bilateral agenda for high-level discussions; encouraging the U.S. legislative branch to be more sensitive to Mexican concerns when drafting new legislation; and, for policymakers, being wary of arguments that a greater military or civilian law enforcement presence on the U.S.-Mexico border is necessarily useful or productive (see Herrera-Lasso, 1999). A recent immigration study (Saxenian, 1999) suggests that the policy debate over immigration should be widened to recognize the positive influence of immigrants to Silicon Valley on trade and economic development in the global economy. Dialogue would encourage recognition that immigration issues are not discrete in nature, but rather are interconnected with a broad range of bilateral policy concerns.

It is clear that the United States can no longer maintain the old status quo: that is, keeping on the books existing immigration laws while relying de facto on undocumented workers to contribute importantly to America's economic progress. New approaches must be considered. They should be studied in the overall context of the need for improved bilateral collaboration, and with the involvement of stakeholders from both countries.

7

Drug Trafficking

The issue of illegal traffic in drugs is an old one in the history of the United States and Mexico, and has had a cyclical character, from bitter disputes to close cooperation, over the years. To some extent, these cycles reflect such external factors as the sharp growth of international drug cartels (e.g., the "French connection" or the "Medellín cartel") and the increasing difficulty, for governments, of controlling the burgeoning traffic.

But other factors have been at work as well, including the lack of clear-cut policies by either country on narcotics control and, importantly, a failure to agree on the proper balance between education and law enforcement for the eradication of narcotics trafficking. This policy uncertainty takes place in a milieu where many conflicting interests in both countries are at work, many with no commitment at all to eliminating drug trafficking and use. Drug enforcement issues often are obscured and good policies hindered by the very nature of the increasingly confrontational political process in Washington, state capitals, and cities around the nation.

While both governments constantly state that they want to eliminate drug trafficking and sales, they are often in disaccord about how to go about this laudable goal. Many Mexicans who hold that the root cause of the problem is unbridled consumption on American streets call on the U.S. government to spend much more on education and drug treatment programs. The Clinton administration, though it has provided modest increases in funds for education and treatment, continues to put great emphasis on the interdiction of narcotics on their way to the United States—either at the source, or in countries on the drug trafficking route (see Figure 7.1 on page 142). Mexico, of course, qualifies in both these categories as the United

States's number-one supplier, inter alia by growing marijuana and opium poppies and by transporting South American cocaine. The connection between official Mexico—both civilian politicians and local military commanders—and illicit drug trafficking is a historical one, and difficult to rupture.

A Historical Perspective

Official U.S.-Mexico cooperation against drug trafficking goes back to the early 1920s, when Mexican president Alvaro Obregón, citing his country's adherence to the 1912 International Opium Convention, issued a series of decree-laws banning opium trade. Later, Plutarco Elías Calles (1924–1928) signed international agreements banning international trafficking in marijuana and heroin and pledged to enact domestic legislation controlling the production and distribution of dangerous drugs. Lázaro Cárdenas (1934–1940) was urged by the U.S. and other foreign governments to follow up on his predecessor's pledges, but other events—such as the nationalization of the oil industry and private American-owned ranches—took center stage during his administration, and little progress was made in drug control discussions.

During World War II, the United States shifted gears and encouraged legal poppy growing and opium production in Mexico to serve the wartime medical needs of the military services. But by 1944 opium production was getting out of hand, particularly in Sinaloa and Sonora. It was clear that the need for morphine (derived from the opium poppy) for military hospitals had been overestimated, and current stockpiles of the drug were more than sufficient. The two countries signed an agreement to cut production and prohibit illegal shipments, which nevertheless continued, though on a fairly modest scale.

The drug issue receded during the 1950s, but reemerged with a vengeance in the 1960s. A new, "turned-on" lifestyle in the United States was creating a vast demand for marijuana—and to a lesser degree, for heroin—and Mexican growers and dealers responded. The U.S. government began, on the one hand, supplying Mexico with aircraft, training, and equipment for drug interdiction and, on the other hand, exerting increasing diplomatic pressure on Mexico to redouble its efforts to destroy opium poppy and marijuana crops and to interdict illicit drugs.

The explosive outcome of this high-pressure diplomacy was predictably counterproductive. Operation Intercept, launched on September 21, 1969, by U.S. law enforcement authorities (who were, in turn, advised by a shadowy figure on President Nixon's staff named G. Gordon Liddy), was the largest narcotics border search-and-seizure operation in history. Operation Intercept caught the Mexican government—and the U.S. State Department—by surprise, and soon created an immense amount of ill will on the part of thousands of innocent Mexicans (and Americans) who were blocked from crossing border points for protracted periods, during which every person and vehicle was meticulously searched.

The Mexican press was highly critical of the operation—especially after the roughing up of a Mexican consul by U.S. agents—and complained that it was more successful in harassing Mexicans than in stopping drug traffic. In fact, very small amounts of drugs were actually seized, as the word quickly spread among *contrabandistas* (smugglers), who simply rerouted their cargoes to more-remote parts of the porous border.

Within days after Operation Intercept was announced, an ad hoc U.S. government interagency committee, composed of State Department and other representatives more interested in cooperation than in confrontation, met and quickly came up with a plan that was both far more effective and, importantly, acceptable to the Mexicans. Operation Cooperation, unveiled October 11, 1969, replaced Operation Intercept and brought U.S. and Mexican agencies together in joint operations designed to reduce drug smuggling. There followed fifteen years of relatively smooth collaboration, including the plant destruction program Operation Condor in the 1970s as well as a number of successful interdiction efforts, many of them based on U.S. global intelligence contacts.

Criticisms of Mexico's antidrug efforts were often based not on the efforts themselves, but on the widespread charges of human-rights abuses and corruption that accompanied them. Federal antidrug police, the subject of numerous complaints to Mexico's Human Rights Commission, were one of the causes of the subsequent abrupt change in command at the top of the Mexican antidrug program. On October 15, 1990, President Salinas named the number-two official in the Interior Ministry, Jorge Carrillo Olea, to be Mexico's new "drug czar" (actually, general coordinator of investigations into drug trafficking).

Carrillo Olea's predecessor, Javier Coello Trejo, had compiled a good record in increasing cocaine and marijuana seizures, but was considered insufficiently responsive to human-rights abuse charges.

The Camarena Case and Aftermath

Carrillo Olea enjoyed a second public-relations advantage over Coello Trejo: he was not involved in the antinarcotics program at the time of the abduction, torture, and murder of Enrique Camarena, an American citizen who served as U.S. Drug Enforcement Agency (DEA) representative at the U.S. Consulate General in Guadalajara. This macabre crime, committed in Guadalajara in February 1985 with the alleged complicity of local Mexican policemen, was bitterly and publicly criticized by senior U.S. officials in Washington and Mexico City, and not only marked the nadir in narcotics trafficking cooperation in the 1980s, but also made the ongoing negotiation of other pressing bilateral issues more difficult.

The fallout of the Camarena case continued into the 1990s, in part because of the forcible apprehension and transfer to U.S. authorities of a Guadalajara physician who was allegedly deeply implicated in the prolonged torture of Camarena. Mexican authorities, noting that the DEA had arranged what amounted to a kidnapping by bounty hunters (a claim the DEA did not deny), insisted that the physician be returned to Mexico. U.S. attorneys argued that, on the basis of international precedent, the physician could be tried in a U.S. court no matter how he came into its jurisdiction. The matter went through the U.S. courts in 1991, and in early 1992 the U.S. Supreme Court ruled in favor of the DEA's actions in this case.

U.S. Assistance to the Mexican Military

In 1995 the United States and Mexico negotiated an agreement for the United States to supply equipment and training to the Mexican military. During the next three years more than seventy helicopters worth about $60 million, four large surveillance aircraft, and two naval frigates were supplied, and hundreds of Mexican soldiers received special-forces training to mount antidrug operations in Mexico, including using the helicopters to descend on clandestine air strips used for the transshipment of drugs from Colombia and elsewhere in South America.

It appears, however, that the equipment and training effort bore few concrete results, and, in at least a few cases, the special-forces soldiers have themselves been involved in criminal activities. Efforts during 1998, then, focused on adjusting the 1995 agreements to cause the least strain on U.S.-Mexico security relations.

Operation Casablanca

Clearly, despite the successes, there have also been low points in the area of U.S.-Mexico narcotics trafficking cooperation throughout the 1990s, including the public identification of top-level Mexicans involved in the anti–drug trafficking field as in the employ of the most notorious drug lords. But the most dramatic low point was probably Operation Casablanca, which surfaced in mid-1998.

Operation Casablanca was a three-year undercover sting operation run by the U.S. Customs Service, which described it as the largest and most successful such effort ever undertaken in this area. In May 1998, U.S. Customs obtained numerous indictments against, among others, the employees of a dozen leading Mexican banks accused of laundering more than $100 million in illegal drug money. Mexican bankers in Mexico City, Ciudad Juárez, and elsewhere, including some linked to the Cali, Colombia, drug cartel, were investigated.

The operation lured alleged Mexican drug traffickers and their bankers to a party in a small Nevada town that was to culminate in a wild evening at a local brothel. It ended, instead, in a mass arrest as U.S. law enforcement agents moved in and spoiled the party. Some 160 arrests were subsequently made, acting on information obtained over the 1995–1998 period, during which Mexican law enforcement and banking authorities were kept in the dark about the operation for "security reasons" to protect the operation from any leaks.

The reaction in Mexico was predictable. Mexicans were outraged, and the ensuing diplomatic uproar brought Mexico's well-known nationalistic sensitivities to the forefront. President Zedillo complained to President Clinton, and stated publicly that no cause "can justify the violation of our sovereignty nor of our laws." Mexico's foreign minister, Rosario Green, added that, "There are a lot of things that we have not accepted, and that we are not going to accept. . . . We Mexicans are very jealous of our national sovereignty" (*New York Times,* May 27, 1998).

The White House response was a carefully worded statement from spokesman Michael McCurry. "President Clinton expressed regret that better prior consultation had not been possible in this case," McCurry noted (White House, May 26, 1998). This statement takes into account two factors: (1) the U.S. law enforcement authorities claimed that at least some preliminary briefings of Mexican officials had taken place; and (2) full consultation would have run the risk of blowing the operation and placing the U.S. agents in physical danger.

On June 3 Mexico officially advised the United States that it might prosecute both U.S. Customs agents and their informants, noting that sting operations such as Casablanca are illegal under Mexican law, and that in any case, the people involved had no permission to be undertaking such an operation in Mexico. Mexico indicated at first that charges might include entrapment, engaging in money laundering, and usurping Mexican legal authority. Mexico subsequently declined to prosecute.

The Drug Control Certification Process

U.S.-Mexico cooperation in resolving the massive problem of illegal narcotics trafficking also has been made more difficult because of the 1986 congressional requirement that the president "certify" countries as cooperating in the narcotics trafficking control effort. This has given rise to an annual process in which the president announces on or before March 1 that he has determined that Mexico, as a drug-producing and transmitting country, has fully cooperated with the United States in efforts to curtail production and trafficking.

These announcements are preceded by a greater or lesser degree of drumbeating in the Congress, which threatens to override the president's certification if Mexico does not shape up. Such threats were more marked in 1998, an election year, than in 1999, when President Clinton's certification, following closely on the heels of a quick visit to President Zedillo in which assurances of new Mexican efforts were forthcoming, met with less criticism. The process leads inevitably to an annual strain on U.S.-Mexico relations.

It is noteworthy that Mexico left as little as possible to chance prior to the 1999 certification. Not only was President Zedillo prepared with the announcement of a new program to combat drug production and trafficking, but also Mexican interior minister Francisco Labastida, then a highly influential cabinet minister, came to Washington in early February 1999 for discussions with Secretary of State

Madeleine Albright, Attorney General Janet Reno, FBI director Louis Freeh, and key figures in the U.S. Congress.

Labastida's message was that Mexican civilian and military leaders were initiating a new program aimed at countering the drug trafficking menace. The $500 million budget covered three years of operations focusing on coordination of satellite communications technology with aircraft, ships, and land vehicles designed to interdict drug smugglers. This would be complemented by better selection and training of antidrug task force personnel and the establishment of a central command center for narcotics trafficking control.

Mexico's Drug Control Record

It is clear that the initiative announced by President Zedillo in early 1999 resulted in part from disappointment in Mexico's performance in 1998 in the critical area of drug seizures. This was particularly notable in heroin seizures, which fell to 280 pounds in 1998, compared with 300 pounds in 1997, and 730 pounds in 1996. Less dramatic declines were noted in cocaine and marijuana seizures as well. Though some key figures escaped extradition, Mexico did extradite twelve fugitives to the United States in 1998, including three Mexican nationals. One of these, Bernardo Velardes López, was sought for the murder of a U.S. Border Patrol agent in a narcotics-related case. While these extraditions were a step in the right direction, the United States continued to press for the arrest and extradition of a number of higher-level figures in Mexico's drug cartels.

A great deal of publicity surrounded the 1998 arrest of Jesús and Luis Amezcua Contreras, who were accused of being major methamphetamine traffickers and leaders of the Colima cartel. Though they were cleared under murky circumstances by a Mexican judge, the United States continued to insist on their extradition. Meanwhile a steady stream of lesser fry, including corrupt military and civilian officials, accounted for some of the 7,250 drug-related arrests in Mexico in 1998. Mexican authorities also obtained the convictions of a number of drug traffickers, including Ernesto "Don Neto" Fonseca Carrillo, already imprisoned for his part in the Camarena murder, who was sentenced to an additional eleven years on other drug-related charges.

To put the Mexican performance in perspective, it is necessary to note that well-entrenched international drug cartels take advantage of the largely unprotected 2,000-mile U.S.-Mexico border to deliver their illegal drugs—including heroin, cocaine, and marijuana—to their sophisticated drug distribution networks across the continental United States. In recent years these cartels have branched out from major cities to smaller cities and rural areas, making them ever harder to interdict. The drug cartels have added methamphetamine trafficking to their list, along with "designer" drugs, illicit steroids, and pharmaceuticals such as Valium and Rohypnol (the infamous "date rape" drug). By mid-1999 Mexico was a major center for the laundering of drug-money (hurt but not destroyed by Operation Casablanca) with ostensibly legitimate businesses on both sides of the border used on a massive scale.

It was in this context that the Mexican government undertook a new and more comprehensive antidrug strategy, including the new $500 million program announced in February 1999. This overall effort was aimed at attacking drug trafficking networks through intelligence sources, eradicating drug crops, reducing money laundering, and interdicting and seizing drug shipments. The focus during 1999 was on the Juárez cartel, the Tijuana cartel, the Gulf cartel, and the Caro Quintero group. Mexican attorney general Jorge Madrazo Cuéllar also moved forward with his attack on corruption within the criminal-justice system both in the police and the courts. Meanwhile, Mexico continues to be a major cultivator of cannabis and opium poppies. The opium poppy production is particularly worrisome given its contribution to heroin production and trafficking in the United States. Mexico is also the principal transit route to the United States for cocaine produced in South America.

The Mexican antidrug effort was facilitated by the establishment in 1996 of a U.S.-Mexico High-Level Contact Group (HLCG) on narcotics control. The HLCG was designed to explore joint solutions to the drug threat, promote cooperation, and agree on performance measures of effectiveness. Among the issues discussed was the Operation Casablanca problem, which was due in part to Mexican laws preventing an investigation of money laundering in the case of individuals who have not had a prior conviction for illegal enrichment or related offenses. Since most drug lords have successfully evaded such convictions, they are exempt from investigation. The Mexican attorney general's office planned during the course of 1999 to send the Congress new legislation resolving this enforcement problem.

In addition to cooperation with the United States, Mexico is an active participant in the United Nations under the authority of the

1998 Drug Convention, the "Anti-Drug Strategy in the Hemisphere" of the Organization of American States, and other international organizations. Mexico frequently uses these international forums to criticize the United States for paying insufficient attention to reducing demand in the massive U.S. market for illicit drugs.

U.S. Drug Control Strategy

At the same time the Mexican interior minister was in Washington, Vice President Al Gore announced from the White House a $17.8 billion antidrug budget proposal to send to the Congress for fiscal year 2000. "Our Administration's National Drug Control Strategy is comprehensive and long-term with more money for drug testing and treatment . . . better drug-law enforcement in our communities, better drug control on our borders . . . and better anti-drug education for young people" (White House, February 8, 1999).

This represented a 40 percent increase in the counterdrug efforts since the Clinton-Gore administration came to office (see Figure 7.1). Among the highlights of the education efforts were $195 million for a media campaign aimed at youth, and $590 million for drug-free schools, in addition to increases in the budget for drug treatment programs. Community policing received $1.3 billion under the proposal, which also called for increases in the DEA, Border Patrol, and drug control liaison activities with Mexico.

U.S. narcotics control policy toward Mexico includes a long-term goal of supporting Mexico's political will to strengthen the institutions that will permit it to take more effective measures against drug production and trafficking and related crimes. It is hoped that this will result in the apprehension and prosecution of leading drug traffickers, the dismantling of their cartels, and the elimination of their money-laundering activities. There is a focus on the development of cooperative activities in which actions on both sides of the border are better coordinated and complement each other's efforts.

Prospects for Bilateral Cooperation

Mexican views. Mexican critics have a strong consensus opinion: They say the United States is putting too much emphasis on interdiction and questionable legal practices while allocating far too few resources to drug prevention programs, particularly in the cities. They

**Figure 7.1   U.S. Federal Drug War Expenditures
(in billions of dollars)**

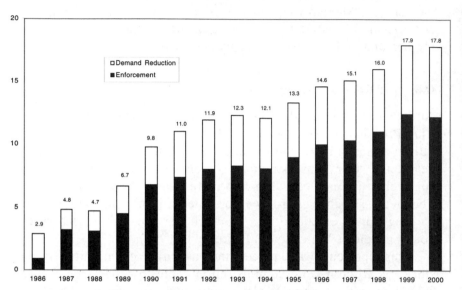

Source: U.S. Office of National Drug Control Policy

ask that the U.S. undertake massive new education and rehabilitation
programs to reduce the seemingly insatiable demand for illicit drugs,
and they call for genuine cooperation rather than unilateral U.S. action—epitomized by Operation Casablanca—in international efforts
aimed at curbing drug trafficking. Mexico welcomes what it sees as
a renewed U.S. effort in 1999 to stress collaboration over secrecy.

Mexicans also point out that the United States could do more in
its own often-sporadic and politically sensitive domestic eradication
efforts. Even though marijuana production is estimated to be the
largest cash crop of Hawaii, Oregon, and California, U.S. growers
seemed largely immune from the kinds of enforcement actions the
U.S. expects of Mexican authorities.

A more recent phenomenon on the antinarcotics scene is the increasing concern of many thoughtful Mexicans that they are beginning to have a drug use problem within their own country. After
decades of being a major supplier of drugs to the United States, and
decrying U.S. demand as the insidious reason for the problem, it is
becoming more and more apparent that drug use, particularly among

Mexican teenagers, should be highlighted and addressed. A report issued by the Mexican Ministry of Health in 1997 showed that cocaine use among Mexico City teenagers had quadrupled, with a 4 percent user rate among the groups studied. Of course, marijuana use was much higher.

Response to what is clearly perceived as increasing drug abuse has been forthcoming among community groups of parents and growing numbers of drug counselors in Mexico City and other major cities and regions in Mexico. These concerns also were reflected by Foreign Minister Rosario Green, who noted that "if you start out on the road of drug abuse and don't stop it on time with truly adequate measures, it could become really dangerous" (*Los Angeles Times,* June 8, 1998).

U.S. views. As the drug certification's March madness drew near in 1999, it was the clear view of President Clinton that it was necessary to certify Mexico as cooperating in the "war on drugs," in order to preserve the overall relationship between the two countries. In the face of disappointing Mexican performance in 1998, the argument had to be that full Mexican collaboration, which might be lost in a decertification battle, was necessary if the U.S. drug control effort was to make any progress.

In 1999 the United States was faced not only with declining figures in drug seizures but also by the failure of Mexican authorities to arrest (and to retain once arrested) some of the most notorious traffickers and, as noted above, the hesitation of the Mexicans to extradite some of these traffickers, despite previous assurances that this would be done. State Department spokesman James Rubin gave a positive interpretation of the situation when he noted that "there is a difference between cooperation and success, and Mexican officials are cooperating more closely with the U.S. at virtually every level than ever before" (U.S. Department of State, February 9, 1999).

This was borne out by the numerous consultations on narcotics issues held by senior U.S. and Mexican officials during 1998 and 1999. Counselor to the president and special envoy for the Americas Mack McLarty made visits to President Zedillo and his most senior advisors, and President Clinton and President Zedillo had several consultations on narcotics trafficking, including personal meetings in June 1998 and February 1999. The HLCG was active during this period as well. Led by Office of National Drug Control Policy director

Barry McCaffrey, Mexican foreign secretary Rosario Green, and Mexican attorney general Jorge Madrazo, the group met in April and December 1998 and in February 1999.

Prospects for 2000 and beyond. It appears that Mexico and the United States will continue on their often bumpy road toward improving cooperative efforts against drug production, trafficking, and abuse. Both governments seem sincere in their declared intentions to accomplish these goals, which include disrupting and dismantling transnational narcotrafficking organizations and the apprehension, prosecution, and conviction of major drug traffickers. Bellwethers of success in the face of conflicting interests and irresponsible partisan politics in both countries will be whether the U.S. president elected in 2000 continues to devote ever-increasing resources to drug education and prevention, and whether a new administration in Mexico has the political will and internal strength to make the institutional changes needed to reduce corruption and improve efficiency. Ultimately, prospects for successful collaboration depend on how well both countries manage the complex and highly interdependent relationship. This will be the subject for further discussion in Chapter 9.

8

Managing Environmental Issues

After years of neglect, environmental issues are now a serious component of U.S.-Mexico relations. This change is in part a result of the general global environmental awareness that began in the 1960s and emerged as an international topic in the 1970s. The other factor responsible for greater environmental awareness between the two countries is the rapidly increasing population in the border region. This increased population has not only contributed to the environmental problems, but has also led to an enhanced concern about ways of confronting environmental issues.

Recent polls in both the United States and Mexico have indicated that people rank environmental issues high on the list of their concerns (see Kiy and Wirth, 1998: 247–248). In both countries, grassroots activists have responded to threats to local air, water, and land quality and to the attempt to locate polluting industries in border areas. Local groups in such places as Tijuana, Mexico, and Del Rio, Texas, have lobbied successfully against the siting of toxic-waste facilities in their communities. State and national governments, too, have addressed environmental issues. The Mexican Congress, for example, enacted legislation—the General Law of Ecological Equilibrium and Environmental Protection (1988, amended 1996)—that allows for greater enforcement of crimes against the environment and provides specific penalties for these crimes. The Mexican Green Party, like its U.S. nongovernmental organization (NGO) counterparts, has also been more influential in both national and local politics. Environmental awareness is now widespread on both sides of the border.

The apparent harmony of these concerns in the United States and Mexico means that increased cooperation on ecological and environmental issues is likely and promising. Mexico and the United States recognized these concerns in the context of NAFTA parallel accords that provide for creation of new institutions, such as the Commission for Environmental Cooperation (CEC), which is helping to standardize environmental laws and resolve conflicts among the member states, including Canada; and the Border Environmental Cooperation Commission (BECC), whose goal is to develop environmental infrastructure projects. These institutions are evidence of the increased cooperation between the two countries on environmental issues.

Environmental Issues and Problems

Mexico and the United States still have a long way to go in addressing their common environmental concerns. A growing population, migration, and the location of industrial enterprises in the border region mean that ecological problems are also increasing. More economic cooperation between the two countries—especially after NAFTA—also has brought greater attention to the border region.

The Evolving Environmental Relationship

The U.S.-Mexico border is nearly 2,000 miles long and passes through a generally arid region. Historically, it was not a region that attracted substantial settlement; agricultural potential was limited due to lack of water, and therefore the population remained small. Irrigated agriculture, ranching, and some extractive industries such as mining provided the basis of the modest economy. Manufacturing was limited or nonexistent and this, together with the small population, kept environmental problems to a minimum. Those industries that did exist were concentrated in specific locales, such as mining and smelters in the El Paso area, for example. In the earlier decades of the twentieth century local populations in both countries were thus generally less aware or concerned about potential or actual ecological problems.

One issue of concern was water. In a desert region, water is life, and both the Mexican and U.S. border population depended—and still depend—on it. The earliest environmental concerns, and earliest environmental cooperation, centered on the availability and quality of the water supply. Attention of the two countries focused on the control of water in the Rio Grande, especially when the United

States as the upstream nation decided in the late nineteenth century to construct the Elephant Butte dam in New Mexico to impound water for agriculture. A similar conflict developed when, about thirty years later, the United States constructed Hoover Dam (then known as Boulder Dam) on the Colorado River and took on the Imperial Valley Project in California. All of these projects reduced the flow of fresh water to Mexico.

Contemporary Issues

In recent decades the number of environmental issues of concern to both the United States and Mexico has grown substantially. Water is no longer the single bone of contention between the two countries. It is part of a constellation of ecological issues demanding attention, money, and other resources from the two governments. As population, trade, and contact have increased in the web that marks the silent integration (Reynolds and Tello, 1983) of the peoples of the United States and Mexico, so too have the environmental issues.

Water. Water rights and quality are still issues calling for effective cooperative management between the two countries (Mumme, 1993), including the quality of water in the three transborder river systems, namely the Rio Grande and the Colorado and Tijuana Rivers. The Colorado River has proven especially contentious. As the downstream neighbor, Mexico receives what is left after seven U.S. states have tapped the river, and this remaining water can be so saline that it is unusable for agriculture. Though Mexico and the United States have signed a treaty guaranteeing the quality of water delivered to Mexico, disputes still linger. Moreover, both the United States and Mexico face depletion of their aquifers (for example, under the El Paso–Ciudad Juárez transboundary area), which could intensify the competition for water in the future.

Both Mexico and the United States must also confront the issue of water pollution and contamination. Intensification of agriculture in the border area means that increasing levels of chemicals, fertilizers, and pesticides are being deposited in watercourses and in groundwater. The issue of sewage is especially problematic. Ciudad Juárez, for example, dumps sewage into the Rio Grande, contaminating river water downstream.

Air. Air pollution was not historically an issue until the advent of the automobile and its widespread use in the rapidly growing cities of the border region, including San Diego/Tijuana, Phoenix, Tucson, El Paso/Juárez, and the cities of the Rio Grande Valley, among others. A growing population requires more power (especially for air conditioners in the U.S. Sunbelt states), which in turn requires power generation, usually through the burning of fossil fuels. The Carbón II power generation facility in Mexico near Big Bend is an example of an inefficient power plant that impacts air quality in the region.

The effects of transborder air pollution are increasingly evident. The extensive wildfires in southern Mexico in 1998 spread haze and smoke as far north as Albuquerque, New Mexico, providing evidence of the long-range transmission of these pollutants. Ordinary automobile exhausts from such cities as Los Angeles and Mexico City are regularly transported by air currents for hundreds or even thousands of miles.

A specific example is the Paso Del Norte region, centering on El Paso, Texas, Ciudad Juárez, Chihuahua, and Sunland Park, New Mexico, an especially problematic area. The nearly 2 million people in this region live in a basin surrounded by mountains. The physical geography of this basin together with the sunny desert climate and low rainfall combine to produce inversion layers noticeable by the hazy brown clouds that regularly settle over the basin. The toxic components of these clouds—including ozone, nitrogen oxides, particulates, and carbon monoxide—regularly exceed emissions standards set by the United States.

Sewage and toxic waste. Land degradation and potential danger to human life are both on the increase due to an increased level of sewage and toxic wastes. The increased industrialization of the border region associated with the development of the *maquiladoras* has led to increased dumping of toxic materials such as heavy metals, chemicals, and radioactive wastes. Not all wastes are properly disposed of and enforcement of proper dumping procedures is often lax, especially in Mexico. The increasing tendency of both national governments to attempt to locate toxic waste dumping and storage facilities—such as the WIPP project in New Mexico—in the border region pose potential problems. Poorer regions, including poorer states such as New Mexico, may become dumping grounds for toxic materials from other states as they attempt to attract job-generating industries to their region.

Land quality issues. In addition to the introduction of toxic materials into the surface and subsurface environments, both Mexico and the United States have witnessed an increase in land degradation including deforestation and overgrazing. Deforestation reduces the ability of the environment to naturally purify the air, and the burning of forest cover to clear land for agriculture in southern Mexico contributes to air pollution, such as the clouds of smoke that were visible in the United States in 1998. Deforestation also contributes to soil erosion, reducing agricultural productivity by washing away topsoil. Loss of forests and the overgrazing of rangeland destroy the natural habitat of wildlife, including endangered species. Deforested and overgrazed lands are slow to recover, and it is doubtful that they will recover to their natural level even if destructive processes are reduced. Land is also being cleared—and agricultural land being converted—for human settlement to accommodate the growing population of Sunbelt and border cities. This land will never be reconverted.

Ecosystem problems. The environmental factors described above all contribute to a general degradation of the ecosystem, including its reduced resiliency to further degradation. The general destruction of ecosystems in the United States and Mexico due to deterioration of the quality of water, air, and land result in habitat loss, potential extinction of species, and problems for migratory species. Migratory species that cross the international border—ranging from butterflies and birds to seals and whales—pose special problems for environmental management, as they depend on a variety of ecosystems often at great distance from one another.

Potential global-change problems. Though information on this topic is limited compared with the increasingly voluminous documentation of the environmental problems noted earlier, it nevertheless warrants consideration. In fact, its very uncertainty makes it especially urgent that the U.S. and Mexican governments make an effort to address the problem sooner rather than later. Global-change problems that could have an impact on the U.S.-Mexico relationship include prolonged drought, shifting cycles of aridity and rainfall, and increased transportation of pollutants over greater distances, and as well as the likelihood of other as yet unrecognized consequences. The impacts of these global-change effects could include reduced food production and crop failures, water shortages, increased spread of pollutants, and shifting patterns of settlement and migration—including perhaps increased undocumented Mexican migration across the border into the United States.

Overall, Mexico and the United States have a host of environmental questions to address. The days of a small, settled population primarily concerned with water availability are no longer with us. Instead, a larger, automobile-dependent and more industrialized population in both countries has generated a set of interconnected environmental problems and issues that increasingly require local, regional, and international cooperation. Differences in the level of economic development in the two countries also have a bearing on environmental questions, as poverty has been linked to ecosystem destruction. Clearly, the underlying economic and social issues that give rise to some ecosystem problems cannot be ignored.

Responses to Environmental Issues

Responses to environmental issues have grown as the problems themselves have multiplied. Historically, responses in both the United States and Mexico have been limited and ad hoc. Today concerted, sustained action is required to address these issues.

Historical Responses

Mexico and the United States share a long history of cooperation in resolving their historic disputes over water rights and water quality. Though the two countries have addressed a number of different environmental issues throughout their historical relationship—including early-twentieth-century agreements on conservation and migratory birds, for example—it has been in the area of water resources that the two countries have focused much of their effort.

Disputes over water were in a sense a natural part of the border relationship—the nearly 2,000-mile-long border between the two countries is either bounded by water or passes through a region of water scarcity. Hence the two national governments have created a variety of institutions to address and resolve water disputes. Chief among these is the International Boundary and Water Commission (IBWC), which has its origins in the commission established in 1889 to address U.S.-Mexico boundary issues. As water became the focus of border concerns, it was later added to the commission.

The International Boundary and Water Commission. No description of U.S.-Mexico environmental and transboundary resource issues would be complete without mention of the IBWC, a binational commission established as a permanent joint entity by a treaty between the United States and Mexico. The IBWC grew out of a mutual effort to survey the international boundary established by the Treaty of Guadalupe Hidalgo in 1848 and the Gadsden Purchase in 1853.

Despite the traumatic events that led to its creation—namely, Mexico's loss of half its territory (and the gain by the United States of one-third of its territory)—the IBWC has served with few exceptions as a model of international cooperation. Undoubtedly, one of the reasons for this is that the commission has been kept as apolitical as possible. Both the U.S. and Mexican commissioners are required by treaty to be civil engineers; their staffs are exclusively professional. Any policy guidance comes from their respective foreign ministries, that is, Mexico's Secretaría de Relaciones Exteriores and the U.S. Department of State.

Among the IBWC's successes has been its important technical contribution to the resolution of the Colorado River salinity dispute. The Colorado River is a major source of water for the southwest United States and northwest Mexico. A huge project to irrigate U.S. farmland was undertaken in the 1950s and completed in 1961. But the diversion of Colorado River water to irrigation and the subsequent drainage of that water—by now having passed through saline farmland—back into the Colorado caused salinity levels to rise in the 1960s. This rendered several thousand acres of Mexicali Valley land south of the border unusable, forcing hundreds of *campesinos* off the land. In the following years, the IBWC worked out an arrangement, signed by both nations in 1973, to build a desalting facility and dispose of unwanted brine.

The IBWC is responsible for the operation of the Rio Grande (Río Bravo) and Colorado River water distribution systems and international dams that control floods, conserve water, and generate electricity along the Rio Grande. It played an important advisory role in the Chamizal Settlement of 1963, helping to resolve a century-old dispute triggered by a sudden shift in the 1860s of the Rio Grande, which marked the boundary between the two border cities of El Paso, Texas, and Ciudad Juárez, Chihuahua. Since the early 1980s, the IBWC has taken on responsibility for growing transboundary waste-water problems (in large part a legacy of the *maquiladora* boom; see Chapter 4), and other emerging environmental issues.

The La Paz Agreement. A specific example of a comprehensive effort to resolve environmental issues in the pre-NAFTA era was the 1983 La Paz Agreement signed by Mexican president Miguel de la Madrid and U.S. president Ronald Reagan. The agreement originated as a U.S. effort to obtain Mexico's assistance in cleaning up the Tijuana River, which flows from northern Mexico into California, bringing Mexican sewage into the city of San Diego. The agreement was later expanded to include other issues such as transborder transportation of hazardous waste, smelters, and urban air pollution (Kiy and Wirth, 1998). The agreement did reduce transborder pollution generated by smelters in the Arizona-Sonora border area through the closure of some smelters and the installation of scrubbers at others. Though the La Paz Agreement provided a general framework and set the stage for later discussions, it did not address many of the environmental issues that have grown in importance since NAFTA.

Contemporary Responses

Though the La Paz Agreement was an important first step in addressing the broader issues of the U.S.-Mexico environmental relationship, it could not anticipate future problems caused by changing circumstances in the United States and Mexico and especially in the border region. For example, by 1990 the number of *maquiladoras* was about twice what it was in 1983, when the agreement was signed. The population in the border area also jumped considerably. As the United States and Mexico began to recognize these facts, and as environmental awareness in general increased, the two governments were prompted to reconsider their environmental concerns. This reconsideration eventually found its way into NAFTA through the medium of the Integrated Border Environment Program (IBEP), developed during 1992–1994. The IBEP created six working groups to address specific issues of concern: air, emergencies, enforcement/compliance, hazardous wastes, pollution prevention, and water.

NAFTA itself was linked with three parallel institutions with an impact on transborder environmental issues. The first of these was the Commission for Environmental Cooperation (CEC), created in 1994 as part of the North American Agreement for Environmental Cooperation, with participation from all three NAFTA countries, including Canada, and headquartered in Montreal. The CEC's role is to address regional environmental concerns, help prevent potential environment and trade conflicts, and promote the effective enforcement of environmental law. Also created in 1994, on a binational basis, were the Border Environmental Cooperation Commission (BECC) and the North American Development Bank (NADBank), with headquarters in Ciudad Juárez, Chihuahua, and San Antonio, Texas, respectively. In addition, some U.S. and Mexican states have also made efforts independent of NAFTA to address ecological concerns by organizing subnational, rather than national, agreements. California and Texas have been especially active in negotiating agreements with their counterparts across the border. Subnational cooperation is limited, however, by the more centralized Mexican political system, in contrast to the highly federal nature north of the border.

Despite the legacy of environmental cooperation and the impetus of NAFTA, transborder environmental cooperation is still a complicated and incomplete matter. As a team of Mexican, U.S., and Canadian scholars have noted (Sánchez-Rodríguez et al., 1998), transboundary environmental management is fragmentary. Though NAFTA and binational agreements are in place, most cooperation is still on an ad hoc basis within the general framework of the agreements. In general NAFTA and the other agreements between the United States and Mexico have not solved or even directly confronted many of the environmental issues faced by the two nations. Rather, they have provided a general grounding as well as institutions in which further debate and discussion can take place. The success or failure of future initiatives cannot be guaranteed by agreements such as NAFTA, but will have to evolve with continued local and regional interest and participation.

Trade and the Environment

Contemporary environmental agreements between the United States and Mexico are connected, directly or indirectly, with the issue of economic interdependence and especially with trade. Indeed, the concept of sustainable development is a conflation of the economic with the environmental. Mexican-U.S. environmental relations cannot be understood apart from the broader issues of the complex economic relations between the two countries. Central to this discussion is whether environment and trade should be understood as two separate issues, or whether they in fact are two sides of the same coin.

Some scholars (for example, Spalding, 1998) have noted that separating trade and environmental issues may be more successful than the linkage alternative, in that trade and environmental regimes are quite distinct. Spalding notes that before the 1990s separation was the common practice. While the Uruguay Round of GATT was under way, numerous separate environmental agreements such as the Montreal Protocol and the Earth Summit took place. Generally speaking, most free-trade advocates prefer separation of the two issues. They feel that environmental regulations as a direct component of trade negotiations reduce the ability of the partners to achieve freer trade.

Linkage, on the other hand, means combining environmental agreements with trade agreements. NAFTA had a side arrangement that addressed environmental issues, and was thus to some degree an example of linkage. Linking trade to the environment may result in greater popular support for free-trade agreements, as the population feels protected by the inclusion of environmental regulations. On the other hand, there is the danger that environmental issues will take a back seat to trade issues in a linked agreement. Nevertheless, environmental groups have often favored linkage as a means of guaranteeing that environmental issues will not be neglected and that economic actors will be aware of the environmental consequences of their actions.

Trade Liberalization: Pros and Cons

Free-traders in academe and the business community argue that free trade is environmentally benign. Trade liberalization increases economic growth, generating the tax revenues that can then be invested and used by the society for environmental protection. Environmental cleanup is costly, and generally paid for by government. With increasing tax revenue due to free trade, funds will be available that can be directed toward the environment. Proponents of trade liberalization also tend to be in favor of separation of trade and the environment and to see these as two issues, rather than one. They argue that trade policy and trade institutions, such as the World Trade Organization (WTO), are not the appropriate venues for dealing with environmental problems. Instead, they assert, international environmental policy should be negotiated separately, and governed by separate treaties and institutional arrangements.

Some environmentalists have suggested that trade liberalization, with its seemingly inevitable consequence of economic growth and development, must necessarily have a negative impact on the environment. They believe that economic growth increases the consumption of natural resources, leading to resource depletion, environmental degradation, and more pollution through the burning of fossil fuels.

The Maquiladoras

In few areas have the clashes between free-traders and environment advocates been more dramatic than in the *maquiladora* industry. Trade proponents have noted that the *maquiladora* manufacturing plants, usually located just across the U.S. border in Mexico and generally in-bond assembly plants for U.S.-made components, are beneficial to both trade partners. U.S. companies can enjoy the lower labor costs in Mexico (and the relatively close proximity of these plants, compared with alternatives in Asia), while Mexican communities benefit from increased employment. Trade advocates have also suggested that U.S. companies operating in Mexico are perhaps more environmentally aware than their Mexican counterparts and thus more likely to protect the environment. Furthermore, U.S. companies will be prompted by their stockholders and by U.S. consumers to maintain their *maquiladora* operations in compliance with environmental regulations.

This is not always the case, according to many environmentalists. Some environmental groups have accused U.S. companies of relocating their operations to Mexico in order to avoid U.S. regulations, and to benefit from the generally poor enforcement of Mexican environmental laws. The U.S. media have documented numerous instances of toxic materials being dumped on land and in water, often in remote areas where dumping is difficult to regulate and control. Some environmental groups thus view the *maquiladoras* as a way for U.S. firms to circumvent environmental regulations in the United States. Even though Mexico has enacted strict environmental laws, they claim that enforcement and compliance with those laws is still substantially below that in the United States.

What is the reality of the *maquiladora* situation? While some unscrupulous operators have indeed dumped toxic materials into transborder waters, others have strictly observed Mexican and U.S. environmental laws and could serve as models of what the *maquiladora* arrangement is supposed to be.

The U.S. division of Philips Electronics, for example, has seven thousand employees in fourteen manufacturing plants in the border region and has not only strictly observed environmental laws, but has also been active in recycling, waste reduction, pollution control, and energy conservation programs (Pizzorusso, 1998). Philips has also been successful in generating a corporate environmental ethos that could serve as a model for other enterprises in the region. On the other hand, the fact that many companies are in violation of environmental regulations clearly demonstrates the need for greater enforcement and monitoring.

Conclusions and Policy Implications

The environment has been transformed from a sideline issue in U.S.-Mexico relations to one of today's key questions. With population surging in the border region, as well as increasing levels of industry, competition over resources, and evidence of pollution and ecosystem degradation, the issue can no longer be ignored.

As we enter the next century, environmental concerns will become even more important. The declining supply and quality of water, already an issue for more than a hundred years, will become even more critical as the population of the two countries continues to grow. Air pollution, especially automobile and industrial emissions, and the dumping of toxic materials on land are becoming more serious. The broader issues of ecosystem dysfunction and the potentially harmful effects of global change did not attract much attention in the twentieth century, but will become critical in the twenty-first.

The United States and Mexico need to continue to monitor and improve existing agreements while exploring new avenues of cooperation. One possible mechanism that has proven successful elsewhere is the use of trust funds or resource indemnity funds to help finance and regulate cooperative measures (Pretes, 1996). In general the United States and Mexico must be not only more aware but also more concerned about these issues. Both countries should come to realize that they have joint responsibility, along with Canada, for the good environmental management of a shared North American continent.

PART 3

Into the Twenty-First Century

9

Trends in the Bilateral Relationship

Traditional Perspectives

During the course of the 1990s, particularly in the latter years of the decade, U.S.-Mexico relations achieved a prominence unusual in the post–World War II era. U.S. foreign policy after World War II had focused on the nation's intense rivalry with the erstwhile Soviet Union. The struggle had direct implications for Europe and much of the developing world. U.S. officials—and the U.S. public as well—viewed the world through the lens of superpower rivalry and judged each country on where it stood in relation to the competing ideologies of East and West.

Given the incredible pace of world events in the 1990s, it is hard to recall that as recently as the early 1980s, Ronald Reagan was attacking the Soviet Union as the "Evil Empire" and describing its dangerous and growing influence in Central America—warning that, "San Salvador is closer to Houston, Texas, than Houston is to Washington, D.C." (White House, May 9, 1984).

As a consequence of U.S. preoccupation with the perceived menace from the Soviets and their satellites, U.S. relations with Mexico in the postwar period were more often than not characterized by (1) a general tendency to ignore the importance of economic and political relations with a country with which we share a 2,000-mile border and a pervasive and growing interdependence; and (2) a failure to understand that the dissimilar foreign-policy perspectives separating the United States and Mexico were based not on any Mexican affinity for the Kremlin leadership, but on Mexico's deep historical roots and interests—which are both very distinct from those of the United States and very important to the Mexican psyche.

In earlier chapters we took a detailed look at these historical roots and learned that they still loom large in the Mexican memory. Mexicans remember the U.S. role in the secession of Texas, along with the loss of half of Mexico's territory in the "War of the North American Invasion" and its aftermath (the Treaty of Guadalupe Hidalgo and the Gadsden Purchase). In the twentieth century, Mexicans' image of their northern neighbor was colored by the occupation of the ports of Veracruz and Tampico by U.S. marines, the "punitive expedition" of General John J. Pershing, and, more recently, U.S. intervention in such nearby countries as Guatemala, the Dominican Republic, Grenada, and Panama.

Mexico's own history and experience led the country to develop a foreign policy and a style of conducting diplomatic relations that are unlike those of the United States. These differences caused problems for both sides.

Mexicans explained that their foreign-policy goals were based on a respect for national sovereignty, territorial integrity, and the right to self-determination. One of the linchpins of this policy has been the Estrada Doctrine, named for former Mexican foreign minister Genaro Estrada, who in 1930 announced that Mexico's policy of nonintervention compelled it automatically to recognize other de facto governments regardless of their ideological position.

This is a policy Mexico has followed with very few exceptions: A staunch supporter of the Spanish Republic, Mexico never recognized the Franco regime in Spain. Also, in solidarity with the Sandinistas in Nicaragua, President López Portillo broke relations with the Somoza government in 1971. In general, Mexico opposes intervention and, in the United Nations and other forums, supports the development of instruments of international law and multilateral political and economic negotiations.

U.S. foreign-policy deliberations are often highly charged and very public, involving the Congress, the administration, the media, special-interest groups, and the general citizenry (the Bosnia and Kosovo debates are examples). But at least until fairly recently Mexican foreign policy was generally made and executed quietly by the president and his team, advice was given in private sessions, and public criticism in the media was relatively muted. This style is changing dramatically, as evidenced by the growing role of opposition party members in an increasingly influential Mexican Congress where the PRI no longer rules, and by better reporting in an improving

Mexican media, both in the press and on television. Even so, foreign-policy issues are still debated less publicly in Mexico than in the United States.

One aspect of Mexico's foreign-policy activity has undergone substantial change in the 1990s. Mexico is more willing to promote its interests by engaging in higher-profile activities in Washington, D.C. By early 1992 President Salinas had almost tripled the size of the professional foreign-service staff, advised by a cadre of lobbyists and assisted by trade experts and other specialists, in the newly expanded Mexican embassy in Washington. In major cities around the United States, a growing number of consular officers are promoting Mexican foreign-trade interests, attracting foreign investment, and joining with their Washington counterparts in promoting Mexican exports and expanded foreign private direct investment in Mexico. The consuls are also charged with establishing through Mexican cultural institutes a closer relationship with the Mexican-American communities in their geographically defined districts, an initiative that has the personal blessing of President Zedillo.

These activities are in stark contrast to the quiet, low-profile path followed by a succession of Mexican ambassadors to the United States over past decades and through the end of the 1980s. Perhaps concerned about establishing a precedent for reciprocal U.S. activities in Mexico, diplomats previously stayed out of the limelight and confined their representational efforts to the State Department, a few other government agencies, and, discreetly, the U.S. Congress.

On substantive issues, Mexico's generaly low-profile style did not prevent it from maintaining its foreign-policy principles against any temptation to side with the United States. For example, in 1962, Mexico—true to the Estrada Doctrine and its conception of sovereignty and self-determination—opposed the passage of the U.S.-supported resolution in the Organization of American States that expelled Cuba from membership. Mexico was the only Latin American country to maintain diplomatic relations with Cuba in subsequent years. Mexico persevered on this course despite U.S. criticism.

Mexico and the World

Not until the presidency of Adolfo López Mateos (1958–1964) did a Mexican administration adopt an active and internationalist foreign policy. Although López Mateos was elected after a campaign filled with leftist rhetoric and with the strong support of former president Lázaro Cárdenas, Mexicans were nonetheless surprised when their new president immediately undertook state visits to such Third World luminaries as Tito in Yugoslavia, Nehru in India, and Sukarno in Indonesia. More important, President López Mateos actively supported the negotiations that led to the Treaty for the De-Nuclearization of Latin America, or the Treaty of Tlatelolco, for which the chief Mexican negotiator, Alfonso García Robles, subsequently shared the Nobel Peace Prize. The treaty negotiations were the chief international initiative of the López Mateos administration.

During the López Mateos administration, Mexico and the United States had sharp exchanges over the breaking of relations with Cuba, the Mexican condemnation of the Bay of Pigs invasion in April 1961, and, later, Mexican concern during the October 1962 Cuban missile crisis. But a truce of sorts was declared in the summer of 1962, when President and Mrs. John F. Kennedy made a historic visit to Mexico City and were greeted by an immense outpouring of popular adulation for "Jack and Jackie" at a number of public ceremonies. Kennedy marked the occasion of his visit by noting in a public statement that "geography has made us neighbors, tradition has made us friends, and economics has made us partners."

There came a brief respite from the international foreign-policy initiatives of López Mateos during the presidency of the quiet, retiring Gustavo Díaz Ordaz (1964–1970), who nonetheless worked tirelessly for the success of the 1968 Summer Olympics held in Mexico City. Unfortunately, those games are best remembered today because of the tragic deaths of students at the hands of army troops at the Plaza of Tlatelolco (Chapter 2).

While eschewing much foreign travel, Díaz Ordaz did meet on a few but not particularly memorable occasions with Presidents Johnson and Nixon. His successor, Luis Echeverría Alvarez (1970–1976), immediately embarked on a highly activist, Third World–oriented series of foreign-policy initiatives. One key reason for this feverish effort is obvious: Echeverría had served as minister of the interior in the previous administration, where as the head of security services he was responsible for the handling of the Tlatelolco massacre. His desire to restore his credentials with leftist Mexican students and intellectuals involved him in a search for a role as a Third World leader.

Echeverría undertook an exceptionally arduous international schedule, visiting many Third World countries as well as Moscow and Beijing. Closer ties and reciprocal visits with Cuba's Fidel Castro and Chile's Salvador Allende were also on the agenda. Mexican activities at the United Nations included successful efforts to seek General Assembly approval of the now-defunct Charter of Economic Rights and Duties of States, opposed by the United States and other developed countries, and Echeverría's ill-advised and costly support for an Arab-sponsored resolution equating Zionism with racism. (The resolution was rescinded in 1991.)

At home, Echeverría pursued a protectionist economic policy. His increased regulation of foreign investment and statist activities (for example, the nationalization of the telephone system) deterred potential foreign investors. At the same time, the public-sector deficit began to soar as, in an effort to stem a growing tide of rural discontent, he undertook a system of subsidies on basic commodities (corn, rice, milk, cooking oil, etc.) and extended rural road systems and electrification projects.

Massive deficit spending caused inflation to grow from an average of 5 percent a year in the previous administration to a then-unheard-of 20 percent during Echeverría's last two years in office. He did accomplish a nationwide crackdown on splinter groups led by former students and teachers who were organizing nascent rural and urban guerrilla organizations. While it is not clear how serious the situation might otherwise have become, his prompt and muscular counter-terrorist campaign, involving a considerable part of the Mexican army, brought an end to these post-Tlatelolco would-be insurgencies.

Later, Echeverría, who had a personal friendship with Chile's socialist president, Salvador Allende, opened Mexican government offices and academic institutions to a wave of leftist exiles who fled Chile following Allende's overthrow and the mysterious circumstances surrounding his apparent suicide in September 1973. The exiles included Allende's widow and other family members. While these advisors and intellectuals were the cause of some irritation to those Mexicans who felt themselves pushed aside, the Chileans nevertheless played at least a modest role in the formation of Mexican government policies in the last two years of the Echeverría administration.

López Portillo: Boom and Bust

There was considerable surprise when the outgoing president picked his aristocratic finance minister, José López Portillo, as his successor. U.S. officials, and indeed the Mexican public in general, believed that López Portillo would usher in a sober, conservative administration in contrast to the international flamboyance of his predecessor. Representatives of international financial institutions such as the International Monetary Fund and the World Bank looked forward to working with López Portillo to undo some of the damage of Echeverría's unwise economic policies.

Unfortunately, it turned out that Mexico would have to wait another six years for an administration interested in the kind of structural reform needed by the Mexican economy and political system. Soon after the beginning of López Portillo's term (1976–1982), the existence of huge new Mexican petroleum reserves was announced.

To get the feel of the early, heady years of the López Portillo administration, it is necessary to go back for a moment to 1960, when Saudi Arabia, Iran, Iraq, Kuwait, and Venezuela formed the Organization of Petroleum Exporting Countries (OPEC). The original motives were quite understandable. Until then, major international oil companies in effect set the price they would pay for crude; the oil-exporting countries concluded, correctly, that they could negotiate better terms with the companies by joining forces.

While OPEC was somewhat successful in negotiations with international oil companies (oil prices rose from about $1 per barrel in 1960 to $3 a barrel in 1973), its attempts to achieve a more significant increase in world prices through a cartel approach were not successful until an exceptional event—the Yom Kippur War of 1973, which pitted Egypt against Israel—galvanized anti-Western sentiment among the Arabs and catalyzed close cooperation within OPEC. Saudi Arabia in particular hoped that the "oil weapon" could be used to threaten the United States and dissuade it from supporting Israel.

The United States, believing that OPEC would never unite behind a Saudi-led embargo on crude-oil exports to the U.S., did not take the Saudi threat seriously. Thus the United States was caught by surprise when, on October 22, 1973, all the Arab countries of OPEC (that is, all OPEC members excepting Iran and Venezuela), declared just such an embargo and cut their production immediately by 25 percent, creating a worldwide oil shortage.

Panic buying on world oil markets ensued, and prices went from $3 a barrel in early 1973 to $11 a barrel in early 1974, a one-year increase of almost 300 percent. While the OPEC embargo was a political failure—the United States continued to pursue a policy of strong support for Israel in the Middle East—the economic effects were considerable. Oil prices climbed steadily, reaching a peak of $37 a barrel in 1981 before dropping back to $31 in 1982 (and much further since). The phenomenal increase in world oil prices had an equally phenomenal economic impact on Mexico. A net oil importer until 1973, PEMEX quickly raised domestic prices for both crude-oil and refined products, and began a rapid expansion program aimed at more intensive exploration and increased production.

The exploration paid off during the early years of the López Portillo administration. In 1977 it was announced that Mexico's proven oil reserves were at least double the previously estimated 6 billion barrels. By 1980, PEMEX's proven reserve estimates had grown severalfold to an astounding (and exaggerated) 72 billion barrels.

It was suddenly very easy for Mexico to negotiate multibillion-dollar development loans from big banks, which were for their part holding vast "petrodollar deposits" from OPEC beneficiaries of the oil boom. Thus López Portillo was able to ignore conventional advice from the IMF and others about the need to address galloping government overspending or the need for basic international trade and investment reforms. He proceeded to go full speed ahead on state-driven industrialization and a host of public-sector projects, many of them flawed by a level of official corruption perhaps previously unmatched in Mexican history.

In 1978, the economy grew by an unstable 8.2 percent—a classic case of overheating, where external funds come pouring into a country and bring about inflation, overvaluation of the currency, and decreased international competitiveness. A staggering debt—approaching $100 billion by the end of the López Portillo administration in 1982—had been added to Mexico's future economic woes.

Meanwhile, López Portillo, elated by the oil bonanza, made little effort to respond cooperatively to U.S. president Jimmy Carter's genuine desire to improve ties. To the contrary, 1979 was a low point in U.S.-Mexico relations. The problems began in February, when

Carter journeyed to Mexico City for a meeting with López Portillo. The result was a series of controversial exchanges, including what Americans considered to be a rude lecture by López Portillo on past U.S. sins and President Carter's infelicitous reference, in a public toast, to "Montezuma's revenge" (a term used to describe traveler's diarrhea). Even though the meeting ended with the announcement of some previously negotiated minor agreements and a mutual display of "friendship" at Carter's airport departure, the visit left both parties wary about the future.

When Carter returned to Washington, he decided to appoint a special coordinator with ambassadorial rank to oversee interagency relations with Mexico. This well-intended effort did not help inter-governmental relations, as Mexicans were both suspicious of the move and uncertain about the chain of command. Was the special coordinator more important than the U.S. ambassador in Mexico? More important than the assistant secretary for inter-American affairs in the State Department? Why did he seem to Mexicans to be more concerned about U.S. business interests than in promoting good relations? These questions were never resolved, and the special-coordinator idea was eventually abandoned.

The penultimate blow to the binational relationship in the ill-fated year of 1979 originated in Carter's efforts to accomplish a two-pronged policy in the troubled country of Nicaragua, long ruled by the dictator Anastasio Somoza. Popular resentment was building, and Somoza's days were numbered. The probable alternative to his rule, however, was hardly ideal. The Marxist-led Sandinistas were the most organized of the opposition elements, so it appeared likely that the Somoza dictatorship of the right would be replaced by a Cuban-style regime of the left. U.S. policy during this period sought to ease Somoza out but, at the same time, to encourage the creation of a ruling coalition of democratic parties and the Sandinistas. Mexico, in a move guaranteed to displease the United States, supported the Sandinistas as the single most effective group in the struggle against Somoza. López Portillo seemed to delight in hosting the insurgent Sandinista *comandantes,* even providing them with the use of his personal aircraft.

The worst was yet to come. In a series of personal telephone conversations, López Portillo had given his word to Carter that Mexico would provide medical asylum to the recently deposed and now ailing Shah of Iran. The United States proceeded on this assurance, only to be informed at a critical moment that Mexico was withdrawing its offer to the Shah. For all practical purposes this act severed personal relations between Carter, who described himself as outraged, and the Mexican president. It was no help when López Portillo, making a triumphal visit to Nicaragua in 1980 after the Sandinistas seized power, took the opportunity to do a little more *yanqui* bashing.

In any case, economic aspects of the two countries' relations grew in importance in the latter part of López Portillo's term. The oil boom had by this time driven the Mexican economy into a red heat, generating substantial borrowing (more than $40 billion from U.S. and other foreign banks) and rapid growth of imports of capital goods in an effort to stimulate manufacturing and diversify exports away from oil dependency. Then came the oil bust of the early 1980s. A rapid deterioration in Mexico's balance of payments, and in its ability to pay interest on its debts, followed. The situation came to a head with the dramatic Washington negotiations in August 1982, which rescued Mexico (and the world's financial markets) from the brink of disaster (see Chapter 3).

Sobering Up with De la Madrid

López Portillo's successor, Miguel de la Madrid (1982–1988), preoccupied by the vast task of achieving domestic economic stability and structural reform, undertook few international initiatives. De la Madrid did, however, play a very constructive role, along with President Oscar Arias of Costa Rica and other South and Central American leaders, in resolving the Nicaraguan civil war and its destabilizing impact on the region. A four-nation "Contadora group" consisting of Mexico, Panama, Venezuela, and Colombia was formed in January 1983 when, at Mexico's initiative, the four countries' foreign ministers met on Panama's Contadora Island to look for solutions to the crisis. Over the next few years, they worked with their Central American neighbors—usually with foreign ministers, but at the presidential level as well—to advance the peace process in a number of ways, including the negotiation of an agreement to avoid incipient war between Honduras and Nicaragua.

When the United States invaded Grenada in October 1983, De la Madrid expressed "profound concern," but without using the rhetoric or the high profile that would have been employed by his immediate predecessors. Mexico joined in when the UN General Assembly voted, 108 to 9, to denounce the invasion. The United States justified its action with the explanation that it was protecting U.S. lives and property. The United States also claimed that Grenada was becoming a Soviet-Cuban base, and pointed ominously to the construction of a new airport whose runway was reportedly too long merely for tourism purposes. Most Mexicans were not convinced, but were too caught up with their own economic problems to make a major issue of the affair.

Perhaps the most dramatic event during the De la Madrid presidency occurred on September 19, 1985: Mexico's worst earthquake ever recorded. It devastated entire sections of Mexico City and left 40,000 dead. The government was caught unprepared, and a rather chauvinist Mexican foreign ministry publicly eschewed the offer of international assistance. This position did not long prevail in the face of the disaster, and soon the United States and many other countries were providing substantial assistance to the victims.

Delays and ineptitude in the government's handling of the disaster resulted in a jump-start for Mexico's civil society, as grassroots neighborhood organizations were formed, and self-help was the order of the day. Many of these groups—often led by students—survived and prospered, and today are considered the precursors of many civil associations and NGOs interested in the environment, community health and welfare, neighborhood security, and other issues.

Nevertheless, De la Madrid is remembered as a quiet and unassertive but ultimately effective president who overcame through persistence and austerity the economic crisis he had inherited from his predecessor. In the end, he had laid the framework for Mexico's necessary opening to the global economy. This was a process now to be led by his successor, Carlos Salinas de Gortari.

The Salinas Presidency

The Salinas presidential campaign began inauspiciously, with a breakaway faction of the government's own party, led by Cuauhtémoc Cárdenas, challenging the PRI in a presidential election. For the first time in decades, the presidential electoral battle was a spirited one. The outcome was at once clear and in doubt. It was clear that Salinas won a plurality of the vote over his two main opponents,

Cárdenas and Manuel Clouthier of the PAN. What was in doubt was whether Salinas won a majority of the votes, as announced several days after the polls closed, with a reported 50.1 percent.

President Salinas may have come into office bearing the burden of a disputed election, but he soon established himself as a forceful president of Mexico. His balanced show of strength in the early weeks of his term—apprehending the notorious head of the state oil agency's corrupt union, and arresting a leading financial figure embroiled in stock exchange chicanery—showed that the new president aimed to be a decisive figure on the Mexican scene.

This helped pave the way for economic and social-reform programs that had a dramatic effect on Mexico's future. These included opening and modernizing the Mexican economy, reducing inflation, initiating such social projects as the multibillion-dollar Programa Nacional de Solidaridad (PRONASOL), and privatizing inefficient state industries. There is no doubt that if presidential elections had been held in 1993 Salinas would have emerged with a clear majority over his PRD and PAN rivals.

Economic and social changes moved ahead during 1991–1993 more briskly than the political reforms President Salinas had promised in his inaugural address, but in 1992 the pace of political reform also began to have an impact. The most visible change was Salinas's willingness to nullify questionable gubernatorial elections in which the PRI candidate had been declared victorious. Three such elections—in the states of Guanajuato, San Luis Potosí, and Tabasco—were nullified after popular protests.

Critics were quick to claim that these actions were taken simply to keep negotiations for the North American Free Trade Agreement (NAFTA) on track, which required that Salinas maintain the credibility he then enjoyed in the United States and Canada (see Chapter 10). Yet the fact remains that the net result was to move the political process in Mexico toward a greater sensitivity to popular will—to move, however hesitantly, in the direction of democratization. Clearly, this growing pluralism is in the best interest of the United States, which has much to gain from a southern neighbor that enjoys the kind of long-term stability only a pluralistic society can, in the end, provide.

In any case, U.S.-Mexico relations in the De la Madrid and Salinas administrations were not a rerun of earlier intense foreign-policy differences during which the United States and Mexico diverged publicly and radically on such issues as Central America, Grenada, and Panama. This period of improved U.S.-Mexico relations in turn fueled negotiations on NAFTA and other economic relations, and a more cooperative approach to migration, control of narcotics trafficking, the environment and transboundary resources, as well as honing each country's perceptions of the other's tastes, culture, and values.

The crises of 1994. Mexico's focus on North America and the world was shattered during 1994 by a number of events, including the Chiapas uprising on January 1, the March 23 assassination of the popular PRI presidential candidate Luis Donaldo Colosio, and the murder in August of PRI secretary general Francisco Ruiz Massieu. These events, and the uncertainties about who the organizers of the killings really were, resulted in a grave loss of public confidence in the economy and the political system. Thus the last year of the Salinas administration turned out to be an unexpected and unwelcome downturn on the Mexican scene, and preceded the peso crisis of late 1994–early 1995 that marked the first weeks of the administration of Ernesto Zedillo Ponce de León.

The Zedillo Presidency

The first weeks of the Zedillo presidency, marked by the Mexican peso crisis (Roett, 1996), soon involved the closest of collaboration between the new president and President Clinton as they tried various schemes together to resolve the peso crisis. After a quick change of finance ministers, the Zedillo administration embarked on an austerity program aimed at reducing public-sector spending and fighting the inflation that threatened to follow the significant devaluation. The new finance minister, Guillermo Ortiz, then began to deal directly with his Washington counterpart and senior White House officials.

President Clinton, House Speaker Newt Gingrich, and Senate leader Bob Dole agreed that Mexico must be given significant help to resolve the crisis that was seen as threatening other Latin American economies as well. But rank-and-file Republicans in the House mounted an unexpected attack, and the collaborative plan was scratched. Clinton then, with tacit support from top congressional leadership, put together a $50 billion loan package, including $25 billion from a little-used U.S. Treasury emergency Exchange Stabilization Fund and matching pledges from international financial institutions and the global banking system. These loans were subsequently paid back in full, and their prompt repayment was highlighted in subsequent presidential state visits by Zedillo to Washington and Clinton to Mexico City. The visits were marked by a growing cordiality in relations between the two presidents.

Several areas of change in Mexico can be seen as affecting U.S.-Mexico relations as the Zedillo administration draws to a close. The diminution in traditional presidential power in Mexico, and an acceptance of electoral results that have given opposition parties, acting together, a majority in the Mexican Congress, is one such change. The U.S. Congress has long been a player in the vagaries of the bilateral relationship, but now the Mexican Congress has a new role as well.

At the same time Mexican opposition parties, notably the PAN and the PRD, are playing a growing role in Mexico's internal debates over the nature and management of the bilateral relationship. For Mexico, the United States is its principal foreign-policy concern, and this was increasingly reflected during the 1990s in Mexican political debate. The growing role of a responsible, independent press in Mexico has contributed to the creation of a national policy forum. Respected newspapers like *Reforma* in Mexico City, *El Norte* in Monterrey, and *Mural* in Guadalajara are giving increasing attention to key issues of international and public policy throughout the nation.

The changes during the closing years of the 1990s are reflected in the growth and development of Mexican industry. Leading Mexican industries had to absorb the shock of entering into competition in the global marketplace, while at the same time enduring the austerity program that followed the peso crisis. Many Mexican firms are increasing their productivity and improving their international marketing skills, determined to take advantage of the opening to the world's largest market provided by NAFTA. Some of the more protectionist U.S. industrial sectors are resistant to foreign competition. This problem will have to be overcome if Mexican firms are to compete fairly in the U.S. market. The Zedillo administration is promoting export diversification to Latin America, Europe, and Asia as well as the United States, but the stark fact is that the United States remains the market for 70–80 percent of Mexican exports.

Another notable change during the Zedillo years has been the tendency toward greater federalism in Mexico. Attempts at state- and municipal-level cooperation in the past have been thwarted by the strong centralization of political and economic power in Mexico City. While U.S. states and even local authorities have a fair amount of leeway in such matters, all too often in the past their counterparts south of the border had to refer proposed local arrangements to the capital.

Over the next decade, U.S.-Mexico relations will encompass a myriad of new transboundary arrangements (e.g., Tijuana–San Diego, Ciudad Juárez–El Paso, Arizona-Sonora) on the environment, trade, and community health, education, cultural, and economic development issues in the border areas that will mark a departure from the past. This is happening at a time when some U.S. border states are becoming increasingly aware of the importance of their economic and social relations with Mexico. While the impact of this burgeoning bilateral relationship extends beyond the border states and is nationwide in impact, it might be useful to focus on one particular border state—California—as a case in point.

California-Mexico Relations

Mexico is fast becoming a key element shaping California's development. The two-way flow of goods, capital, information, technology, and people has expanded dramatically since the 1980s. This was particularly noticeable when the Asian crisis in the late 1990s resulted in a 15 percent drop in California's trade with Japan, Taiwan, and Singapore, and a 37 percent drop in California's exports to South Korea. During the years of the Asian crisis, California's exports to Mexico continued to rise. For example, exports increased to $13.3 billion in 1998, representing an increase of 16 percent over 1997. California exports to Mexico continue to increase, suggesting that by 2001 or 2002 Mexico could surpass Japan as California's top trading partner.

While the Asian crisis was a good reason in itself to improve economic and social relations with Mexico, there were other factors that made it an imperative for California's new governor, Gray

Davis, who took office in January 1999. California's relations with Mexico had fallen to a historic low under Davis's predecessor, Pete Wilson, due to a combination of what was perceived as anti-Mexican sentiments expressed by Wilson during his hard-fought 1994 gubernatorial campaign and his subsequent neglect of key California-Mexico border and other issues. California businessmen were concerned that Governor Wilson's great unpopularity in Mexico could have adverse effects on their business relationships with potential Mexican clients. During the 1998 campaign, Davis promised to improve relations with Mexico as one of his highest priorities.

The new governor followed through in February 1999 with a highly successful visit to Mexico City and the industrial hub city of Monterrey, Nuevo León, in northern Mexico. He had cordial meetings with President Zedillo and his cabinet, and spoke on several occasions with Mexican lawmakers and businessmen. After meeting with President Zedillo, Davis noted at a press conference that "I have long believed that California cannot succeed if Mexico does not succeed," adding that "we are tied together by a common history and a common tradition . . . the President of Mexico and I agree that we should work as allies to solve common problems" (*San Francisco Chronicle,* February 10, 1999).

While trade, education, and science and technology areas are important in the California-Mexico relationship, the core issue is immigration, which has played a key role in the relationship over many decades (Lowenthal and Burgess, 1993). In fact, Latinos, mostly of Mexican origin, now make up more than one-quarter of California's population, and 40 percent in Los Angeles County. By the year 2010, one in three persons in California will be of Latino origin.

The Immigration Dimension

California will continue to face immigration as one of the most important of many international/domestic—sometimes called "intermestic"—issues in this decade and into the next century. Currently two-thirds of immigrants residing in California are from Mexico. The traditional bilateral concerns with which much of this volume has dealt—in fact the very process of improving the management of the U.S.–Mexico relationship—are impacted by what in the past would have been called "domestic" issues.

This is in part the case because since the 1980s in the United States there has been a devolution of resources and responsibilities away from the federal level, and directed toward the states, counties, and cities. The federal government has mandated social-welfare entitlements to all residents, while failing in some cases to make the funding available to fulfill these entitlements to the state and local authorities that people look to for social, education, and health benefits. In fact, federal support in these areas actually declined in the 1980s, with the largest cuts for California being in health and human services, housing and urban planning, and public education, all areas strongly affected by Mexican immigration, both documented and undocumented.

How is Mexican immigration affecting California, especially the urban areas of southern California? What is the true nature of the health, educational, and social status of Mexican immigrants, and how has it been perceived by the general public?

The erosion of a stereotype. In order to answer such questions, it must be understood that the traditional profile of the typical Mexican immigrant is changing rapidly. For a decade after the *bracero* program of contract labor importation ended in 1964, Mexican immigration consisted of mostly young, undocumented males who left their immediate relatives behind in order to work temporarily in the United States, usually for six months or less. Most came from a small subset of Mexican rural communities, located in seven Mexican states, and worked in seasonal U.S. agriculture. As we saw in Chapter 6, recent evidence from both sides of the border shows a much more heterogeneous flow of migrants. They tend to originate from more diverse Mexican areas, are increasingly female, and tend to work in urban areas.

The shift has also occurred from a temporary to a more permanent Mexican immigrant population, as changes in the California economy have affected the demand for Mexican immigrant labor. Economic restructuring has produced millions of assembly jobs in light industry, electronics, furniture, clothing, and a host of other fields. These can easily be filled by recently arrived migrant workers. At the same time, the rapid advance of service industries, from building maintenance (often contracted out to immigrant labor agencies) to hotels, restaurants, and fast-food franchises, has generated a huge number of additional low-wage jobs that are unattractive to many U.S. workers. Even sharp recessions have failed to reduce this demand for Mexican labor in California. In fact, the strength and persistence of this demand is one of the most salient features of the California economic and social scene as reflected in the immigration phenomenon of the 1990s.

It should be remembered that California has absorbed approximately half of the total Mexican immigration to the United States. Agriculture, the sector that used to absorb the majority of Mexicans arriving in California, has lost ground to manufacturing, construction, and a rapidly expanding urban-services sector. Agricultural workers—who used to be in the majority among Mexican immigrant laborers—now make up only about 10–15 percent of Mexican documented and undocumented workers.

This "Mexicanization" of certain jobs, firms, and agencies is part of a fundamental process of economic change in the United States, the aging of the native-born work force, and the changing U.S. role in the global economy. If U.S. firms cannot compete successfully against Asian and other transnational corporations, then they will be unable to export. Immigrants provide a ready and willing work force that allows many U.S. firms to compete without moving their entire operations abroad, or going out of business.

This reality suggests a different conception from the one that is often articulated: that the United States in general and California in particular are absorbing Mexican immigrants at levels exceeding the requirements of the economy. The fact is that California (and the United States) will continue in the new millennium to face shortages of entry-level workers. History tells us that these young workers will continue to come from Mexico, which in the next ten years will be providing California with more than half of its new young workers.

Composition of migrants to California. Increasing numbers of Mexican females are migrating to California. Female workers are especially likely to originate in urban areas in Mexico, and to find work in urban service sectors, for example as domestic servants; service industry jobs, including hotels and restaurants; janitorial services; and as assembly plant workers in electronics and other such industries. The Immigration Reform and Control Act of 1986 (IRCA), discussed in detail in Chapter 6, also gave impetus to female migration by encouraging whole families to emigrate from Mexico. IRCA legalized approximately 3 million illegal immigrants, mostly Mexican, and allowed them to bring wives and families to the United States, which they did.

The trend away from a temporary male agricultural work force (1940s to 1970s) to a more socially heterogeneous, long-term urban immigrant community (1980s to 1990s) is unlikely to be reversed, and raises new questions about the social and economic effects of Mexican immigration on certain highly impacted local communities in California. The shift to urban employment has increased the visibility of Mexican immigrants, and some Californians seem unprepared to accept the notion of a settled, visible, and growing Latino presence.

The political role of anti-immigrant activists. There has been a growing need for increased federal assistance and for greater cooperation among federal, state, and local authorities to ensure that all California residents receive needed health, education, and welfare services. Unfortunately, this real need for increased assistance was exploited for anti-immigrant purposes by national and local organizations active in the early 1990s in Sacramento and in such cities as San Diego and Los Angeles. They organized efforts to oppose immigration, using as a wedge undocumented immigrants—or "illegal aliens," their preferred term.

California governor Pete Wilson, running for reelection in 1994, was trailing in the polls by more than 20 percentage points at the beginning of that year. He leaped on the "illegal alien" issue as one way of regaining popularity among California's voters. Wilson first joined San Diego's sheriff John Duffy in calling for U.S. marines along the border to "prevent" illegal immigration and twisted perfectly legitimate concerns about adequate federal funding for community services into what essentially became—whether or not Governor Wilson intended it to be so—an anti-immigrant campaign.

Governor Wilson was able to gain political advantage over his opponent on the eve of the November 1994 elections by blaming Mexican illegal immigrants for many of California's economic and social ills. He conveniently overlooked the nationwide recession from which California was just recovering, the significant loss in defense jobs following the end of the Cold War, and his own administration's mismanagement of California's economic recovery. Wilson's decision to use the "anti-illegal-immigrant" theme in his reelection campaign may have been based in part on 1993 polls that showed 63 percent of Californians surveyed thought that there were "too many" immigrants in California, and an astounding (and ill-informed) 78 percent felt that immigrants on balance posed a financial burden on the state—this despite the fact that in the last three decades, with only intermittent demonstrations of concern, California has integrated millions of documented and undocumented immigrants into its economy and society.

Thus, two diametrically opposed views were contending during 1994 for control of the California immigration debate. On the one side were the restrictionists who favored bolstering the Border Patrol, creating a new state (or national) identity card, and drastic reductions or outright elimination of social benefits to undocumented immigrants. On the other side of the debate were advocates of more open immigration policies who wanted to uphold current levels of legal immigration, and to seek humane ways of controlling illegal immigration.

Proposition 187: History and consequences. The restrictionist view in the California immigration debate is best demonstrated by the now-infamous Proposition 187, which was approved by California voters by a wide margin on November 8, 1994. The progress of Proposition 187 through the California campaign was closely and emotionally followed by the Mexican media and Mexicans in general, and is worthwhile to review.

Proposition 187 was drafted by restrictionist interests, assisted by members of the Wilson administration, staff of conservative state legislators, and other special-interest groups. If ever effectively administered, it would deny public education, nonemergency medical care, and other state and locally funded benefits to illegal immigrants. Wilson made support for Proposition 187 a central theme of his successful reelection campaign, as did the unsuccessful Republican senatorial candidate, Michael Huffington, who was narrowly defeated by Senator Dianne Feinstein, an opponent of Proposition 187. Others in opposition to Proposition 187 were President Clinton and key members of his administration, and such conservative Republicans as former secretary of education William Bennett and former secretary of housing and urban development Jack Kemp.

The immediate, direct consequences of Proposition 187 were insignificant, despite the incredible amount of adverse publicity it generated in Mexico and elsewhere. This was in part because several legal challenges were filed in the federal courts immediately after the vote. Restraining orders were issued blocking the implementation of all of the important provisions of 187. The orders blocked those sections of the proposed law that require schools, hospitals, and social-service agencies to turn away "suspected" illegal immigrants and report them to state and federal officials. Subsequently there were about a dozen additional lawsuits filed challenging 187. The issue was not finally resolved, however, until mid-1999, when Governor Davis agreed to drop any plans to challenge the restraining orders by means of further, and probably useless, appeals.

Understanding the facts about Mexican immigrants. What is the real nature of the health and social status of Mexican immigrants in California, and what are the costs and benefits for California from this immigration? Mexican immigrants, even undocumented, are not a homogeneous group. That means that the impact of Mexican immigrants on any particular local or regional area must be understood within the context of their incorporation into the local labor market, and hence the degree of their positive contribution to that particular receiving community. Probably the most beneficial group of immigrants are the young males who come primarily to work, and who plan to return to Mexico at some point. They are healthy, work long hours, and are unlikely to seek out health or social services, though they do pay taxes that are withheld from their salaries or go to a Social Security account number they have presented to an employer. Undocumented workers here for a longer time, or who more or less permanently settle in a community, both work and pay taxes, and utilize educational and social services very much the way documented migrants and U.S. citizens do, and their tax contributions outweigh social-welfare costs. Job displacement by undocumented immigrants of citizens and legal residents is generally temporary, and the net effect is to add productivity and to expand the total number of jobs in the community.

Conclusions. Over the past two centuries in the United States, newcomers have benefited immeasurably from the nation's public-education system—English, Irish, Scots, Poles, Italians, Jews, Scandinavians,

Germans, Asians, Latin Americans—the list is endless. The public schools, which many restrictionists would now deny to the new wave of immigrants, have been a key source of integration and upward movement. Higher-skilled jobs mean higher-wage jobs, and these must not be closed off to new immigrants if the California economy is to grow and to remain globally competitive.

U.S.-Mexico National Security Issues

The United States and Mexico have historically held far different views about the definition of national security. For the United States, particularly in the Cold War era, national security was defined as protecting the United States and its allies from the nuclear threats of the Soviet Union and its allies. For Mexico, internal security issues and protection of its southern border were the primary concerns of the Mexican military and the civilian leadership of the country. Neither country has had an interest in militarizing the border, making the U.S.-Mexico (and U.S.-Canada) frontiers the longest undefended ones on earth.

The most serious security threat that the United States and Mexico share in the 1990s is the scourge of narcotrafficking (see Chapter 7). Mexico fears that robust drug cartels might penetrate its public- and private-sector institutions (including civilian law enforcement, the military, and banking and industry) and subvert Mexican society (Schulz, 1997). The battle lines are drawn on this front, and the outcome of the struggle is uncertain. There is no evidence that the narcotraffickers have reached Los Pinos (the Mexican presidency) during the term of President Zedillo, who is given high marks for personal honesty. Unfortunately, the same cannot be said for his predecessor.

Whatever the eventual outcome of the controversial trials, convictions, and appeals of Raúl Salinas or the investigation of other members of the Salinas clan, it is clear that narcotraffickers reached to high levels in the Salinas presidency. This is not a total surprise, given the fact that illegal drug exports are running around $30 billion a year, according to an official in the Mexican attorney general's office (*Washington Post,* April 28, 1996).

The Mexican military has become increasingly involved in anti–drug trafficking in recent years. The army is now responsible for several state offices of the federal police, with senior army officers taking charge in such states as Chihuahua and Baja California Norte. Public-security issues are more and more a joint concern of the military and such civilian authorities as the Federal Judicial Police, who themselves have been given better training, some of it provided by the United States.

Mexico's second-most-important national-security concern is control of guerrilla activity. The most obvious example is the Ejército Zapatista de Liberación Nacional (EZLN), which has been active in Chiapas since January 1994 and is publicly represented by the popular Subcomandante Marcos (see Chapter 3). Other guerrilla activity has cropped up in Guerrero, Oaxaca, and other states. These groups, known by such acronyms as PROCUP, PDLP, and EPR, finance their activities in part through kidnappings and robberies. While they do not enjoy widespread popular support, they can and do pose a threat to the Mexican military and civilian police, given their ability to mount isolated acts of violence. Further socioeconomic decline, political crises, and the like could increase opportunities for these often well-organized groups to create real security problems. The United States, though, would be well advised to steer clear of any involvement in Mexico's non-drug-related internal security issues. Indeed it should do everything possible to ensure that the support given to the Mexican military for narcotrafficking suppression is not misused in situations where the United States has no business being involved.

The Future of U.S.-Mexico Relations

Many challenges are ahead if the management of U.S.-Mexico relations is to be improved and strengthened. Mexico has undergone dramatic economic and political transformation, and taken steps toward openness and pluralism. How will these changed political, economic, and social conditions in Mexico impact the complex process of U.S.-Mexico relations? What are some of the policy and institutional adjustments that should be made, and concrete steps taken, to improve the management of the complex bilateral relationship? A few are outlined below.

Adjusting to Changing Realities in Mexico

Perhaps the most dramatic impact on the traditional management of the relationship is the new lack of certainty in Mexico's political process. Gone are the days when the Mexican president enjoyed almost complete control over foreign and economic policies. Failure by U.S. policymakers to recognize this change dooms the effective management of the relationship. The long-term interest of the United States demands that any ambivalence over the old stability versus the new democratization be resolved in favor of the latter.

While the conventional wisdom is that the PRI will win the presidential elections in 2000 under the leadership of party regular and former minister of the interior Francisco Labastida, other outcomes must be considered as well. It is possible that Vicente Fox, the PAN candidate and former governor of Guanajuato, or even Cuauhtémoc Cárdenas, the PRD candidate and former mayor of Mexico City, could score an upset victory. The point is that U.S. policymakers must be more flexible, and become more adept at establishing links with a wider variety of players on the emerging Mexican political scene. Among those who should be included in these efforts are state and local government officials and political leaders of all three major parties, as Mexico moves toward decentralization. The failure to carry out this objective, or an appearance of U.S. favoritism—intentional or not—toward the PRI, will cause a backlash that will make good relations more difficult.

Finally, the process of decentralization within Mexico gives U.S. and Mexican state and local authorities along the U.S.-Mexico border better opportunities to settle their mutual problems with a minimum of national government intervention. The new role of NGOs is a factor to be taken into account in the process of bilateral relations, particularly in such areas as the environment, public health, conservation, and sustainable rural and urban development.

Improving the Management of the Relationship

The critical day-to-day management of U.S.-Mexico relations could be greatly improved by the creation of a Bureau of North American Affairs within the State Department, which would encompass Canada and Mexico as well as related regional economic and political affairs. For decades Mexico fell under the Bureau of Inter-American Affairs and Canada under the Bureau of European Affairs (Smith, 1992). In recent years, a Bureau of Western Hemisphere Affairs was created that simply tacks Canada onto Latin America and the Caribbean. This may be some small improvement, but what is really needed is a separate bureau in the department that concerns itself with North America. This would give our closest neighbors the attention they deserve, and would clearly advance U.S. interests by focusing and improving the policymaking process. A caveat: Creating a Bureau of North American Affairs in the State Department would not be as effective unless it were matched by a similar organizational change on the National Security Council (NSC) staff.

Closely allied with this organizational change is the need to pay far closer attention, beginning at the White House, to filling promptly the ambassadorial post in Mexico when it becomes vacant. Mexicans are very aware of and sensitive to the fact that, for example, there was no U.S. ambassador in Mexico City from June 1997 to August 1998. On a practical basis, a good, well-respected ambassador can play an important role in focusing Washington's attention on matters crucial to the bilateral relationship, and in representing the United States at the highest levels of the Mexican government.

Establishing a "Pre-Crisis" Economic Assistance Group

Lessons that could be learned from the Mexican crisis of 1994–1995 include establishing institutional framework to provide for early warning and timely handling of emerging concerns in the Mexican economy. Mexico's stability is too important for the U.S. to let that country "sink or swim." The December 1994 crisis caught Washington almost completely by surprise. Steps to assist the Mexicans, although ultimately successful, were less timely and effective than they might have been if there had been an established interagency framework to handle such emergencies. While the Treasury Department should probably do the heavy lifting in these cases, input from State, NSC staff, and other agencies is important. Perhaps the existing but underutilized Inter-Agency Working Group (IWG) mechanism could be adapted for this purpose. Such an arrangement would facilitate consultation and cooperation with partners in the assistance effort, such as the IMF and other international banks and financial institutions. A special unit of the IWG or similar mechanism might serve as a focus for the analysis of intelligence information that could provide an earlier warning of economic crises. The failure to properly evaluate such advance information was a factor in delaying the U.S. response to the emerging Mexican peso crisis in 1994.

Tipping the Balance on Antidrug Policy

We saw in Chapter 7 that about 70 percent of the U.S. federal drug control budget goes for enforcement, and about 30 percent for education, prevention, and treatment. Given the growing evidence that a stronger public-health and education approach would be more effective (see Eldredge, 1998; Gray, 1998; Massing, 1998), it is time for the United States to conduct a high-level, bipartisan reassessment of budget priorities, with a good look at giving greater emphasis to education, prevention, and treatment over crime and punishment.

Meanwhile, any supplementary funds in the federal drug control budget should go to drug education, prevention, and treatment. As two experts have noted, "A serious antidrug policy would call for an equally serious federal investment in drug treatment, which research has consistently found to be cost-effective, with a focus on hard-core users. . . . It would require appropriate treatment for criminals, expand court-mandated treatment, and revise restrictive sentencing laws to make possible more treatment in prison, after prison, and instead of prison." They add that "the federal government's prevention campaigns should be sustained, with a more aggressive effort to reach children at risk, and increased support for broad community antidrug efforts" (Kleber and Rosenthal, 1998).

The certification process debate. Under a law passed by the U.S. Congress in 1986, the president must certify by March 1 every year whether certain countries are "cooperating" in combating drug trafficking. The president has a range of options: to deny certification and impose economic sanctions; to deny certification but suspend sanctions as being in the national interest; or to certify that the country is cooperating. In late February 1997, and again at about the same time in 1998, the president announced that Mexico should be certified. In February 1999 the president issued a statement acknowledging

President Zedillo's "efforts in Mexico's interests to root out the scourge" of narcotrafficking (*New York Times,* February 16, 1999). Even though Mexico has continued to be certified each year, the process is clouded by congressional criticisms of Mexico. It involves much time and intense attention on the part of senior Mexican officials, who work for certification while at the same time asserting that the certification process is an infringement to Mexico's sovereignty. It is unclear that the certification process has any positive impact on the achievement of bilateral efforts to combat narcotraffickers. It is entirely clear that the process is a significant irritant in the overall management of U.S.-Mexico relations. It is interesting to note that an independent panel sponsored by the Council on Foreign Relations decided that the certification process acts as a corrosive force in U.S.–Latin American relations (Falco et al., 1997).

The Helms-Burton Act

Perhaps equally corrosive on U.S. relations with Mexico and its other trading partners is the Helms-Burton law, passed in 1996, which would apply a secondary boycott to foreign companies that do business with Cuba. The European Union claims that this tactic is in violation of U.S. obligations as a member of the World Trade Organization (WTO), and Canadians and Mexicans believe it may be a violation of NAFTA as well. The Helms-Burton threat of direct punishment of Mexican, Canadian, and other foreign firms has had an adverse impact on U.S. trade interests.

The legislative history of Helms-Burton is interesting. It was passed just after the Cuban air force destroyed two civilian U.S.-based anti-Castro aircraft flying in international airspace, but dangerously close to the Cuban coast. While it is likely that under other circumstances President Clinton might have vetoed the bill, the fallout from the Cuban destruction of the civilian planes was such that he felt compelled by perceived popular sentiment to sign it into law. Subsequently, Clinton maneuvered to delay implementation of some of the more onerous provisions of the law, and the State Department has been slow to enforce provisions of the law suspending U.S. visas of business executives (and their families) who undertake certain trade or investment projects in Cuba. Nevertheless a great deal of unfavorable criticism has come from America's major trading partners.

For many Mexicans, Helms-Burton is only one aspect of a failed U.S. policy to continue the embargo of Cuba imposed during the Cold War. They believe that the political leader who has the most to fear from a dramatic U.S. lifting of the sanctions is Cuban president Fidel Castro, who would no longer be able to use the United States as the scapegoat. They believe that if Castro were to oppose an opening of the Cuban economy following the lifting of sanctions, he would then bear the full responsibility for his actions as the Cuban economy continued to deteriorate.

Bilateral or Multilateral Approaches? Pros and Cons

As we review the broad range of U.S.-Mexico policy issues, including economic issues (trade, labor, investment), migration, narcotics trafficking, the environment, transboundary resources, health and education in border communities, and differing views on foreign policy, it becomes clear that the management of these complex relations requires that solutions be devised that fit the specific issues. While it is generally agreed that in most cases a unilateral approach by either country is the least effective, the trade-off between bilateral or multilateral efforts is not always as clear. As an initial exercise, let's look at a few of these issues on a case-by-case basis.

Trade, labor, and investment disputes. When two countries are becoming closer partners in the global economy, disputes regarding trade, labor, and investment issues are bound to arise. The framework for institutional settlement of these issues exists, and needs to be strengthened. Institutions inspired by NAFTA have been designed to take on many of these disputes, and the World Trade Organization (WTO) plays a similar role. Unilateral actions by either country—such as the U.S. House of Representatives' passage in early 1999 of a bill to restrict steel imports—make this process more difficult. If the U.S. steel import bill ever became law, it would clearly violate both NAFTA and WTO agreements.

Migration issues. Greater efforts by both sides should be made to break with the unilateral approach to migration as essentially a sovereign, domestic issue. This could do much to defuse incipient problems in the relationship. The work of ad hoc bilateral commissions could be expanded, and greater attention paid at cabinet-level meetings of U.S. and Mexican officials.

Drug trafficking. While bilateral cooperation is vital to the success of antidrug efforts, there is a role here for multilateral actions as well. One possibility would be to create, perhaps within the framework of the Organization of American States, a hemisphere-wide standing commission on antidrug enforcement, which inter alia would supersede the unilateral drug certification process now mandated by the U.S. Congress. Within the OAS, each country's performance would be assessed on an annual basis with a view to improving overall cooperation. The United States would come under scrutiny in this forum, and such items as resources devoted to and success of demand reduction programs could be assessed.

Environmental issues. Fortunately, in the area of the environment, much work is already being done in multilateral institutions, and the situation appears promising (see chapter 8). Organizations such as the Commission for Environmental Cooperation (CEC) and the Border Environmental Cooperation Commission (BECC) are working to standardize laws and develop environmental-infrastructure projects. The International Boundary and Water Commission (IBWC) does an exemplary job on transboundary water issues. These organizations are linked to a myriad of NGOs on both sides of the border that are working to improve the management of environmental problems.

Strengthening interparliamentary links. There is a long, history of interparliamentary contacts, often desultory, between the legislative branches of the United States and Mexico. Annual meetings have been lackluster and unproductive. Perhaps this is not too surprising considering that until the 1990s the Mexican Congress was largely a rubber stamp for a powerful Mexican executive. That is far from the case as the 1990s come to a close. It is important that a new, dynamic approach be taken to revive and give impetus to a broad range of interparliamentary activities involving appropriate members of the two legislative bodies. Some steps are already under way, but this could be a fruitful avenue for improving the understanding of issues of great concern to both countries.

Multilateral education initiatives. It is heartening to note that border-state governors have begun to take a closer look at improving educational collaboration in the K–12 area, and other organizations have worked to improve links among higher-education institutions. One such effort is trilateral. It is the North American Initiative in Higher Education, announced at the tenth anniversary of the North American Institute (NAMI) in Santa Fe, New Mexico, in August 1998. This effort will "facilitate the creation of successful strategic alliances between institutions of higher education and the private sectors across North America and serve as a clearinghouse for information about best practices and successful models of strategic partnership," according to the NAMI announcement. This is but one example of how NGOs can work collaboratively to advance the cause of improved educational opportunities across borders. It is also a good example of how issues once considered purely domestic-policy concerns—such as education—are now taking on an "intermestic" dimension.

Conclusion

Two new presidents—one American, the other Mexican—face a myriad of policy decisions in 2001 as they address themselves to the complexities of U.S.-Mexico relations. The profound transformations that took place in Mexico during the 1990s, and changing circumstances in the United States as well, call for a major transition in the management of the bilateral relationship. We have seen that some of the longtime characteristics of the Mexican system—presidential power over the legislature, courts, states, and military; the PRI's corporatist domination of the political scene; and the strong influence of government bureaucracy over the private sector—have all weakened dramatically. We have seen that these changing conditions are a challenge to the way in which the United States has traditionally approached the management of the relationship. We are beyond the eras of intervention and benign neglect. Both countries must now work together with mutual trust and respect to build a strong and successful partnership.

10

Prospects for NAFTA and Beyond: Toward a Free-Trade Area of the Americas?

NAFTA: Origins and Prospects

The first step toward NAFTA was taken in 1965, when a U.S.-Canada pact provided for freer trade in automotive components between the two countries. This agreement resulted over time in an almost complete integration of automobile component manufacture and assembly at plants located in Canada and the United States, thus accomplishing economics of scale and making the industry more competitive in world markets. Mexico's liberalization of investment policies in the 1970s and 1980s made that country, too, an important player in automobile manufacture and assembly.

As early as 1965, Mexico's *maquiladora* industry was taking advantage of modifications in the U.S. tariff schedule that favored goods assembled in Mexico with U.S. components. U.S. tariffs apply only to the value added abroad by, for example, Mexican assembly-line labor. Intermediate products can be brought into Mexico on a duty-free basis for labor-intensive processing. The *maquiladora,* or assembly, industry consists of plants usually located just south of the U.S.-Mexico border. The number of Mexican *maquiladora* plants has soared from twelve in 1965 to three thousand in 1998, and total *maquiladora* exports to the United States have grown from $3 million in 1965 to $45 billion in 1998. During this period, the number of Mexicans employed in *maquiladoras* has reached more than a half million. These plants, which employ relatively low-wage workers (predominantly women), often provide the flexibility U.S. employers need to stay competitive in a difficult international market, permitting these companies to sustain parallel manufacturing and sales operations in the United States rather than moving their plants overseas.

In 1987 the United States and Mexico signed an agreement paving the way for mutual sector-by-sector reductions in tariffs and nontariff barriers to trade. The agreement also established procedures for handling disputes that arise when one country, convinced that another country's government is subsidizing the production cost of an imported item, assesses a countervailing duty designed to offset the alleged subsidy. In effect, these were the first steps toward a comprehensive free-trade agreement, although few realized how far and how fast these steps would come.

Parallel to the advancing U.S.-Mexican trade negotiations, moreover, were efforts to improve trade relations between Canada and Mexico. Several accords were signed similar to those between the United States and Mexico covering the environment, agriculture, and trade issues. Yet another trade link—one that involved intense and divisive political debate in Canada—was the signing of the United States–Canada Free Trade Agreement, which went into effect on January 1, 1989. These pacts led to the negotiation of the North American Free Trade Agreement (NAFTA), which was to create a market of some 360 million people with a combined output of $6 trillion— somewhat larger than that of the European Union (EU).

The North American Market

In February 1991, Presidents Bush and Salinas and Canadian prime minister Brian Mulroney formally announced that their governments were preparing to negotiate a historic free-trade agreement that would be a catalyst for hemispheric economic growth led by increased investment, trade, and jobs. The timing of the announcement appeared ideal for all concerned. All three countries needed economic stimulation—particularly the United States and Canada, which were suffering from unexpectedly persistent recessions. And although Mexico was enjoying a fairly comfortable rate of real growth thanks to recent economic reforms, its recovery was just beginning and was therefore somewhat uncertain.

As talks got under way in June 1991, trade negotiators for the three countries were assigned four major tasks: (1) reduction of all tariffs to zero over the next few years; (2) elimination of pesky nontariff barriers to North American trade; (3) ensuring an open climate for private direct investment among the three countries; and (4) full protection of intellectual property rights such as patents, trademarks, and copyrights.

One of the greatest challenges to the NAFTA negotiators arose from the fact that the three economies were highly asymmetrical: In 1991 the gross national product of the United States was about $5.3 trillion, while Canada's ($460 billion) and Mexico's ($200 billion) were far more modest. Population patterns were also quite different: In 1990 the United States had 260 million people, Mexico 88 million, and Canada only 26 million.

But the aggregate figures for a North American economy were impressive: a gross product of nearly $6 trillion and a population of 362 million. These figures compared favorably with those of the European Union, which had an output of less than $5.5 trillion and a population of 350 million. It was anticipated that NAFTA would provide advantages—employment gains, higher incomes, and improved international competitiveness through production sharing, technology transfer, and economies of scale—equal to or better than Europe's.

The successful conclusion to the NAFTA negotiations among executive-branch teams of experts from the three countries was a necessary but insufficient step. While legislative-branch approval of the NAFTA agreement was easily accomplished in the Canadian Parliament and Mexican Congress, it was a different story in the United States. Not only did the U.S. Congress have to approve the agreement, but a new president, coming into office in January 1993, had expressed reservations about NAFTA during the campaign (though some of his worries were presumably allayed by the undertaking of negotiation of NAFTA side agreements on environment and labor). President Bush, along with his Mexican and Canadian counterparts, signed the basic agreement in December 1992.

During early 1993, however, there was much uncertainty about the priority President Clinton was giving to the passage of NAFTA, and the inclination of key members of Congress, particularly from labor districts, to pass it. The AFL-CIO kept up a drumbeat of opposition to NAFTA during these months, and there was little response from pro–free traders in the Congress, the private sector, or the White House. Finally, with the side agreements negotiated, Clinton did send the package to Capitol Hill in September 1993. After a good deal of intense political activity (see Pastor and Fernández de Castro, 1998) the package was approved by the U.S. Congress in November 1993, and came into effect on January 1, 1994.

NAFTA at Five

After five years, the effects of NAFTA can be judged favorably. Most economists, and private-sector business and industry, point to clear benefits, whereas NAFTA's critics blame the agreement for causing the loss of U.S. jobs in certain sectors and, by the very growth in economic activity resulting from NAFTA, exacerbating environmental problems. Recently these issues have tended primarily to be the concern of business and labor special-interest groups. For the general public a myriad of other domestic and foreign issues have moved to the front pages and the TV news.

Economic statistics continue to give a positive cast to NAFTA (see Figure 10.1). Trilateral trade has grown from $225 billion in 1992 to $683 billion in 1998, tripling in size. Since more than one-third of U.S. economic growth comes directly from exports, companies from all over the United States are gaining jobs as a result of NAFTA. It is clear from these figures that NAFTA is a success in terms of trade expansion and job creation. It is also reported that the NAFTA trade dispute mechanism, though it suffered from an uncertain start, is playing a growing role in settling troublesome trade problems (Leycegui et al., 1995).

Prospects for a Free-Trade Area of the Americas

During the first Summit of the Americas in 1994 it was agreed by the chiefs of state of thirty-four Western Hemisphere nations that negotiations to complete the creation of a Free-Trade Area of the Americas (FTAA) by 2005 should get under way immediately. The understanding was that NAFTA would expand, starting with Chile and proceeding with the Central American Common Market (CACM), and the Caribbean Common Market (CARICOM), and eventually move south and include negotiations with the Common Market of South America (MERCOSUR). It was agreed at that time that NAFTA should provide the scope and model for the FTAA.

Figure 10.1   North America: Population, GNP, and Trade, 1998

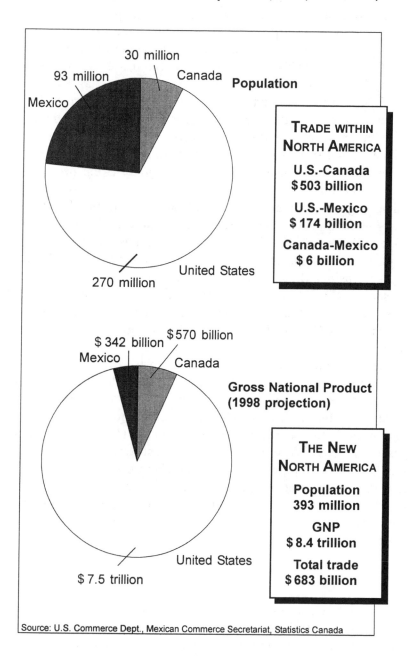

30 million
Canada   **Population**

93 million
Mexico

**TRADE WITHIN
NORTH AMERICA**

**U.S.-Canada
$503 billion**

**U.S.-Mexico
$174 billion**

**Canada-Mexico
$6 billion**

United States
270 million

$342 billion $570 billion
Mexico   Canada

**Gross National Product
(1998 projection)**

**THE NEW
NORTH AMERICA**

**Population
393 million**

**GNP
$8.4 trillion**

**Total trade
$683 billion**

United States
$7.5 trillion

Source: U.S. Commerce Dept., Mexican Commerce Secretariat, Statistics Canada

Some of the enthusiasm, however, particularly in the United States, was soon dampened by the Mexican peso crisis in 1995, when the attention of senior U.S. policymakers was diverted to assisting the Mexican government in its subsequent economic recovery. Critics of NAFTA in particular, and free trade in general, seized on the Mexican crisis as grist for their protectionist mill.

Elsewhere in the hemisphere there was still considerable momentum in favor of the FTAA. In preparation for the Santiago Summit meeting of chiefs of state in April 1998, hemisphere economic ministers met in San José, Costa Rica, to establish working groups on market access; investment; services; government procurement; dispute settlement; agriculture; intellectual property; subsidies, antidumping and countervailing duties; and competition policy. Their plans were approved at the Santiago Summit, and the hemisphere-wide trade negotiations began. However, and as a reflection of waning U.S. leadership, it became increasingly clear that NAFTA was no longer considered the automatically preferred model. U.S. efforts to pursue the NAFTA model were rebuffed by Brazil and others, and it was decided that the FTAA "negotiations will be an open process in which MERCOSUR and other subregional groupings will receive their full due" (Roett, 1999).

This action by Brazil and others surprised senior U.S. participants in the Santiago Summit, but it was preceded by several years of uncertainty and sporadic involvement in Latin American free-trade issues by the Clinton administration, which certainly played a role in the Latin American leaders' response. The administration inherited the NAFTA initiative from its predecessor and, to its credit, finally got NAFTA through a reluctant Congress. But the subsequent lack of effective trade expansion leadership wrought what may well be a long-term change in the dynamics of U.S.–Latin American economic relations, with Brazil taking on a more important role as the most influential member of MERCOSUR.

Fast Track and Free Trade

The United States suffered a particularly hard blow in relations with its hemisphere trading partners with the failure of the Clinton administration to gain approval for what until recent years had been fairly routine congressional approval for fast-track authority. What is fast track, and why is it important?

"Fast track" is authority that Congress grants the president to negotiate trade agreements with the stipulation that Congress may subsequently accept or reject an agreement, but not amend it. This gives U.S. trade negotiators a tool they must have to come to final agreement with their counterparts in other countries and regions. Lacking fast-track authority, any agreement the U.S. side might reach would be subject to arbitrary modification by Congress. Obviously, no serious U.S. trading partner is interested in negotiating first with the executive branch, only to have to renegotiate the whole deal with congressional committees.

Fast-track authority is thus a vital first step in pursuing the U.S. goal of opening markets worldwide, whether through bilateral, regional, or global trading arrangements. Exports are an increasingly important component of U.S. job growth, and account for one out of every three jobs created in the U.S. economy. These are not low-paid service jobs, but are good jobs created by an expanding export industrial sector, including high technology. In order to sustain prosperity in the United States, we must continue to open markets abroad, and this is crucially hampered by the absence of fast track.

The Millennium Round. The Europeans have proposed that a new round of global trade negotiations—the "Millennium Round"—open in 2000. These negotiations would reform World Trade Organization (WTO) regulations in such areas as agriculture, intellectual property rights, and services. As the world's largest exporter of goods and services, the United States has a vital interest in these emerging areas. Fast track is indispensable if the United States is to play a role, along with the other trading nations of the world, in reforming the WTO mechanism in these sectors.

The FTAA. We have already seen how the United States is losing momentum and fading from its traditional leadership role in the Western Hemisphere as a result of the lack of congressional authority to conduct meaningful trade negotiations. Thus fast-track authority is needed not only for global trade negotiations, but for regional arrangements as well.

European countries have moved in briskly in the absence of U.S. commitment to trade expansion in the Western Hemisphere. Europe's trade with MERCOSUR more than doubled in the 1994–1998 period, and many European firms have discovered that with the negotiation of new trade arrangements they have a competitive advantage over U.S. firms in trading with MERCOSUR countries, and, even more dramatically, with Chile. In addition to the European Union (EU), every major country in the Western Hemisphere has gained duty-free access to the Chilean market—with the exception of the United States. This puts U.S. workers in such sectors as textiles and construction equipment at a disadvantage—even as most U.S. union leaders oppose the fast-track authority that would give U.S. workers a level playing field in the world economy.

NAFTA and the Global Economy

In January 1999, as NAFTA embarked on its sixth year, the world's multilateral trading system was celebrating its fiftieth anniversary. The achievements of the GATT in reducing tariffs and nontariff barriers to trade, and of its successor, the WTO, in settling trade disputes, were duly noted in a series of events in Geneva and elsewhere. At the same time, preliminary discussions were under way to embark in 2000 on the Millennium Round and further reforms aimed at freer trade and greater economic benefits to the global community. It was clear that there was a valuable lesson to learn from a half-century's experience of liberalizing trade through multilateral rounds undertaken every decade or so. The more of the global economy that is included, the greater the scope for putting together deals that will be mutually beneficial and hence acceptable.

Does that mean regional trade arrangements like NAFTA are less desirable? Not necessarily. A regional group like NAFTA can support forward movement globally if it is open to trade to the rest of the world, and does not discriminate. It is more important, then, that the United States, Canada, and Mexico resist internal protectionist pressures and stay on the course to trade liberalization both regionally—for example in NAFTA and the FTAA—and globally in the Millennium Round itself. How are the countries coping with these protectionist pressures? What role are they likely to play in Millennium Round and FTAA negotiations during the 2000–2005 period?

The U.S. Record

The failure of U.S. will following the Mexican peso crisis of 1995 and the resulting difficulties with Congress on crafting the necessary support package for the Mexicans had serious consequences. The result was in a serious dilution of the administration's efforts to obtain fast-track authority for NAFTA enlargement, the FTAA, and even the new WTO round.

During the middle- and late-1990s, domestic protectionists argued that reducing foreign imports somehow protects American jobs, its manufacturing base, its technological edge, and even its very sovereignty. These arguments were inadequately answered by an often embattled Clinton team. In all fairness, it must be noted that private-sector leadership in the struggle for freer trade was at times notably absent. And trade liberalization's natural allies in Congress, including many Republicans, and Democrats not threatened by a major labor union constituency, were also largely silent.

Agenda for 2000 and beyond. New leadership is needed to make the clear argument in favor of trade liberalization and to gain the public support required for effective U.S. participation in multilateral and global trade negotiations over the next several years. The FTAA represents a key opportunity to undertake this task, and to enable the United States to strengthen cooperation with its neighbors while acting as an engine of growth for the hemisphere. Armed with fast track, a necessary but insufficient achievement, the United States could regain at least part of its traditional leadership role in hemisphere interministerial trade meetings. As trade liberalization should be seen in both a regional and global context, much care must be taken to ensure that, as the FTAA evolves, its work is complementary to the activities of the WTO and the Millennium Round beginning in 2000. This view is not typically held by the leadership in all Latin American trade arrangements, especially in the case of MERCOSUR. U.S. negotiators must be alert to discourage FTAA arrangements that could be counterproductive in terms of global trade liberalization.

Perhaps the original idea, criticized at the Santiago Summit, of creating an FTAA more in the original NAFTA mold will become more attractive as MERCOSUR loses some of its economic strength with the Brazil crisis, problems in Argentina, and the realization that relations with the EU may not in 2000 and beyond be as fruitful as envisioned. In any case, the new U.S. administration taking office in January 2001 will have a splendid opportunity to recapture America's traditional positive role in leading the world toward trade liberalization and its abundant and indisputable benefits. It would be a tragedy indeed if this opportunity were lost.

How Canada Copes

After completing the NAFTA negotiations, and observing that the United States was going to be unable or unwilling to expand NAFTA to include Chile, the Canadian government concluded bilateral free-trade agreements with Chile and Israel, both similar to NAFTA, but with some new wrinkles. One change limits antidumping and countervailing duty remedies, and the other protects "Canadian culture." This latter provision in particular is problematic, because it essentially protects Canadian magazine owners from having to compete with more popular U.S. publications.

Canada has also moved, in separate legislation, to prevent Canadian firms from advertising in U.S. magazines that have special editions (split runs) destined for Canada. Since the U.S. magazines would lose money without the Canadian advertising, this effectively bars them from distribution in Canada. More tentative are suggestions to tax U.S. films shown in Canada (a discriminatory tax clearly prohibited by the WTO) and to limit U.S. foreign private direct investment in Canada. But, on balance, Canada has a rather good record on supporting trade liberalization and is likely to be able to defeat most protectionist measures originating in its provinces and to play an important and useful role in both FTAA and WTO trade negotiations.

The Mexican Case

Mexico's policy in multilateral and global trade negotiations will be determined in part by trends in the Mexican economy and in institution building, stability, and democratization. Economic indicators in 1999 looked satisfactory, though GDP dropped from 4.8 percent in 1998 to about half that in 1999. Trade continued strong, as did foreign private direct investment. The public-sector budget was expected to benefit from an important external factor—rising world oil prices. The political process continued with its occasional surprises, but in general reflected a trend toward firmer institutions and a more pluralistic political system. If these trends continue in 2000 and beyond it will bode well for Mexico's ability to play an important role in FTAA and Millennium Round negotiations.

Meanwhile, Mexico is attempting to reduce its overwhelming dependence on U.S. trade (more than 80 percent of Mexico's trade is with the United States). Mexico has negotiated a trade pact with the European Union for signature in 2000. This could make Mexico a "hub" country, with opportunities to play a more important role with its "spokes"—other hemisphere countries with which it enjoys special trade relations. It is also hoping that the pact will reverse Mexico's consistent trade deficit with the EU. In any case, Mexico seems poised to join its NAFTA partners in continuing the vital process of trade liberalization by working with them on an array of regional and global issues, including but not limited to the FTAA and WTO.

NAFTA and Prospects for Dollarization

The European Monetary Union (EMU) and the growing use of euros in EU transactions has sparked interest in the possibility of a monetary union in the Americas, or in such regional groupings as the South American countries (MERCOSUR) or those of North America. However, analysts have been quick to note that there are important differences between Europe and the Western Hemisphere (see Suttle, 1999). The most obvious difference is that the United States is the dominant force in the hemisphere's economy, and is unlikely to be interested in any arrangement that would reduce its economic-policy space to accommodate a regional situation. Other asymmetries in the economies of Latin America are more marked than those in Europe. And, the United States aside, the fragile nature of the bigger hemisphere economies, such as Brazil, would seem to militate against any sort of EMU-type arrangement, either in the MERCOSUR or FTAA contexts.

While prospects are dim for any Western Hemisphere monetary union in the foreseeable future, there has been considerable discussion about the possible advantages of an intra-NAFTA currency area. This would not involve the creation of any sort of North American Monetary Unit (NAMU), which would be of no interest to the United States, but would involve instead the creation of an Argentine-style currency board, in which America's NAFTA partners would peg their currency to the U.S. dollar, or even the full dollarization of their economies, using the U.S. dollar as legal tender in their countries. There are reasons for such considerations. Both Canada and Mexico conduct 80 percent or more of their trade with the United States, and trade with the United States accounts for some 30 percent of their GDP. Both the Mexican and Canadian currencies have fluctuated over recent years, leading to thoughts that perhaps trade would be encouraged and facilitated by some form of dollarization. But there are significant differences between the Canadian and Mexican cases as well. We shall examine some of them below.

The Canadian situation. Canadian analysts have identified several areas that are most important to the consideration of shifting Canada's exchange rate policy from its current flexibility to some form of dollarization. They include monetary and fiscal discipline; costs of currency risk; benefits of flexibility; the resource sector; manufacturing sector productivity; transition costs; and sovereignty (McCallum, 1999). In reviewing these areas, McCallum concluded that Canada already enjoys a suitably high degree of monetary and fiscal discipline; that it is difficult to demonstrate that manufacturing sector productivity is significantly linked to the exchange rate; and that none of the other advantages that might accrue would be worth Canada's loss of sovereign control over its own monetary and fiscal policies. In any case, he notes, "For the citizens of Canada I suspect that such a policy would be a very hard sell indeed, whatever the balance of economic costs and benefits" (McCallum, 1999). This statement by a leading Canadian analyst (McCallum is senior vice president and chief economist of the Royal Bank of Canada) is a convincing indication that the prospect for Canada's moving away from its flexible exchange rate regime is very slight.

The Mexican situation. It is no surprise that some Mexicans are looking longingly at the prospect of the dollarization of the Mexican economy. The sharp devaluations of the Mexican peso since 1976 have come all too frequently, and at great cost to Mexican workers and to the middle class, as the peso has lost more than 90 percent of its value. Advocates of dollarization, whereby the U.S. dollar would become legal tender in Mexico, point out that with dollarization these devaluations would cease. Inflation and interest rates should over time converge to near U.S. levels. Mexican politicians and bankers would not be able to pursue unwise monetary policies. Capital flight would be a thing of the past. Mexicans would have in the dollar a reliable store of value for their savings. (For a full exposition of this case, see Salinas-León, 1998.)

These and other possible benefits must be matched by Mexicans, however, against some of the same criteria set up by the Canadians. They must ask themselves whether, in fact, Mexico's flexible exchange rate policies have not served Mexicans well in recent years. They must examine carefully whether the apparent benefits might not be outweighed by other factors, not least being the loss of sovereignty that is inevitably involved. They must recognize that dollarization is not a step toward any kind of NAMU; the United States almost certainly will not, in the foreseeable future, give up any control over the activities of the Federal Reserve Board (though it might allow observers, assist in helping Mexico set up better banking supervision, and the like). In sum, this would be a vitally important decision to be taken by Mexico, and it must proceed with extreme caution.

Entering the Twenty-First Century

Mexico, the United States, and Canada share a continent and are bound together by a complex web of economic and social transactions that occur millions of times a day in the interlocking worlds of trade, finance, tourism, education, and culture. The question is not whether or not that interdependence is going to continue to grow. It will. The question, rather, is whether the three countries, as a North American community, can guide this growing interrelationship in a way that most benefits all of their peoples.

A first test of that ability was the successful conclusion of NAFTA, which came into effect in 1994. NAFTA has served the peoples of the continent well in expanding economic opportunities. In 1998 Mexico became the second largest market for American exports, surpassing Japan. This means that the NAFTA countries are one another's best trading partners. During the first five years of NAFTA, U.S. merchandise exports to Mexico almost doubled, with trade in 1999 expected to exceed $180 billion. The NAFTA partnership has helped protect the continent from the worst effects of financial market turmoil in Asia, Russia, and Brazil.

Meanwhile improved effectiveness in resolving trade disputes, closer cooperation in facing environmental concerns, and the creation of a better mechanism for addressing labor issues, all as envisaged in the NAFTA side agreements, has helped to resolve outstanding issues. Privatization and economic liberalization have opened new opportunities for U.S. and Canadian investment in Mexico's railroads, ports, banks, and airports. President Zedillo's initiative, announced in 1999, to privatize the electricity sector holds out the prospect of providing Mexico with expanded and more efficient sources of electrical power.

With NAFTA providing freer trade in goods and promoting direct investment in industry, what might be the next economic area to be explored? A good candidate is the expansion of NAFTA into a customs union. At present, tariffs are being phased out and nontariff barriers to trade (NTB) are being eliminated, but each country employs its own antidumping and countervailing duties, laws and regulations. It would be useful, early in the new century, to form trilateral working groups to study the pros and cons of transforming NAFTA into a customs union, with a common trade policy and a common external tariff. This would mean the three countries would have to give up a bit more sovereignty, but traditional reluctance to do so might be reduced in the face of rapidly changing global conditions (see Weintraub in Baer et al., 1996).

Another candidate for trilateral discussions might be promoting the freer flow of labor, though as we have seen (e.g., in Chapter 6) this is a very sensitive political issue. In such an asymmetrical labor market as North America's, it is important to keep in mind that freer labor movement, like free trade, is not a zero-sum game, where one side's advantage is at the cost of another. Rather, it is a positive-sum game, in which trade, investment, and labor flows combine to produce greater productivity, efficiency, and higher standards of living for all.

We have seen that through the process of "silent integration" the United States already benefits from the flow of both documented and undocumented labor migration from and through Mexico in such areas as services, agriculture, and manufacturing operations, including high technology. But the benefits would be greater, and more mutual, if this labor pool integration were to be legitimized by formal intergovernmental agreements facilitating the flow of human resources in both directions; that is, not only would the more traditional south-north flows be documented and rationalized, but also the more developed partners—the United States and Canada—would more easily be able to send research and development specialists to work with Mexican counterparts in product design, worker training, quality control, and environmental-impact studies. Increasing the percentage of documented (as opposed to undocumented) workers in the United States would also help ensure that migrants' working conditions were improved, and would relieve the current fears of undocumented workers threatened with the denial of social services or deportation.

These economic issues, although they are usually given the greatest weight in the discussions about NAFTA and beyond, are not the only—nor even in the long run, perhaps, the most important—link in the North American relationship. We also need to create better understanding among the peoples of the three nations. Efforts in the field of education, such as the initiative announced by the North American Institute (NAMI) in Santa Fe, New Mexico, in 1998, should promote free movement of educators and students among educational institutions in Canada, the United States, and Mexico and try to achieve common admission requirements and enhanced transferability of academic credit. Public resources and private philanthropy could support vastly increased programs of scholarships and other support for the North American educational enterprise, including science and technology, with a focus on science policy and environmental concerns. The resulting dense network of educational exchanges, visiting scholars, and collaborative research on North American economic and social problems would inform the vision of an emerging North American community (see Earle and Wirth, 1995).

All this can and should be accomplished by strengthening, not diminishing, the myriad cultural identities throughout the countries of North America. The era of the "melting pot" is long behind us. Each of the nations of North America enjoys a rich diversity within its own borders. As a whole, North America forms a fascinating mosaic of languages, literature, music, art, and aspirations. The future lies in our ability to accommodate—and celebrate—our cultural pluralism while forming a mutually beneficial civil and political society.

Chronology

1810   Mexican war of independence begins.

Father Miguel Hidalgo y Costilla proclaims Mexican independence from Spain on September 16.

1811   Hidalgo captured and executed by Spanish. José Maria Morelos assumes leadership of the struggle for independence.

1821   Conservative forces led by former Spanish officer Agustín de Iturbide secure Mexican independence from Spain.

1822   Iturbide crowned Emperor Agustín I.

Mexico annexes Central America.

Texan politician Stephen Austin granted permission to settle U.S. colonists in Texas.

1823   Iturbide forced to abdicate. Central America secedes from Mexico.

1824   First constitution drafted. Guadalupe Victoria elected first president of Mexico.

1829   Mexico abolishes slavery in attempt to discourage Anglo settlement of Texas.

1830   Mexican government bans further American settlement of Texas.

1834   Texas secedes from Mexico.

1836   Mexican general Antonio López de Santa Anna arrives in Texas with an army. He storms the Alamo but is defeated and captured at San Jacinto by rebellious Texans and forced to grant Texas independence.

1845   United States annexes Texas.

1846   Border skirmishes lead to U.S. declaration of war on Mexico.

1847   Gen. Zachary Taylor decisively defeats Mexican forces at Angostura.

        U.S. Army expeditionary force under Gen. Winfield Scott lands at Veracruz and then takes Mexico City.

1848   Mexico signs Treaty of Guadalupe Hidalgo. In exchange for $15 million, Mexico cedes California, Nevada, Arizona, New Mexico, Utah, and part of Colorado to the United States, and gives up all claims to Texas.

1853   United States purchases large tract of southern New Mexico and southeastern Arizona from Mexico for railroad expansion. Known as the Gadsden Purchase.

1857   Mexico's liberal government adopts a new constitution, limiting Church power and broadening individual freedoms.

        Conservatives stage a revolt and take Mexico City.

        Benito Juárez leads liberal forces in the War of the Reform.

1860   Liberal victory: Juárez recaptures Mexico City and becomes first full-blooded Indian president of Mexico.

1861   Spanish, British, and French forces jointly occupy Veracruz demanding repayment of debts.

1862   Britain and Spain withdraw troops, but French drive inland and are defeated on May 5 (Cinco de Mayo) at Puebla.

1863 Reinforced French troops drive Juárez from Puebla and the Mexican capital.

1864 France installs Maximilian as emperor of Mexico.

1867 Juárez leads the fight against the emperor. Maximilian defeated and executed; Juárez reelected president.

1876 Juárez's successor, Sebastián Lerdo de Tejada, overthrown by Gen. Porfirio Díaz.

Díaz begins thirty-four-year rule (except for 1880–1884). Extensive U.S. investment in Mexico, especially in railroads and mining.

1910 Moderate Francisco Madero proclaims Plan of San Luis Potosí, calling for revolt against Díaz and for free elections. Beginning of Mexican Revolution as rebellions break out in the north and in Puebla.

1911 After thirty-four years of rule, Díaz resigns in the face of expanding rebellions and sails to France.

Madero returns from exile in the United States and is elected president.

Emiliano Zapata, in south, declares Madero a traitor and drafts Plan of Ayala, calling for land redistribution.

1913 Ten Tragic Days, February 8–18. Madero and Vice President Jesús María Pino Suárez arrested and killed on orders of Gen. Victoriano Huerta. U.S. ambassador Henry Lane Wilson, a critic of Madero, is indirectly implicated. President Woodrow Wilson refuses to recognize Huerta's government and brings economic and diplomatic pressure on Huerta.

Pancho Villa and Venustiano Carranza, in north, and Emiliano Zapata, in south, all take up arms against Huerta.

1914 U.S. naval forces seize Veracruz to deprive Huerta of arms shipments, and stay for seven months.

Huerta flees Mexico, and Carranza's forces under Gen. Alvaro Obregón take Mexico City. (Huerta dies two years later in an El Paso jail.)

Revolutionary convention at Aguascalientes adopts Plan of Ayala.

World War I begins in Europe in August.

U.S. soldiers withdraw from Veracruz.

1915   Villa defeated at Celaya, but continues to fight.

Carranza recognized by the United States as chief of government forces.

1916   Villa raids town of Columbus, New Mexico. U.S. sends punitive force under Gen. John Pershing into Mexico in search of Villa.

Carranza's forces invade Morelos, center of Zapata's support.

1917   Pershing withdraws from Mexico, having failed to find Villa.

Carranza's government adopts the Constitution of 1917, providing for labor and land reform.

Carranza elected constitutional president.

United States enters World War I in April.

German foreign minister, Arthur Zimmerman, sends telegram to Carranza offering to restore all territories lost to the United States in Mexican War in exchange for Mexico's support. Carranza rejects offer.

1919   Last U.S. incursion into Mexico, after Villa attacks Ciudad Juárez.

1920   Carranza's regime toppled; he flees Mexico City and is killed.

Obregón becomes president.

Villa ends his rebellion.

1921   José Vasconcelos becomes minister of education and starts cultural and literacy campaigns.

1923   United States and Mexico sign Bucareli Agreements, guaranteeing sanctity of U.S. property in Mexico in exchange for U.S. recognition of Obregón's government.

Villa assassinated.

1924   United States gives Obregón arms to suppress a coup.

Mexico recognizes the Soviet Union.

Plutarco Elías Calles elected president.

1926   Calles's anticlerical policies lead to the Cristero rebellion, an uprising of ultraconservatives, priests, and peasants.

1927   Ambassador Dwight Morrow is sent to Mexico to negotiate petroleum disputes; he also helps in mediation of church-state conflicts.

1928   Calles succeeded by Obregón; Obregón is assassinated in July.

Calles begins six-year reign as *jefe político,* selecting functionary presidents, the first of whom is Emilio Portes Gil.

1929   Founding of Partido Nacional Revolucionario (PNR), precursor of the PRI.

Cristero rebellion suppressed.

1930   Foreign Minister Genaro Estrada announces Mexico policy of strict nonintervention and routine recognition of de facto governments (the Estrada Doctrine).

1934   Lázaro Cárdenas becomes president, with support of workers, peasants, and leading elements of military.

1936   Cárdenas sends Calles into exile. The president arms 60,000 peasants to support his sweeping land reforms.

1938   Cárdenas nationalizes oil industry. United States responds with economic sanctions.

1939   Partido Acción Nacional (PAN) founded by Manuel Gómez Morín.

1940   Manuel Avila Camacho becomes president, promotes closer ties with the United States.

1941   United States enters World War II in December.

1942   Mexico enters World War II on Allied side in May.

United States and Mexico initiate *bracero* program, allowing Americans to contract Mexican agricultural labor.

1945   Inter-American Conference on Problems of War and Peace at Chapultepec.

1946   Miguel Alemán elected president.

Mexican industrialization intensifies.

Ruling party renamed Partido Revolucionario Institucional, or PRI.

1947   Harry Truman visits Mexico; Alemán tours Washington, D.C., New York, and Kansas City.

1952   Adolfo Ruiz Cortines succeeds Alemán.

United States deports illegal Mexican workers, so-called "Operation Wetback."

1958   Adolfo López Mateos elected president.

U.S.-Mexico trade and investment grow.

1964   Mexico and United States settle Chamizal boundary dispute, which arose in 1864 when the Rio Grande changed its course and passed 440 acres of Mexican territory to the U.S. side of the river.

1965   Border Industrialization Program created by Mexican government. *Maquiladora* industry is to grow from twelve plants in 1965 to three thousand in 1998.

1968   Prior to Mexico City's hosting of Olympics, government brutally cracks down on leftist student demonstrations; in October, demonstrators massacred at Tlatelolco.

1970   Luis Echeverría elected president. His foreign policy activism and "Mexicanization" investment policies stimulate a significant downturn in U.S. relations with Mexico.

1974   Mexico joins Venezuela in creating a Latin American economic system.

1976   José López Portillo assumes presidency. During the early years of his term, high oil revenues bring record growth to Mexican economy and stimulate massive borrowing by government.

1977   The government launches electoral reform in face of growing voter apathy and criticism about the country's "one-party democracy." Chamber of Deputies increased to 400 seats to make room for opposition parties.

1979   Mexico breaks off relations with Nicaraguan dictator Anastasio Somoza and sides with Cuban-supported Sandinistas; also breaks previous promises and refuses to admit the terminally ill Shah of Iran following his ouster by fundamental Islamic forces. The two actions rankle the administration of U.S. president Jimmy Carter.

1980   After long negotiations, President López Portillo suddenly decides that Mexico will not join the General Agreement on Tariffs and Trade (the GATT).

1981   Oil prices plummet late in year.

1982   Mexico forced to suspend payments on principal of $100 billion foreign debt in August. Mexico's economic crises weaken Mexico's freedom to differ with Washington over economic and international issues.

López Portillo nationalizes banking system.

Miguel de la Madrid elected president. Mexico's massive foreign debt forces him to implement an economic stabilization program with austerity measures and to begin an extensive restructuring program. The peso is devalued.

1983   A wave of local victories by the center-right PAN raises new questions about the invincibility of the PRI government.

1985   Mexico City hit by devastating earthquake on September 19; 40,000 left dead.

Slaying of DEA agent Enrique Camarena in Mexico strains U.S.-Mexico relations.

1986   Another electoral reform, designed in part to increase the government's credibility, increases the number of Chamber of Deputies seats to 500, but conditions for effective multiparty democracy still not met.

Mexico joins the GATT, ushering in a new era of trade liberalization.

1987   Mexico and the United States sign bilateral framework agreement for trade and investment.

A PRI faction called the Democratic Current leaves the party after the selection of technocrat Carlos Salinas de Gortari as presidential candidate. The Democratic Current, led by Cuauhtémoc Cárdenas, goes on to form Frente Democrático Nacional (FDN) to contest the 1988 presidential elections.

1988   Salinas defeats opposition candidate Cárdenas in presidential elections. Accusations of fraud lead to massive protests.

1989   Partido Revolucionario Democrático (PRD) formally founded, succeeding the FDN electoral coalition led by Cárdenas.

Mexico and the United States undertake bilateral Trade and Investment Facilitation Talks.

PAN wins first governorship, in Baja California (Norte).

Constitutional amendment paves the way for electoral reforms.

Year-end agreements with multilateral lenders and commercial banks reduce Mexico's commercial debt and ease debt service schedule.

1990   Presidents Bush and Salinas issue joint statement in June in support of negotiations for free-trade agreement.

1991   Canada joins negotiations in February for the establishment of a North American Free Trade Agreement (NAFTA).

U.S. Congress allows fast-track NAFTA negotiations to proceed in June.

Large PRI plurality in 1991 midterm elections restores official party's stronghold in Mexican Congress.

1993   NAFTA is approved by three legislatures; takes effect January 1, 1994.

1994   Guerrillas of the Zapatista Army of National Liberation (EZLN) launch a major uprising in Chiapas on the day NAFTA goes into effect. A tentative peace accord reached in March does not hold; negotiations are to continue sporadically for years.

Luis Donaldo Colosio, the PRI presidential candidate, assassinated in Tijuana, Baja California, in March. Assassin is arrested, but motives and authors of crime remained unresolved.

Ernesto Zedillo Ponce de León, the candidate chosen to replace Colosio, elected in August in fair elections. Outgoing president Salinas is seen as next president of the newly created World Trade Organization. Mexican economy appears sound.

Zedillo inaugurated on December 1. Finance minister announces projected 4 percent GDP growth and only 4 percent inflation in Mexico for 1995. Foreign investors pleased with new president and his team.

Fissures in economic structure quickly appear. Ineffectual attempts by new Zedillo administration's economic team—15 percent devaluation fails, peso allowed to float, sharp reduction in international reserves, lead to peso crisis with international repercussions.

1995   U.S. government announces rescue plan for Mexico. Plan succeeds, and Mexico soon begins to recover, and to repay loans ahead of schedule.

PAN wins electoral victory in Guadalajara, Jalisco.

Zedillo embarks on judicial-reform program. Creates new supreme court. Faces tough battle on public-security issue as crime rises.

1997   Midterm elections in Mexican Congress give opposition parties a majority in the Chamber of Deputies, though PRI maintains plurality in Chamber and control of Senate. Cárdenas becomes first elected mayor of Mexico City.

1998   PRI candidate, running as opposition to entrenched PAN in Chihuahua, wins upset election in gubernatorial race. Other results mixed. PRI wins in Durango, Quintana Roo, and Hidalgo, loses to PRD in Zacatecas, Oaxaca, Veracruz, Tlaxcala, and Baja California Sur.

Zedillo announces programs to focus on extreme poverty, health, and education (Progresa).

Mexicans protest to the United States over "Operation Casablanca," a drug sting operation that netted several Mexican bankers and narcotraffickers. Mexican concerns revolve around sovereignty issue and insufficient prior consultation.

1999 Year begins with dramatic visit of pope to Mexico; millions of Mexicans attend many public events. Pope calls for hemispheric solidarity of the faithful.

Clinton visit to Mexico in February highlighted by his support of Zedillo record on drug cooperation, and assurances that Mexico would be certified to Congress as cooperating in the war on drugs.

Decline in world oil prices affects Mexican public-sector budget and requires series of budget cuts to keep deficit under control. Situation alleviated somewhat as oil prices increased significantly through the balance of the year.

Visit to Mexico City and Guadalajara by newly inaugurated governor of California begins dramatic turnaround in California-Mexico relations, which had suffered under previous state leadership. Followed up by President Zedillo's successful visit to California.

Zedillo announces 1999 foreign private direct investment goal of $10 billion.

Labor Secretary José González Fernández elected secretary general of PRI. Seen as favorite of Zedillo.

PRI holds open primary for party's presidential nomination. Former interior minister and party regular Francisco Labastida wins handily and begins his campaign against Vicente Fox of the PAN and Cuahtémoc Cárdenas of the PRD in a three-way race for the presidency.

Guide to Further Reading

I encourage interested readers of this book to extend their knowledge of Mexico, U.S.-Mexico relations, and the emerging North American community by going on to the publications listed below. I have tried to be particularly selective in commending these, with the understanding that readers should also consult the much more extensive bibliography that follows. In the recommendations listed below I have noted only the author or principal editor; the full citations are in the bibliography.

As an introduction and general background to the field of Mexico and U.S.-Mexico relations, I recommend *The Labyrinth of Solitude* (Paz, 1985a), *Many Mexicos* (Simpson, 1952), *Mexico and the United States: Managing the Relationship* (Roett, 1988), *Marriage of Convenience: Relations Between Mexico and the United States* (Weintraub, 1989), *The Course of Mexican History* (Meyer et al., 1998), *Mexico: A History* (Miller, 1985), *Mexico: Biography of Power: A History of Modern Mexico, 1810–1996* (Krauze, 1997), *A New Time for Mexico* (Fuentes, 1996), *Foreign Policy in U.S.-Mexican Relations* (Green and Smith, 1989), *The United States and Mexico* (Vázquez and Meyer, 1985) and *U.S.-Mexico: The New Agenda* (Fernández de Castro et al., 1999). Among the volumes that deal with a single aspect of the Mexican experience, I recommend the masterful *Life and Times of Pancho Villa* (Katz, 1998) and a brilliant account of the Tlatelolco tragedy, *Massacre in Mexico* (Poniatowska, 1991).

A number of volumes also are recommended for readers with more specialized interests. For an in-depth understanding of recent key international economic issues I suggest *NAFTA: An Assessment* (Hufbauer and Schott, 1993), *NAFTA at Three: A Progress Report*

(Weintraub, 1997), and *The Mexican Peso Crisis: International Perspectives* (Roett, 1996). Migration and border issues are covered in such volumes as *Mexican Migration to the United States: Origins, Consequences, and Policy Options* (Cornelius and Bustamante, 1989), and *The U.S.-Mexico Border: Transcending Divisions, Contesting Identities* (Spener and Staudt, 1998). The issues of drug trafficking and national drug control policies are taken up in *Ending the War on Drugs: A Solution for America* (Eldredge, 1998) and *Rethinking International Drug Control: New Directions for U.S. Policy* (Falco et al., 1997). Finally, managing environmental issues is the subject of such recent publications as *Environmental Management on North America's Borders* (Kiy and Wirth, 1998) and *Environment and Trade: A Framework for Moving Forward in the WTO* (Sampson, 1999).

Bibliography

Aguilar-Camín, Héctor, 1997. "A Transformation for the Millennium." *Los Angeles Times*, October 22.

Aguilar-Zinser, Adolfo, 1997. "Will Congress Maximize Its Power?" *Los Angeles Times*, October 6.

Baer, M. Delal, and Sidney Weintraub, 1994. *The NAFTA Debate: Grappling with Unconventional Trade Issues*. Boulder and London: Lynne Rienner Publishers.

Baer, M. Delal, et al., eds., 1996. *NAFTA and Sovereignty: Trade-offs for Canada, Mexico, and the United States*. Washington, D.C.: Center for Strategic and International Studies.

Baer, M. Delal, and Roderic Ai Camp, eds., 1997. *Presiding Over Change? Zedillo's First Year*. Washington, D.C.: Center for Strategic and International Studies.

Bailey, John, and Sergio Aguayo, eds., 1996. *Strategy and Security in U.S.-Mexican Relations Beyond the Cold War*. La Jolla: University of California San Diego.

Baker, George, 1995. "The Concept of Virtual Economy in Mexico's Energy Sector: The Legal Challenge," in *NAFTA: Law and Business Review of the Americas* 1, no. 3 (Summer).

———, 1999. *Notes on Mexico's Crude Oil Reserves*, Baker & Associates report, March 2.

Bean, Frank D., Rodolfo O. de la Garza, Bryan R. Roberts, and Sidney Weintraub, eds., 1997. *At the Crossroads: Mexico and U.S. Immigration Policy*. Lanham, Md.: Rowman and Littlefield Publishers, Inc.

Bean, Frank D., Jurgen Schmandt, and Sidney Weintraub, eds., 1989. *Mexican and Central American Population and U.S. Immigration Policy*. Austin: University of Texas Press.

Bean, Frank D., Georges Vernez, and Charles B. Keely, 1989. *Opening and Closing the Doors: Evaluating Immigration Reform and Control*. Santa

Monica, Calif., and Washington, D.C.: The RAND Corporation and the Urban Institute.

Bethell, Leslie, 1991. *Mexico Since Independence.* Cambridge: Cambridge University Press.

Bilateral Commission on the Future of U.S.-Mexico Relations, 1989. *The Challenge of Interdependence: Mexico and the United States.* Lanham, Md.: University Press of America.

Bosworth, Barry P., Susan M. Collins, and Nora Claudia Lustig, eds., 1997. *Coming Together? Mexico-U.S. Relations.* Washington, D.C.: Brookings Institution.

Brandenburg, Frank R., 1964. *The Making of Modern Mexico.* Englewood Cliffs, N.J.: Prentice-Hall, Inc.

Camp, Roderic Ai, 1993. *Politics in Mexico.* Oxford: Oxford University Press.

———, 1996. "The Zedillo Legacy in Mexico." Washington, D.C.: Center for Strategic and International Studies, October 3.

Castañeda, Jorge G., 1996. *The Mexican Shock: Its Meaning for the United States.* New York: The New Press.

Centeno, Miguel A., 1997. *Democracy Within Reason: Technocratic Revolution in Mexico.* University Park: Pennsylvania State University Press.

Cline, Howard F., 1965. *The United States and Mexico.* New York: Athenaeum.

Coatsworth, John H., and Carlos Rico, eds., 1989. *Images of Mexico in the United States.* La Jolla: University of California San Diego.

Cook, Maria Lorena, Kevin J. Middlebrook, and Juan Molinar-Horcasitas, 1994. *The Politics of Economic Restructuring in Mexico.* La Jolla: University of California San Diego.

Cornelius, Wayne, and Jorge Bustamante, eds., 1989. *Mexican Migration to the United States: Origins, Consequences, and Policy Options.* La Jolla: University of California San Diego.

Cornelius, Wayne, Judith Gentleman, and Peter H. Smith, eds., 1989. *Mexico's Alternative Political Futures.* La Jolla: University of California San Diego.

Cornelius, Wayne, Ann L. Craig, and Jonathan Fox, 1993. *Transforming State-Society Relations in Mexico: The National Solidarity Strategy.* La Jolla: University of California San Diego.

Diamond, Larry, Juan Linz, and Seymour Martin Lipset, eds., 1989. *Democracy in Developing Countries: Volume 4, Latin America.* Boulder and London: Lynne Rienner Publishers.

Earle, Robert I., and John Wirth, 1995. *Identities in North America.* Stanford: Stanford University Press.

Eisenstadt, Todd A., and Cathryn L. Thorup, 1994. *Caring Capacity vs. Carrying Capacity: Community Response to Mexican Immigration in*

San Diego's North County. La Jolla: University of California San Diego.

Eldredge, Dirk Chase, 1998. *Ending the War on Drugs: A Solution for America.* Bridgehampton, N.Y.: BridgeWorks.

Falco, Mathea, et al., 1997. *Rethinking International Drug Control: New Directions for U.S. Policy.* New York: Council on Foreign Relations.

Fernández de Castro, Rafael, et al., eds., 1999. *U.S.-Mexico: The New Agenda.* Austin: University of Texas Press.

Foweraker, Joe, and Ann L. Craig, eds., 1990. *Popular Movements and Political Change in Mexico.* Boulder and London: Lynne Rienner Publishers.

Fuentes, Carlos. "After Living in a Bad Novel, the Voters Write Their Future," *Los Angeles Times,* July 2, 1997.

―――. 1992. *The Buried Mirror: Reflections on Spain and the New World.* Boston, New York, and London: Houghton Mifflin.

―――. 1996. *A New Time for Mexico.* New York: Farrar, Straus & Giroux.

Glade, William, and Cassio Luiselli, eds., 1989. *The Economics of Interdependence: Mexico and the United States.* La Jolla: University of California San Diego.

Globerman, Steven, and Michael Walker, eds., 1993. *Assessing NAFTA: A Trinational Analysis.* Vancouver: Fraser Institute.

González, Guadalupe, and Marta Tienda, eds., 1989. *The Drug Connection in U.S.-Mexican Relations.* La Jolla: University of California San Diego.

Gray, Mike, 1998. *Drug Crazy: How We Got into This Mess and How We Can Get Out.* New York: Random House.

Grayson, George, 1997. *Mexico: Corporatism to Pluralism.* New York: Harcourt-Brace.

Green, Rosario, and Peter H. Smith, eds., 1989. *Foreign Policy in U.S.-Mexican Relations.* La Jolla: University of California San Diego.

Haber, Stephen, ed., 1997. *How Latin America Fell Behind: Essays in the Economic Histories of Brazil and Mexico.* Stanford: Stanford University Press.

Hansen, Roger D., 1971. *Mexican Economic Development: The Roots of Modern Growth.* Washington, D.C.: National Planning Association.

Hart, John Mason, 1988. *Revolutionary Mexico: The Coming and Process of the Mexican Revolution.* Berkeley: University of California Press.

Herrera-Lasso, Luis, 1999. "The Impact of U.S. Immigration Policy on U.S.-Mexico Relations," *Voices of Mexico.* Mexico City: National Autonomous University of Mexico, January–March.

Hufbauer, Gary, and Jeffrey J. Schott, 1993. *NAFTA: An Assessment,* (rev. ed.). Washington, D.C.: Institute for International Economics.

Johnston, Bruce, et al., 1987. *U.S.-Mexico Relations: Agriculture and Rural Development*. Stanford: Stanford University Press.

Kandell, Jonathan, 1988. *La Capital: The Biography of Mexico City*. New York: Random House.

Katz, Friedrich, 1998. *The Life and Times of Pancho Villa*. Stanford: Stanford University Press.

Kiy, Richard, and John D. Wirth, eds., 1998. *Environmental Management on North America's Borders*. College Station: Texas A&M University Press.

Kleber, Herbert D., and Mitchell S. Rosenthal, 1998. "Drug Myths from Abroad," in *Foreign Affairs*, September-October.

Krauze, Enrique, 1997. *Mexico: Biography of Power: A History of Modern Mexico, 1810–1996*. New York: HarperCollins.

———. 1998. "In Memory of Octavio Paz (1914–1998)," in *The New York Review of Books,* May 28.

Levy, Daniel, and Gabriel Székeley, 1983. *Mexico: Paradoxes of Stability and Change*. Boulder, Colo.: Westview Press.

Leycegui, Beatriz, et al., eds., 1995. *Trading Punches: Trade Remedy Law and Disputes Under NAFTA*. Mexico, DF: Instituto Tecnologico Autonomo de Mexico.

Loaeza, Soledad, 1997. "The Church Is Just Another Player," *Los Angeles Times*, July 16.

Lowenthal, Abraham F., and Katrina Burgess, 1993. *The California-Mexico Connection*. Stanford: Stanford University Press.

———, 1998. "United States–Latin American Relations at the Century's Turn: Managing the 'Intermestic' Agenda." Los Angeles: Pacific Council on International Policy, September.

Lustig, Nora, 1992. *Mexico: The Remaking of an Economy*. Washington, D.C.: Brookings Institution.

Magaloni, Beatriz, 1997. "Judicial Reform Starts at the Top," *Los Angeles Times*, July 25.

Markiewicz, Dana, 1993. *The Mexican Revolution and the Limits of Agrarian Reform*. Boulder and London: Lynne Rienner Publishers.

Massing, Michael, 1998. *The Fix*. New York: Simon & Schuster.

McCallum, John, 1999. "Seven Issues in the Choice of Exchange Rate Regime for Canada." Toronto: Royal Bank of Canada, February.

Meissner, Doris M., et al., eds., 1993. *International Migration Challenges in a New Era*. New York: The Trilateral Commission.

Mexico–United States Binational Commission, 1997. *Mexico-U.S. Binational Study on Migration*. Mexico City and Washington, D.C.: Ministry of Foreign Affairs and U.S. Department of State.

Meyer, Lorenzo, 1997. "Downsizing the Presidency," *Los Angeles Times,* August 27.

Meyer, Michael, et al., 1998. *The Course of Mexican History,* 6th ed. Oxford: Oxford University Press.

Middlebrook, Kevin J., 1995. *The Paradox of Revolution: Labor, the State, and Authoritarianism in Mexico.* Baltimore: The Johns Hopkins University Press.

Miller, Robert Ryal, 1985. *Mexico: A History.* Norman: University of Oklahoma Press.

————, 1989. *Shamrock and Sword: The Saint Patrick's Battalion in the U.S.-Mexico War.* Norman: University of Oklahoma Press.

Mishel, Lawrence, Jared Bernstein, and John Schmitt, 1999. *The State of Working America.* Ithaca and London: Cornell University Press.

Morris, Stephen D., 1995. *Political Reformism in Mexico: An Overview of Contemporary Mexican Politics.* Boulder and London: Lynne Rienner Publishers.

Mumme, Stephen, 1993. "Innovation and Reform in Transboundary Resource Management: A Critical Look at the International Boundary and Water Commission, United States and Mexico," in *Natural Resources Journal* 33, no. 1 (Winter).

Nadelmann, Ethan A., 1998. "Commonsense Drug Policy," in *Foreign Affairs,* January-February.

Orme, William A., Jr., 1993. *Continental Shift: Free Trade and the New North America.* Washington, D.C.: The Washington Post Co.

Oster, Patrick, 1990. *The Mexicans.* New York: Harper & Row.

Pastor, Robert, and Rafael Fernández de Castro, eds., 1998. *The Controversial Pivot: The U.S. Congress and North America.* Washington, D.C.: Brookings Institution.

Pastor, Robert, and Jorge Castañeda, 1988. *Limits to Friendship: The United States and Mexico.* New York: Knopf.

Paz, Octavio, 1985a. *The Labyrinth of Solitude,* Edition E-811. New York: Grove Press.

————, 1985b. *One Earth, Four or Five Worlds: Reflections on Contemporary History.* New York: Harcourt, Brace, Jovanovich.

————, 1972. *The Other Mexico: Critique of the Pyramid.* New York: Grove Press.

————, 1988. *Sor Juana de la Cruz.* Cambridge: Harvard/Belknap Press.

Pizzorusso, Ann C., 1998. "The Maquiladoras and the Environment," in Kiy and Wirth.

Poniatowska, Elena, 1991. *Massacre in Mexico.* Columbia: University of Missouri Press.

————, 1997. "Women's Battle for Respect Is Fought Inch by Inch," *Los Angeles Times,* September 8.

Pretes, Michael, 1996. "Managing Resource Wealth in North America: A Trust Fund Approach," in *NAMINEWS* (Santa Fe, N.M.), no. 18 (Summer).

Purcell, Susan Kaufman, 1997. "The Changing Nature of U.S.-Mexico Relations," in *Journal of Interamerican Studies & World Affairs* 39, no. 1 (Spring).

Purcell, Susan Kaufman, and Luis Rubio, eds., 1998. *Mexico Under Zedillo.* New York: Americas Society.

Reavis, Dick J., 1990. *Conversations with Moctezuma: Ancient Shadows over Modern Life in Mexico.* New York: Morrow.

Reynolds, Clark W., and Carlos Tello, eds., 1983. *U.S.-Mexico Relations: Economic and Social Aspects.* Stanford: Stanford University Press.

Reynolds, Clark W., Leonard Waverman, and Gerardo Bueno, eds., 1991. *The Dynamics of North American Trade and Investment: Canada, Mexico, and the United States.* Stanford: Stanford University Press.

Riding, Alan, 1984. *Distant Neighbors.* New York: Random House.

Roett, Riordan, ed., 1988. *Mexico and the United States: Managing the Relationship.* Boulder, Colo.: Westview Press.

————, 1988. *Political and Economic Liberalization in Mexico: At a Critical Juncture?* Boulder and London: Lynne Rienner Publishers.

————, 1991. *Mexico's External Relations in the 1990s.* Boulder and London: Lynne Rienner Publishers.

————, 1995. *The Challenge of Institutional Reform in Mexico.* Boulder and London: Lynne Rienner Publishers.

————, 1996. *The Mexican Peso Crisis: International Perspectives.* Boulder and London: Lynne Rienner Publishers.

————, 1998. *Mexico's Private Sector: Recent History, Future Challenges.* Boulder and London: Lynne Rienner Publishers.

————, 1999. *MERCOSUR: Regional Integration, World Markets.* Boulder and London: Lynne Rienner Publishers.

Rubio, Luis, 1997. "The New Entrepreneur Class Writes Its Own Ticket," *Los Angeles Times,* July 30.

Salinas-León, Roberto, 1998. "Give Mexicans a Choice between Pesos and Dollars," *Wall Street Journal,* October 16.

Sampson, Gary P., 1999. *Environment and Trade: A Framework for Moving Forward in the WTO.* Washington, D.C.: Overseas Development Council.

Sánchez-Rodríguez, Roberto A., et al., 1998. "Dynamics of Transboundary Environmental Agreements in North America," in Kiy and Wirth, 1998.

Saxenian, AnnaLee, 1999. *Silicon Valley's New Immigrant Entrepreneurs.* San Francisco: Public Policy Institute of California.

Schulz, Donald E., 1997. "The United States, Mexico, and the Agony of National Security." New York: Bildner Center for Western Hemisphere Studies, CUNY, April.

Silva-Herzog, Jesús, 1987. *Beyond the Crisis: Mexico and the Americas in Transition.* Stanford: Americas Program, Stanford University.

Simpson, Lesley Byrd, 1952. *Many Mexicos.* Berkeley: University of California Press.

Smith, Clint E., 1992. *The Disappearing Border: Mexico–United States Relations to the 1990s,* Stanford: Portable Stanford Press.

———, 1996. "International Perspectives on the Mexican Peso Crisis," in Roett.

Spalding, Mark J., 1998. "Things Are Going to Get Far Worse Before They Get Any Better: Environmental Issues Associated with U.S.-Mexican Economic Integration." Paper presented at the "Mexico and the U.S. in the Next Decade" conference, University of California San Diego, May 11, 1998.

Spener, David, and Kathleen Staudt, 1998. *The U.S.-Mexico Border: Transcending Divisions, Contesting Identities.* Boulder and London: Lynne Rienner Publishers.

Suttle, Philip, 1999. "Monetary Union in the Americas," Morgan Guaranty Trust Company Research Report (New York), February 12.

Toro, María Celia, 1995. *Mexico's "War" on Drugs: Causes and Consequences.* Boulder and London: Lynne Rienner Publishers.

U.S. Government, 1999. *The National Drug Control Strategy.* Washington, D.C.: Government Printing Office.

———, 1997. Press release by the Immigration and Naturalization Service (Washington, D.C.) September 5.

Vásquez, Carlos, and Manuel García y Griego, 1983. *Mexican-U.S. Relations: Conflict and Convergence.* Los Angeles: UCLA Press.

Vázquez, Josefina Zoraida, and Lorenzo Meyer, 1985. *The United States and Mexico.* Chicago: University of Chicago Press.

Wager, Stephen J., and Donald E. Schulz, 1994. *The Awakening: The Zapatista Revolt and Its Implications for Civil-Military Relations and the Future of Mexico.* Carlisle, Pa.: U.S. Army War College.

Weintraub, Sidney, 1989. *Marriage of Convenience: Relations Between Mexico and the United States.* Oxford: Oxford University Press.

———, 1995. *NAFTA: What Comes Next?* Washington, D.C.: Center for Strategic and International Studies.

———, 1997. *NAFTA at Three: A Progress Report.* Washington, D.C.: Center for Strategic and International Studies.

Weintraub, Sidney, and Christopher Sands, eds., 1998. *The North American Auto Industry Under NAFTA.* Washington, D.C.: Center for Strategic and International Studies.

Whiting, Van R., Jr., 1992. *The Political Economy of Foreign Investment in Mexico: Nationalism, Liberalism, and Constraints on Choice.* Baltimore: The Johns Hopkins University Press.

Wilkie, James, ed., 1990. *Society and Economy in Mexico.* Statistical Abstract of Latin America Supplement Series, Los Angeles: UCLA.

Wilkie, James W., and Clint E. Smith, eds., 1999. *Integrating Cities and Regions: North America Faces Globalization.* Los Angeles and Guadalajara: UCLA and the University of Guadalajara Press.

Index

About the Book

This concise, accessible volume astutely describes the complex
Mexico-U.S. relationship from the beginning of the nineteenth century through the end of the twentieth.

Smith begins with a brief history of early U.S.-Mexico relations,
focusing on the Texas Secession, the Mexican War, and the Gadsden
Purchase. By 1853, one-half of what used to be Mexico had become
one-third of what is now the United States, and for a full century,
strained ties between the two countries were more the rule than the
exception. But, Smith observes, the lopsided algebra has been transformed, and today we see a growing web of interrelationships that
has created an inevitable partnership.

This evolution is explored in a series of chapters on contemporary issues affecting the partnership: globalization, the process of democratization in Mexico, Mexican immigration to the United States,
illegal narcotics trafficking, and a myriad of trade, labor, and environmental issues. Then, looking forward, the book concludes with a
discussion of trends in Mexico-U.S. relations, including the impact
of domestic changes in both countries and of the proposed Free
Trade Agreement for the Americas (FTAA).

Clint E. Smith is senior research associate at the Stanford Institute
for Economic Policy Research, Stanford University. He is author of
The Disappearing Border, as well as numerous articles on Mexico,
Mexico-U.S. relations, and emerging economic regions in North
America.